Praise for *Change Management Masterclass*

"This book covers the complex subject of change management in a highly readable way. It provides an invaluable resource for managers or MBA students wanting to learn how to manage change successfully."
Dr Tim Hughes, Bristol Business School

"A thoroughly practical and straightforward change management handbook, full of useful ideas and handy tips."
Chris Bones, Principal, Henley Management College

"An excellent practical read. It consolidated my existing learning, and at the same time introduced me to some new and useful models, which I shall use."
Anjali Arya MBA, Organizational Development Consultant

"*Change Management Masterclass* provides a structured way to navigate through the complex subject of change management. Students and operational managers alike should benefit from this useful book, that combines relevant theory, experience and best practice."
Philip Lawrence MBA, Programmes Manager, Alcatel Lucent

"This brings together everything on change management I can ever remember reading or studying into a very structured and logical framework, and presents a clearly balanced view of academic models and commercial insight, drawing from organization examples and management experience. I would see this book being valuable to students or senior business leaders either as a framework to read completely for a comprehensive learning of the subject, or as a reference guide by using selected elements of the 'task and process framework' from which you could build specific knowledge and ideas."
Deborah Bateman MBA, Manager, Business Support & Development, Halifax

"*Change Management Masterclass* is an excellent guide for both managers and students to learn how to manage change better within their organizations. The well-organized structure and case study approach makes the subject very accessible to the reader. I have really enjoyed reading this book and would highly recommend it."
Maria Jesus Fernandez-Gutierrez, Enterprise Core Voice Proposition Manager, Vodafone UK

"It illustrates clearly that there isn't just one answer or approach to managing change successfully. The key message from this book for senior managers of large organizations is the importance of developing strong and adaptable leadership capabilities to support and align every phase of the change process."
Pascoe Sawyers, Director, Leadership Academy, Improvement & Development Agency

CHANGE MANAGEMENT
MASTERCLASS

A Step by Step Guide to
Successful Change Management

Mike Green

**KOGAN
PAGE**

London and Philadelphia

Publisher's note

Every possible effort has been made to ensure that the information contained in this book is accurate at the time of going to press, and the publishers and author cannot accept responsibility for any errors or omissions, however caused. No responsibility for loss or damage occasioned to any person acting, or refraining from action, as a result of the material in this publication can be accepted by the editor, the publisher or any of the authors.

First published in Great Britain and the United States in 2007 by Kogan Page Limited

120 Pentonville Road
London N1 9JN
United Kingdom
www.kogan-page.co.uk

525 South 4th Street, #241
Philadelphia PA 19147
USA

© Mike Green, 2007

The right of Mike Green to be identified as the author of this work has been asserted by him in accordance with the Copyright, Designs and Patents Act 1988.

ISBN-10 0 7494 4507 6
ISBN-13 978 0 7494 4507 2

British Library Cataloguing-in-Publication Data

A CIP record for this book is available from the British Library.

Library of Congress Cataloging-in-Publication Data

Green, Mike, 1959–
    Change management masterclass : a step by step guide to successful change management / Mike Green.
        p. cm.
    Includes bibliographical references and index.
    ISBN-13: 978-0-7494-4507-2
    ISBN-10: 0-7494-4507-6
    1. Organizational   change–Management.   2. Organizational   change–Management–Case studies. I. Title.
    HD58.8.G724 2007
    658.4'03–dc22
                                    2007001972

Typeset by Saxon Graphics Ltd, Derby
Printed and bound in India by Replika Press Pvt Ltd

Contents

Acknowledgements

Many people have contributed to this book in many ways. I would first and foremost like to thank the managers from all the organizations who willingly gave of their time to discuss how they managed change. In all cases they were open with what worked and what didn't. Interestingly, they all learnt from what didn't as much as what did! So thank you Jørgen Jørgensen from Aarhus; Richard Kitson, John Heffer and John Spens from Aster; Christoph Boelling and John Watson from Biogen Idec; Leslie Boydell and Jane Wilde from the Institute of Public Health in Ireland; Jane, Barbara, Paul and Wendy from the British Council. Also thank you to Nicky and Nick and the other contributors to the case studies.

A special thank you to my colleague Richard Lacey who took the trouble to look at the manuscript and offer some wonderful suggestions. Thanks also to Esther Cameron for her continued support and challenge on all matters relating to change management.

I have received an enormous amount of support from both students and colleagues at Henley Management College and also all those involved with the I&DeA's Leadership Academy.

This book wouldn't have been possible without the kind forbearance of my partner Jane and her continued encouragement even when it seemed to take over our lives. A special thank you to my daughter Brigit for her wonderful drawings which appear throughout this book.

The Myers-Briggs Type Indicator (MBTI®) is a registered trade mark of the Myers-Briggs Type Indicator Trust.

About the Author

Mike Green has been involved in facilitating change for over 20 years. Working in both the public and private sectors he's seen what works and what doesn't when it comes to change and has clear ideas of what approaches have a chance of success and those doomed to failure!

In previous lives Mike has been a finance manager, a trade union negotiator and a psychotherapist, but now prefers the relative calm of helping others manage change.

Mike runs Transitional Space, specializing in individual, team and organizational development. He facilitates organizational learning and performance enhancement through a variety of personal, interpersonal and systemic interventions.

Mike is also a Visiting Executive Fellow at Henley Management College, where he tutors in people management, personal development and business transformation.

Mike can be contacted via mike@transitionalspace.co.uk and www.changemanagementmasterclass.com

Introduction

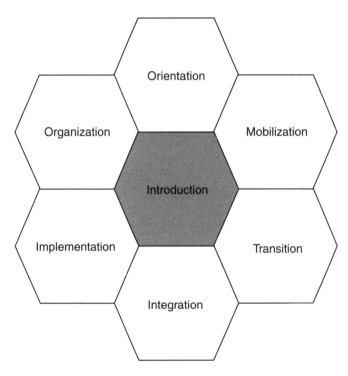

There is nothing more difficult to take in hand, more perilous to conduct, or more uncertain in its success, than to take the lead in the introduction of a new order of things.
(Niccolo Machiavelli, *The Prince*, 1532)

Out of the earth to rest or range
Perpetual in perpetual change,
The unknown passing through the strange.
(John Masefield, 1878–1967, *The Passing Strange*)

There's nothing constant in the world,
All ebb and flow, and every shape that's born
Bears in its womb the seeds of change.
(Ovid, 43BC–AD17, *Metamorphoses*)

The Edge

It doesn't have to be terrifying.
Sometimes it's simply curling your toes
over the end of the high dive,
bending your knees and lightly bouncing
up and down, as if your wings were fluttering.

Or it might be the moment when you're waiting –
dawn-at the border –
for the man in the blue uniform
to hand back your passport,
to say it's all right to leap
from the train to the platform.

And after the flying and the splash,
after you haul your bag up on your shoulder,
it's safe to say that before long
you'll come to the edge of something
and have to leap again.

Maybe it's someone you didn't see
by the pool, wearing a flowered bathing suit –
maybe the love of your life.
or maybe it's a museum with one painting
that finally explains everything.

And even if death is waiting,
you can still love
the perfect fit of the doorknob
in your hand as you open the door.
You can still search for the immortal
painting and buy postcards of it
to send all over the world.

You can leap
and let the water hold you,
throwing one hand over the other,
hoisting yourself up
to dry your body in the sun.

You can lift your rucksack –
the road rolling away before you –
and walk on joyfully,
going forward, forever leaping,
loving the high dive as well as the bottom stair,
loving the held breath, loving the tired feet.
(Richard Jones, 'The Edge', from *The Blessing: New and Selected Poems*.
Copyright © 2000 by Richard Jones. Reprinted with the permission of
Copper Canyon Press, www.coppercanyonpress.org)

Introduction to change management

Change Management Masterclass seeks to introduce the concept of change
management through looking at why organizations need to change;
discussing the different ways of approaching change; describing a process for
successful change management; and learning what works and what doesn't
when managing change.

This book is designed to lead you through the change process in a relatively orderly fashion – looking at the different phases of the change process;
introducing tools and models and ways of tackling issues at each stage; giving
examples of what has worked and what hasn't; drawing on both academic
research and people's experiences in the thick of change.

One of the key tests of the various models is whether they are practical
tools for mapping, analysis, insight and action in the world of organizational
change. Throughout this book I have tried to test them out through their
application in a variety of different organizational settings. I have drawn
from my own experiences as a change practitioner, from that of colleagues
and of course from published research. There are a number of organizations
that I have observed as they have managed their change initiatives and I have
drawn out some of the key findings which hopefully will enlighten our
discussions.

One objective of this book is to present a way of looking at and managing
change, drawing on different models that have stood the test of time and
have demonstrated their usability, and combining them with current
thinking on, for example, emergent change, systems and complexity theory.
Principally though, I would wish to suggest a way that students and
managers alike can make sense of change and manage it more effectively by
using some or all of the concepts in this book.

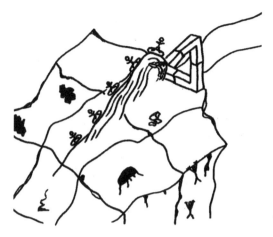

Given the new competitive landscape around the world, with more countries from Eastern Europe entering the European Union, the explosion in manufacturing capability in the Indian sub-continent and China, and similar trends emerging in South America; given the growth in outsourcing, off-shoring and shared services; given the continuing and increasing possibility of global culture clashes, and the escalation of local and national conflicts; all with a backdrop of global warming, climate change and mass movements of people, there seems to be little let up in the exponential growth in change. And of course on an organizational level, whichever industry, whichever country, there will be the responses to these trends and a developing awareness of diversity issues and corporate social responsibility.

How well do organizations manage change?

> Gartner estimates that less than 10% of enterprises and their Chief Information Officers have attempted to institutionalize change management in even the most basic way: by training managers, by creating a program management office (PMO) or by any other means... We've all heard the stats. The specific numbers vary but the fact remains: most large-scale projects that fail to achieve their stated objectives are dramatically over budget or are delivered late. According to Gartner, a full 66% of projects meet at least one of these parameters.
>
> (*CIO Australia's Magazine for Information Executives,* 5 June 2006)

A recent McKinsey survey (2006) suggested that only 6 per cent of change management projects were completely successful (with a further 32 per cent 'mostly' successful). During the changes the mood of the organization was characterized by:

	Successful projects (%)	Unsuccessful projects (%)
Anxiety	44	51
Confusion	22	43
Frustration	23	44
Fatigue	24	34
Resistance	24	28

On the positive side there was a marked sense of focus, enthusiasm, feelings of momentum, hope and confidence in those organizations successfully managing change.

Worrall and Cooper (2006), in an organizational change management study, found that over 90 per cent of managers in all organizations were affected by change, with that figure rising to over 97 per cent in public-listed companies and public sector organizations. They highlighted that:

> The proportion of managers affected by three or more forms of change increased from 45% to 53%. The triad of cost reduction, the use of contract staff and culture change increased... to more than half the managers responding... This triad has had significant implications for the attitudes and behaviour of many managers: as a result of change, their loyalty and morale have declined and their sense of job security and well-being has plummeted:
>
> Percentage of managers feeling that change had negatively affected their:

Motivation:	51%
Sense of employee well-being:	48%
Loyalty:	47%
Morale:	61%
Sense of job security:	56%

Change

Kurt Lewin introduced his concept of organizational change during the middle of the last century (Lewin, 1951). His work was deeply embedded in looking at how human systems operate and the different dynamics at play. His central model comprises three stages: unfreezing, effecting change and then refreezing. Starting with a status quo, you move things and then continue with the new status quo. Some critics have suggested that this is too linear a model of change for these turbulent times of exponential change – that there is no initial 'stable equilibrium' that needs to be unfrozen to allow change to occur. Likewise there's no promised land of a renewed equilibrium position where we can all rest, recuperate and not worry any more.

There are however certain key tenets of Lewin which are true for all change scenarios:

● change doesn't operate in a vacuum but within an interactive system which itself is within a wider environment;
● any human system will have a variety of forces at play which can help and/or hinder movement. These forces need to be addressed; and
● the change process is helped through a process of observing or being in the system and exploring what works and what doesn't.

So what Lewin was suggesting was that in any human system there are different states of dynamic equilibrium and to move from one state to another the forces at play within the system need to be redirected to achieve movement towards the preferred state. We sometimes try to treat change as if it were a discrete object which has clear definable boundaries as if nothing went before and nothing comes after, frozen in time and space.

Change doesn't just start at page one but in fact in countless thoughts, ideas, experiences, conversations, incidents and motivations stretching back many years. Likewise it doesn't necessarily stop once put in motion. However, we can take some snapshots of change in motion, see some action replays and make some predictions based on the lines of trajectory as to where it may lead.

Similarly this book is a staging post for people, managers and students who want to further their thinking and develop their change management skills. The aspiration is to enable you to manage change better in the future with, I hope and trust, a consequential knock-on effect of improving organizational and individual performance and well-being.

The philosopher of comparative religion, Alan Watts, once famously drew the universe as a squiggle across a page and then explained that what humankind does is put some sort of grid across it in an attempt to make sense of it, create some order out of chaos, and perhaps gain some control over it.

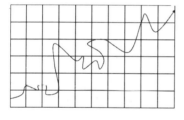 This book is such an attempt – to look at the change process in a relatively ordered and structured way. This isn't to say that change is a straightforward thing or process, rather that if you come at it in a structured and ordered way you may have a greater chance of dealing with the unpredictability and emergent themes along the way.

Format of the book

 Despite my tenet about the nature of the universe, in the actual setting out of the book I will try to approach change in a relatively orderly way, even if the nature of change itself is not so well planned.

The following is a straightforward model of change which captures both the task and process sides of change:

- *orientation* is the direction, positioning and preferences for change;
- *organization* is the more formal arrangements, systems and formulations of the change process;
- *mobilization* is the process of involving, engaging and catalysing the stakeholders affected by the changes;
- *implementation* is the process of carrying out or executing the changes;
- *transition* is managing the passage of people through the changes;
- *integration* is the embedding of the changes and the realizing of the transformation to produce a qualitative step change.

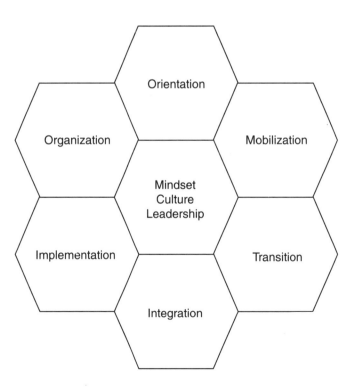

Figure 0.1 Tasks and processes in change management

Central to the change process and interactive at all times are the fundamentals of:

- the *mindsets* we have when we approach the change arena;
- the organizational *culture* within which we operate; and
- the *leadership* at all levels and at all stages to make the change a successful one.

This book comprises three parts. Part I sets the scene and direction and explores why we need change in the first place and how the way we conceptualize change affects how we manage change. Part II describes eight organizational change case studies drawn from different public and private sector settings. Part III looks at the process of change from different angles through a number of stages.

A useful accompaniment to change

Things which are put together are both whole and not whole, brought together and taken apart, in harmony and out of harmony; one thing arises from all things, and all things arise from one thing.

(Heraclitus, 540–475BCE)

A relatively straightforward model for approaching change 'in the moment' as you progress along the change process outlined above is one that I and my colleagues have tested over the years with various managers, and indeed with political leaders. There are many choices with many dynamics and I've found it useful to appraise any situation by applying this model of leadership of change (see for example, I&DeA, 2006; Leadership Development Commission, 2003).

- Managers are in the business of achieving certain outcomes or at least gaining tangible results. For this to happen there needs to be clarity about what it is that needs to be achieved and the structures, systems and strategies in place to attain that.
- No matter how well planned, structured and organized the intervention is it is unlikely to work unless you pay particular attention to three further aspects of the change process.
- The emotional component of change cannot ever be divorced from the change itself. To make a change is to disturb the equilibrium of individuals, of teams and of the organization. Indeed that is most likely what you want to do! As Heifetz and Laurie (1997) say, 'Followers want comfort and stability, and solutions from their leaders. But that's

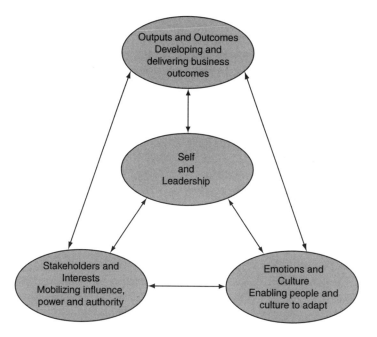

Figure 0.2 Leading outcomes, interests and emotions

babysitting. Real leaders ask hard questions and knock people out of their comfort zones. Then they manage the resulting distress.'

- There will inevitably be a number of stakeholders in the change – those who will have a view; those who will want a say; those who will be affected; those who will need to change or adjust; those who will win; those who will lose; those who will have an interest; those who will have some energy; those who will have some commitment; those who will not. Managing change successfully will need to take account of the voices and positions of these stakeholders, and agents of change will need to negotiate their way through the often competing and conflicting needs and wants of the stakeholders.

- Right in the middle are those who are the prime movers of the change – be they the CEO, the project manager, the change team or a team leader in a remote part of the organization. The way this person or group enacts the change is all so crucial. How much they attend to the task; how much they attend to the people; how much they plan; how much they allow to emerge; whether they're autocratic or democratic, authoritative or affiliative – all these things impact the probability of achieving successful outcomes, the level of communication and engagement with stakeholders, and the emotional well-being of those affected.

So we enter the world of change with a process, a route map; a set of key dimensions to be looking out for; an understanding that our own personalities affect how we respond to and manage change; and a flexible enough mind and attitude to allow for some emergences if not emergencies along the way.

PART I

1. Approaching Change

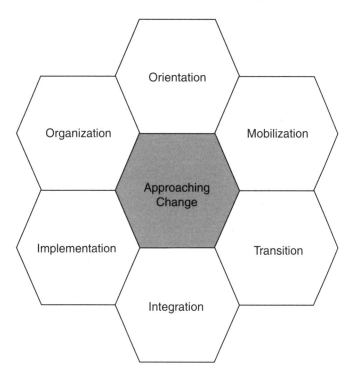

Wisdom lies neither in fixity nor in change, but in the dialectic between the two.
(Octavio Paz, b. 1914, Mexican poet)

Things do not change; we change.
(Henry David Thoreau)

Like a man who has worn eyeglasses so long
that he forgets he has them on,
we forget that the world looks to us the way it does
because we have become used to seeing it that way
through a particular set of lenses.
(Kenich Ohmae)

Introduction

We all approach change in different ways. That's partly because of our different personalities and it's partly because of our individual histories. We see the world in different ways and also react to it in different ways. The whole area of change management is one where these ideas have a particular relevance and resonance.

If we conceptualize change in a particular way then perhaps we will try to manage it in a way that is seemingly logical within our reality, whilst leaving no room for the idea that it's just our reality or certainly just one way of looking at the world.

In this chapter we will look at our assumptions about how organizations work and our assumptions about change. We can then see how these assumptions might shape some of the approaches to change, hopefully leading to a more comprehensive and flexible set of interventions.

Metaphors and paradigms

In *Making Sense of Change Management* (Cameron and Green, 2004) we drew upon Morgan's (1986) book, *Images of Organization* to suggest that we can view organizations in four different ways – and those different ways can lead us towards a greater understanding of organizational dynamics and what might or might not work when it comes to trying to change the organization:

1. organizations as machines;
2. organizations as political systems;
3. organizations as organisms; and
4. organizations as flux and transformation.

Table 1.1 Metaphors, beliefs and assumptions

Metaphor	Key beliefs	Key assumptions
Machine	Each employee should have only one line manager	The organization can be changed to an agreed end state by those in positions of authority
	Labour should be divided into specific roles	
	Each individual should be managed by objectives	There will be resistance, and this needs to be managed
	Teams represent no more than the summation of individual efforts	Change can be executed well if it is well planned and

Table 1.1 Metaphors, beliefs and assumptions *continued…*

Metaphor	Key beliefs	Key assumptions
	Management should control and there should be employee discipline	well controlled
Political system	You can't stay out of organizational politics. You're already in it. Building support for your approach is essential if you want to make anything happen You need to know who's powerful, and who they are close to There is an important political map which overrides the published organizational structure Coalitions between individuals are more important than work teams The most important decisions in an organization concern the allocation of scarce resources ie, who gets what, and these are reached through bargaining, negotiating and vying for position	The change won't work unless it's supported by a powerful person The wider the support for change the better this It's important to understand the political map, and to understand who will be winners and losers as a result of this change Positive strategies include creating new coalitions and renegotiating issues
Organism	There is no 'one best way' to design or manage an organization The flow of information between different parts of the systems and its environment is key to the organization's success It's important to maximize the fit between individual, team and organizational needs	Changes are made only in response to changes in the external environment (rather than using an internal focus) Individuals and groups need to be psychologically aware of the need for change in order to adapt The response to a change in the environment can be designed and worked towards Participation and psychological support are necessary strategies for success

Table 1.1 Metaphors, beliefs and assumptions   *continued...*

Metaphor	Key beliefs	Key assumptions
Flux and transformation	Order naturally emerges out of chaos Organizations have a natural capacity to self-renew Organizational life is not governed by the rules of cause and effect Key tensions are important in the emergence of new ways of doing things The formal organizational structure (teams, hierarchies) only represents one of many dimensions of organizational life	Change cannot be managed; it emerges Managers are not outside the systems they manage; they are part of the whole environment Tensions and conflicts are an important feature of emerging change Managers act as enablers; they enable people to exchange views and focus on significant differences

Source: Cameron and Green, 2004

Organizations as machines

This metaphor reflects upon the idea that an organization functions like a machine – if all the parts are properly constructed and connected and force applied in the right place and right direction then the machine will start to move and continue to move until it needs repair or replacement or encounters resistance. It feeds into the notion that it is possible to design a perfect well-oiled machine and to plan a change that will take the organization from state A to state B in clearly defined stages with the likelihood of success as long as everyone does what's in the plan. You can see this as the ideal metaphor for a simple project management approach to change where everything not only can be put onto a Gantt chart but everything and everyone will perform as if it really were a piece of machinery.

Of course the organization as a machine metaphor has its place because many products and services rely on clear, predictable, reliable and compliant processes:

> Fast-food restaurants and service organizations of many kinds operate... with every action preplanned in a minute way, even in areas where personal interactions with others are concerned... Even the most casual smile, greeting, comment, or suggestion by a sales assistant is often programmed by company policy and rehearsed to produce authentic results.

> (Morgan, 1986)

Organizations as political systems

This metaphor suggests that everyone who inhabits an organizational space is in the midst not only of a human system but one where there are competing forces and pulls on scarce resources and where different players have different degrees of power. It is the awareness and management of these forces and these players that allow work to be achieved. There is an understanding of who is an enabler and who is a disabler; who stands to gain and who stands to lose; who is supporting you and who might be against you. These are all factors you need to consider when you want to effect change and enter this reality:

> organizational goals, structure, technology, job design, leadership style, and other seemingly formal aspects of organizational functioning have a political dimension as well as the more obvious political power plays and conflicts.
>
> (Morgan, 1986)

Organizations as organisms

This metaphor posits that organizations are not discrete singular entities but are composed of a number of internal subsystems operating in an external environment and there are flows and interaction throughout. It is an open-systems approach as defined by Von Bertalanffy (1968). Operating within this metaphor an organization would be organizing itself around the changing environment – the more turbulence in the environment the greater the need for adaptability. Its internal subsystems – structural, human, managerial, informational – would all need to be capable of receiving data from the environment and other parts of the system and responding intelligently:

> organizations are open systems and are best understood as ongoing processes rather than as collections of parts... Thus, we see strategy, structure, technology, and the human and managerial dimensions of organization as subsystems with living needs that must be satisfied in a mutually acceptable way.
>
> (Morgan, 1986)

Organizations as flux and transformation

Entering into the metaphor of flux and transformation can be a disconcerting experience. We are moving into a world where we need to review our understanding of what an organization actually is. Rather than a machine or a social system of power bases, or an organism that interacts symbiotically with the environment, it is a place that has form and movement but events which cannot be predictable. There is a dynamism that can lead to equilibrium or disequilibrium depending on factors or 'attractors' at play:

organizations are characterized by multiple systems of interaction that are both ordered and chaotic. Because of this internal complexity, random disturbances can produce unpredictable events and relationships that reverberate throughout a system... despite all the unpredictability, coherent order always emerges out of the randomness and surface chaos.

(Morgan, 1986)

So we can see quite early on that when approaching change it may be that you are operating within one particular metaphor and you will attempt to enact change through that particular lens, regardless of the circumstances prevailing at the time. Or it may be that the organization is operating within one particular metaphor and will only accommodate one way of thinking about change and what needs to be done.

Paradigms of change

de Caluwé and Vermaak (2004) have categorized approaches to change in a somewhat different way. Reviewing the literature they have identified five different ways in which we can conceptualize what happens when we want to make change interventions (see Figure 1.1). They have given colours to each of these approaches. Some of them relate to the four organizational models and indeed to the three-ball model of outputs, interests, and emotions and culture that we met in the introduction.

Blue – change through design – is most often the one we see occurring in organizations. It is the project management approach to change and involves careful planning and detailed analysis before the change happens. It links quite well with the machine metaphor of organizations and leading outcomes in the three-ball model. It is very much about the rational way to enact change. If we have done the initial analysis well enough and can plan the steps and stages comprehensively enough then the inputs that we make will produce the outputs that we want.

Yellow – change through addressing interests – addresses the political aspect of organizations, recognizing that there are winners and losers in all change situations and that directly addressing the different wants and needs of the various stakeholders is a necessary element in getting positive movement forward in the driving forces for change and a useful way of attending to those forces that are restraining or against the change. This is most closely aligned to the political metaphor and also leading interests in the three-ball model.

Red – change through people – recognizes that change in an organization is predominately done through people, and for the outcome of any change initiative to be successful it will not only need to have addressed the concerns of the organization's people but to have engaged with them in order for new

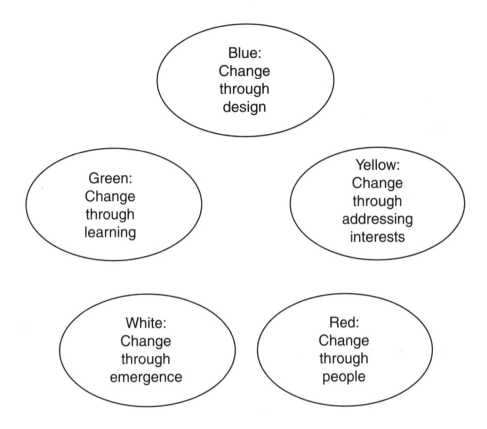

Adapted from de Caluwé and Vermaak, 2004

Figure 1.1 Five approaches to change

attitudes, skills and behaviours to have been acquired or learnt and certainly demonstrated.

White – change through emergence – is about creating the conditions for change to occur without specifying the exact nature of the changes. Drawing on the flux and transformation metaphor it suggests that we cannot logically and rationally design, plan and manage change in a linear way. What is required is an enabling environment, people to make sense of what is happening, and to spot where the organizational energy is and take steps to removing hindrances and obstacles. Perhaps requiring a leap of faith, this approach is based around the belief that systems will self-organize and, even in the midst of chaos, order and evolution will occur.

Green – change through learning – is concerned with change happening as a direct result of learning. Here we are talking about individual and team learning and also the concept of the learning organization. The key focus is on creating the environment necessary for individuals and teams to acquire the necessary knowledge, skills and experience to step into the new state and also how collectively the organization can embed any new knowledge for sustained performance. This also covers the single-loop and double-loop learning of Argyris (see Chapter 9) and ways in which the organization can monitor and evaluate itself throughout the changes.

Implications and different roles of leaders and change agents

Entering into a change process when operating within one of the four change metaphors or five paradigms has implications for how you construct your change process and what sort of role you need to play.

Using the machine metaphor or the 'change through design' paradigm will entail a rigorous project management approach with a leadership style that is one of architect and grand designer. The terrain is about efficiency and effectiveness of project planning processes and their well-oiled implementation. It's about an unambiguous mapping out of the plan to get from A to B and the careful planning, managing, monitoring and controlling of this process.

The political metaphor and 'change through addressing interests' will require a greater focus on managing stakeholders, the informal organization and ensuring that key players are brought on board, and potential winners are motivated enough and potential losers' needs are managed. The terrain for the change agent within this paradigm is all about power and the harnessing of it. The change agents themselves have to have perceived power as well as requiring powerful sponsors.

The organism metaphor requires the change agent to be monitoring the environment and taking the pulse of the organization. A key focus will be to create an enabling environment where people can learn to become responsive to the environment and the changes that are needed. It is also necessary to be aware of the process in order for responses, reactions and adaptations to be factored in as the change proceeds.

The flux and transformation metaphor and the 'change through emergence' paradigm recognize that change cannot be explicitly managed, but rather needs to emerge. The tensions, the conflicts and the hot spots within the organization and those on the boundary are where the change agent is focused. Once again the role is one of enabling emergence rather than directing and controlling it. The concepts of setting parameters, acting as a container and reminding people of core values are critical to this process.

The 'change through learning' paradigm draws on the key ideas from the organizational development movement originating in the 1960s, and the writers and researchers of the learning organization. Coaching, training and group and team facilitation are all ways of providing opportunities for learning to take place.

The 'change through people' paradigm is situated between the learning paradigm and the interest paradigm. It recognizes the need to include, involve and engage with all stakeholders, but principally managers and staff in order to create solutions that address the important issues. Given that change happens through people, winning the hearts and minds of the people is clearly a key factor in this. Affiliative and democratic management styles, human resource management and a collaborative culture are strong indicators of change agents operating within this paradigm.

Types of change

When approaching change it is also useful to be able to understand the extent of the changes that you are facing or are going to initiate.

Balogun and Hailey (2004) have segregated the nature of the change (incremental and 'big bang') from the end result (transformation and realignment), which results in four fundamental types of change:

1. *Adaptation* – is a 'non-paradigmatic change implemented slowly through staged initiatives'.
2. *Reconstruction* – is also a 'non-paradigmatic change to realign the way the organization operates, but in a more dramatic and faster manner'.
3. *Evolution* – is a 'transformational change implemented gradually through different stages and interrelated initiatives'.
4. *Revolution* – is 'fundamental, transformative change... but it occurs via simultaneous initiatives on many fronts, and often in a relative short space of time'.

Stace and Dunphy (2002) distinguish a number of levels of change on a continuum:

- *Level 1 – Fine tuning*. Addressing and improving the fit between strategy and the organizations people, processes and structure, for example, policy and process changes; continuous improvement teams; development of reward mechanisms and training programmes tied into strategy. Refining, clarifying, interpreting group norms and operating procedures.
- *Level 2 – Incremental adjustment*. Relatively modest changes around the organization in the light of external drivers for change. Typically changes involving strategy, structure and management process. Shifting the scale and scope of the operation; changing the product or service mix; addressing production inefficiencies; evolving the structure so that it's fit for the purpose of the refined strategy.
- *Level 3 – Modular transformation*. Major restructuring and realignment – focusing specific parts of the organization rather than the organization in its entirety. For example, a restructuring of the marketing department around distribution channels rather than product lines, or a decentralization of the HR department into business units (or more likely a centralization of HR into shared services); appointment of different key personnel; significant shift in the strategy of a cost or profit centre; introduction of new information systems that redefine key business processes.
- *Level 4 – Corporate transformation*. Fundamental shift in organizational business strategy involving new statement of vision, mission and/or values; major restructuring that changes the power bases within the organization; radical changes to structure, systems and processes across the whole organization; key appointments recruited from outside the organization.

Top-down/bottom-up – planned/emergent

Higgs and Rowland (2005) when looking at approaches to change categorized them along two axes: a uniform approach (top-down) as against a more disseminated or differentiated approach (bottom-up) and change as a predictable phenomenon (planned) as against change as a more complex phenomenon (emergent). Their research suggested that when there was large scale change an emergent approach was more successful – 'change is a complex activity' – and the more that change was planned as a simplistic machine metaphor then the less successful was the outcome. Indeed there was a negative correlation between effectiveness and the directed approach.

An emergent approach which was not overly dictated by top management was shown to be more effective than the other approaches. It is important to note here that the authors state:

> it was apparent that the emergent approach occurred in the context of a change framework that was more planned and structured. It is feasible, from this data, to propose that the emergent approach describes how change actually happens as opposed to how change is articulated.

What this could mean is that there's a crucial role of senior managers or change agents to frame the changes in an overarching vision or set of guiding principles but then to create an enabling environment for more local change agents to initiate and implement change. This recognizes fully the emergent nature of change.

Kahane (2004) looked at three types of complexity in change situations:

1. *dynamic,* where the questions is whether to focus on the whole system or just a specific part;
2. *generative,* where the question is whether to take a planned or emergent approach; and
3. *social,* where the question is who to involve in the change.

When there are low levels of complexity you can see causal effects more clearly and it is probably worthwhile focusing on one part of the organization at a time. If the strategic and operational environments are relatively predictable and have low turbulence then it is easier to plan a whole change approach. When the organization and its stakeholders are fairly well aligned and have shared vision, values and assumptions, then if the leader has his or her finger on the pulse, he or she can perhaps involve fewer people in the decision.

However, when the level of complexity is relatively high a different set of solutions might be appropriate. When the causal links are harder to make, a whole system approach might be indicated. If the strategic and operational environment is more turbulent or rapidly changing then a planned approach may not work so well, with a more emergent, organic approach to change indicated. The greater the level of complexity the more you might need contributions from around the organization – horizontally and vertically and from external stakeholders too.

Culture

Like individuals, organizations have their own identity – a way of being and behaving which differentiates them from other organizations. Culture is sometimes defines as 'the way we do things around here'. It captures the general feel, but culture is more complex than that. Trompenaars and Hampden-Turner (2001) see that:

> Every organization has its own unique culture even though they may not have consciously tried to create it. Rather it will have been probably created unconsciously, based on the values of the top management or the founders or core people who build and/or direct that organization… [you can] regard culture as referring to the shared assumptions, beliefs, values and norms, actions as well as artefacts and language patterns. It is an acquired body of knowledge about how to behave and shared meanings and symbols which facilitate everyone's interpretation and understanding of how to act within an organization.

If we want to manage change within specific cultures and if indeed we want to change the cultures themselves as a way of changing strategy or enhancing performance it is essential to understand what culture is and how culture itself changes.

Schein (1999) identified three different levels of culture with three different levels of difficulty in changing it:

1. *Artefacts* – are the things that you will encounter as you enter the organization and move around: what you see, what you hear, what you feel about the place. There may be car parking spaces reserved right by the front door for the most senior managers whilst other staff don't have any car parking at all. In others there are no allocated spaces. Some organizations will be very formal and people wear suits and smart clothes. Other organizations will be somewhat ramshackle and people work in jeans. Some organizations will be open plan, others will have individual offices. In some organizations drinks are 'on tap', whereas others will have pay machines.

2. *Espoused values* – at this level of culture you will find out some of the meaning behind what you have encountered, the organizational rules – either made public and lived, or tacit and followed as the norm. There may be a stay late culture even though the working times are clearly set out. There may be an acknowledgement that in order to get something through the decision-making process you have to network it round the key players first. Often

these rules are laid out in a set of organizational values and sometimes translated into behavioural imperatives. Everyone knows what the deal is. Sometimes the espoused values are not the value-in-practice (Argyris, 1990) and although teamwork is valued people are rewarded for individual effort; or integrity is a core principle but if you can get away with something then that's ok too.

3. *Basic underlying assumptions* – this level deals with the core of the organization's identity and can be related back to its history and how it came to be successful or survived due to the values, attitudes and beliefs of the key people in its history. Schein says, 'the essence of culture is these jointly learned values, beliefs, and assumptions that become shared and taken for granted as the organization continues to be successful. It is important to remember that they resulted from a joint learning process.'

Schein goes on to suggest that there are six different ways in which culture evolves. Some of these can be influenced by leaders and change agents and some cannot:

1. a general evolution in which the organization naturally adapts to its environment;
2. a specific evolution of teams or subgroups within the organization to their different environments;
3. a guided evolution resulting from cultural 'insights' on the part of leaders;
4. guided evolution through encouraging teams to learn from each other, and empowering selected hybrids from subcultures that are better adapted to current realities;
5. planned and managed culture change through the creation of parallel systems of steering committees and project-oriented task forces; and
6. partial or total cultural destruction through new leadership that eliminates the carriers of the former culture (turnarounds, bankruptcies, etc). (Cameron and Green, 2004)

There are a number of models you can use to help identify your culture. In the context of change the key point is using a model that illuminates where the organization is now and highlights a range of different cultures that might potentially better fit the preferred end state.

Harrison's four cultures

Charles Handy's four types of culture are well known – cultures based around the concept of power, role, task and person. He based his ideas on those of Harrison (1972):

1. *A power culture* is one where decisions are based around the sources of power within the organization and are often centrally controlled. From entrepreneurial companies to organizations with strong charismatic leaders the operating paradigm is based around ensuring you have the necessary people 'on side' and have the power and authority to make decisions relatively quickly without any particular bureaucratic hindrances.
2. *The role culture* on the other hand tries to fit the workings of the organization into clearly defined structures and roles, with accountabilities being aligned to the role and each person in their role knowing where they fit into the system. Large bureaucratic institutions would typically display the characteristics of a role culture.
3. *Task culture* is characterized by getting things done, and power and authority emanate from the ability to achieve the tasks in hand. What is rewarded is not necessarily position but task accomplishment, with systems and structures designed to enable that to happen. Project management organizations and meritocracies would often have a task culture.
4. *A person culture* would have the needs of the people pretty central to its ethos. This might be at the expense of the overarching aims of the organization. Academic or professional associations or partnerships might display elements of the person culture, with decision-making more consensual and explicit displays of power being shunned.

Goffee and Jones's 'character of a corporation'

Goffee and Jones (2000) teased out the differences in culture through looking at the degrees of sociability and solidarity within an organization. Sociability is the degree to which people are friendly with each other and work towards a social cohesion within the organization. Solidarity is in their words, 'a measure of a community's ability to pursue shared objectives quickly and effectively, regardless of personal ties'. The resulting matrix describes four possible cultures:

1. *Networked (high sociability, low solidarity).* The networked culture is one where cohesiveness across the organization is valued, with people encouraged to use both formal and informal networks to achieve their objectives and have a fulfilling time. Relationships form an important

part of the work environment, with the giving and receiving of support a key aspect.

2. *Fragmented (low sociability, low solidarity)*. The fragmented culture on the other hand doesn't value social cohesion and relationships within the work environment. People are that much harder to get to know (for friendship and for work accomplishment). Individualism, autonomy and freedom are valued, with individual efforts and achievements being rewarded.

3. *Communal (high sociability, high solidarity)*. The communal culture is both cohesive and collaborative, with people committed to each other, the organization and the products and services the organization provides. Often a very 'values-based' company with high levels of passion commitment and teamwork.

4. *Mercenary (low sociability, high solidarity)*. The mercenary culture is high on task focus, low on people process. There is little movement towards cohesiveness though high degrees of collaboration when a task needs achieving. As a result relationships tend to be transactional with people being used for their abilities to help the task, not for who they are. Communication will tend to be on a need to know basis.

An understanding of culture is crucial during change for three reasons:

1. knowing whether the culture you are in will be the best for the end state;
2. knowing how the culture will aid or detract from the change effort; and
3. being aware that the culture you are in will consciously or subconsciously shape your thoughts, ideas and decision-making processes when engaged in discussing change.

Personality

The Myers-Briggs Type Indicator (MBTI®) is one of the most widely used personality profilers in the world today. Based on initial work by analytical psychologist Carl Jung in the early part of the 20th century, the MBTI was devised by Katherine Briggs and daughter Isabel Myers and has been well documented and researched over the past 60 years.

MBTI® identifies four different personality dimensions (giving eight preferences) that we all use at different times. However, each person will have a preference for one combination over the others. This generates a possible 16 different 'types'.

Two things are of interest to us in exploring change: different personalities approach, address and respond to change in different ways; and organizations themselves can be seen to exhibit the personality traits of their individuals, which in turn affect how they will respond to change.

 Depending where you are on the extroversion–introversion dimension you will be more outgoing, externally oriented and more likely to be enthusiastic about getting things done (extraversion), or more likely to think things through, spend time planning and be more cautious about taking action (introversion).

Some of us will naturally be more practical and pragmatic, searching for tangible results and focusing specifically on what needs to be done. Others of us will want to see how things fit into the bigger picture, be inspired by clear visions of the future and be less interested in the detailed implementation (sensing-intuition).

The thinking-feeling dimension separates those who approach change in an analytic, logical, objective way ensuring that the business case sets out the costs and benefits clearly, from those people who make decisions based on their values, or the values of the organization. They will be sure to factor in the potential impact on the people that the change will be affecting.

The judging-perceiving dimension will sort people into those who are structured and organized in their approach to life and those who like to keep their options open and are more at ease in ambiguous and less well defined situations.

The net result is that those with particular preferences are more or less likely to react to change in different ways – whether they initiate it or whether they receive it.

Grouping the MBTI® types into four categories, we have four types of personality, which will be found in all organizations, exhibiting significant differences in behaviour:

1. *The thoughtful realists* will want to know why there's a need for change and will require some good evidence-based arguments. When initiating change they will adopt the view that if it isn't broken why would they want to change it. They therefore might be seen as more cautious when it comes to change; not necessarily against change, but needing some time to think it through.
2. *The thoughtful innovators* also need time to think things through but not from the viewpoint of retaining things, more ensuring it fits with the bigger picture, the wider strategy and that all the component parts are interlinked.

3. *Action-oriented realists* are happy to kick-start the changes and get things moving. Their natural energy and enthusiasm will create the momentum but they do need to have a clear focus and that focus needs to be practical and based on improving efficiency and effectiveness – what, why, how, who and by when would be typical questions.
4. The final group are the *action-oriented innovators* who are similar to the action-oriented realists in their energy and enthusiasm but also are more like the thoughtful innovators in their focus on the future and different ways of changing and the possible different scenarios.

The implications of personality run throughout all aspects of change and particularly in the initial framing of the change, the implementation plan and the communication to and engagement with the stakeholders. A project team with all four personality types would have the capability of being able to complement each others preferences – unfortunately there would also be the possibility of a recipe for conflict.

A particular case worth mentioning is the management team. Management teams both in the United States and the UK are skewed from the natural distribution of Myers-Briggs types within the whole population. Typically they are composed of more managers with the thinking and judging types. This can result in management teams making decisions about change by valuing a logical, analytical, 'business case' approach rather than spending time on how the decisions tie in with core values and what the impact on people is going to be. You can see the result of this in many change programmes across organizations today.

There can also be a tendency to want to close things down, having made a decision, rather than keeping options open and living with an element of uncertainty but also with the possibility of enhancing and improving on the changes. The most commonly used management tool is strategic planning:

> For the past 12 years, Bain & Company, a firm of consultants, has asked companies around the world how much they use such tools, and how satisfied they are with them. Its latest analysis, out this week, shows that strategic planning, used by almost four out of every five companies, is currently the most popular.
>
> (*Economist*, 9 April 2005)

Yet, all the evidence shows strategic planning doesn't work! 'Realized strategy is only 10% to 30% of the intended (ie planned) strategy' (Grant, 2003).

The realized strategy emerges from the way in which managers (change agents) implement the plans based on their own experiences, their capabilities, the capabilities of the organization and the extent to which external events let them implement the strategy. An individual's interpretation of a plan will be affected by all his or her experiential influences as well as preferences and attitudes and, of course, the actual resources available (as opposed to the planned resources) – together with his or her attitudes, experiences, etc – and the external constraints and opportunities prevalent at the time of implementation.

Groupthink

Irving Janis looked at significant decisions made by people in authority which turned out to be disastrous. He established that a phenomenon he defined as 'groupthink' occurs in certain situations and when certain criteria are met. He defines groupthink as 'a mode of thinking that people engage in when they are deeply involved in a cohesive in-group, when the members' striving for unanimity overrides their motivation to realistically appraise alternative courses of action' (Janis, 1972).

In hindsight decisions such as the Bay of Pigs invasion of Cuba, the Chernobyl nuclear plant disaster and the Challenger space shuttle disaster were seen to suffer from the type of decision making that Janis highlighted. More recently the fruitless search for illusionary weapons of mass destruction, the subsequent invasion of Iraq, and the consequent failure to predict and prepare for the ongoing insurgency has been blamed on groupthink.

Janis (1972) described some of the attitudes and behaviours in a group suffering from groupthink:

- an illusion of invulnerability, shared by most or all the members, which creates excessive optimism and encourages taking extreme risks;
- collective efforts to rationalize in order to discount warnings that might lead the members to reconsider their assumptions before they recommit themselves to their past policy decisions;
- an unquestioned belief in the group's inherent morality, inclining the members to ignore the ethical or moral consequences of their decisions;
- stereotyped views of enemy leaders as too evil to warrant genuine attempts to negotiate, or as too weak and stupid to counter whatever risky attempts are made to defeat their purposes;
- direct pressure on any member who expresses strong arguments against any of the group's stereotypes, illusions, or commitments, making clear that this type of dissent is contrary to what is expected of all loyal members;

- self-censorship of deviations from the apparent group consensus, reflecting each member's inclination to minimize the importance of his or her doubts and counterarguments;
- a shared illusion of unanimity concerning judgements conforming to the majority view (partly resulting from self-censorship of deviations, augmented by the false assumption that silence means consent);
- the emergence of self-appointed 'mindguards' – members who protect the group from adverse information that might shatter their shared complacency about the effectiveness and morality of their decisions.

Summary

When we approach change we do so with a particular mindset of how change will work. By using Morgan's metaphors and de Caluwé and Vermaak's paradigms we can begin to understand some of our own assumptions about change and what might or might not be appropriate in this particular organization for this particular change. The most appropriate of Morgan's metaphors are the machine, the political, the organism, and flux and transformation.

De Caluwé and Vermaak's paradigms are change through design; addressing interests; people; emergence; and learning.

Different researchers have identified different types of change. Balogun and Hailey identified change along the axes of incremental–big bang and transformation–realignment. This resulted in four types of change: adaptation, reconstruction, evolution and revolution.

Stace and Dunphy saw change on a continuum from minimal change through to a fundamental shift: Level 1 – fine tuning; Level 2 – incremental adjustment; Level 3 – modular transformation; Level 4 – corporate transformation.

Change can also be classified between planned and emergent with some management researchers highlighting the fact that the more complex the change the more likely that an emergent approach would be more effective.

Culture was seen as a critical component when managing change by identifying the current culture and how change can be managed within that culture; and by identifying the preferred culture that would more likely be able to sustain the new corporate strategy.

On an individual basis we saw how four basic personality types might approach and respond to change. On a team basis the cautionary phenomenon of groupthink was highlighted.

2. Orientation

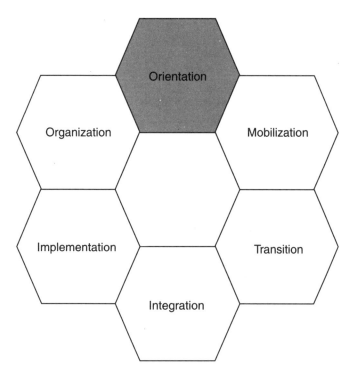

If we do not learn from history,
we shall be compelled to relive it.
True.
But if we do not change the future,
we shall be compelled to endure it.
And that could be worse.
(Alvin Toffler)

I cannot say whether things will get better if we change; what I can say is
they must change if they are to get better.
(G C Lichtenberg)

The future is ever a misted landscape, no man foreknows it,
but at cyclical turns there is a change felt in the rhythm of events.
(Robinson Jeffers, 1887–1962, poet)

The best way to be ready for the future is to invent it.
(John Sculley)

Introduction

This chapter looks at how the organization can become oriented towards change. We will first look briefly at the need for change and at how our approaches to change will influence our orientation; establish what some of the key things are that you need to do to orientate your organization to change: and discuss a number of frameworks which may help in this process.

There are many excellent texts on corporate strategy (Johnson *et al*, 2005; Sadler, 2003a; Thompson, 2005) and we will not be going over too much old ground but sketching out the processes whereby we can arrive at a place in time where we can consider our strategic options enough to plan and implement the change processes that the rest of the book will describe. It is important when you're stuck in the midst of change that you remember what it was that you wanted to change in the first place. The whole purpose of the change will be to respond to changing circumstances in the external or internal environment. We will not know whether we have managed change successfully unless we can compare what we end up with to where we started from.

The need for change

The need for change can come from within the organization or from without. It can be imposed by regulatory bodies or made necessary by the actions of competitors. It can emerge from a perceived need within the organization as a result of a planned process of strategic review, as a result of a crisis or a change in leadership. It is important to understand what drives change in order to ensure that the aims and objectives for change are well framed and referred to when initiating and implementing change. This section looks at the drivers for change and some of the tools and techniques used to ascertain what needs to change and why. Often the eventual success or failure of the change will be seeded in this initial analysis. Crucially, what needs to change emerges from these analyses.

Direction

At any discrete point in time, an organization will have a direction and a momentum of its own. How the direction and the momentum were arrived at can be traced back through various iterations of cause and effect, sometimes influenced by external events, sometimes by internal events, more often than not through a combination of the two. The direction of the organization will, in a rational world, be articulated through its vision, mission, objectives, strategy and tactics (VMOST). These might be quite explicit – published and in the public domain – or they might be implicit – inferred from the activities of the organization over time.

The organization's momentum – the speed at which it is moving towards its objective – can be seen to be a combination of three factors:

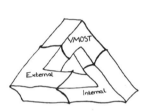

Vision

The organization's vision is a description of what it aspires to be, where it is heading and in the future where it wants to be.

Visions need to be lofty and strategic, compelling and engaging to have any worth for the stakeholders in the organization

Mission

The organization's mission defines what the organization's purpose is – its raison d'être – what it is in existence for.

Objectives

Aims and objectives are more specific realizable goals that can be quantified and qualified and which you'll know when you achieve them as they are measurable.

Strategy

The strategy is the plan of how you are seeking to get from here to there – the realization of the vision. This might be the actual plan or the perspective or position that you'll be adopting to realize the plan.

Tactics

The tactics are the shorter-term plans and behaviours for achieving milestones within the overall strategy.

Values

Not necessarily part of the VMOST, an organization's values are the set of explicit or implicit rules, conventions and guidelines within which people in the organization operate in order to maintain the organization's integrity in achieving its goals. Values reflect what the organization and its employees hold dear.

1. the clarity and congruence of the VMOST;
2. the ease with which the organization's external environment enables progress to be made; and
3. the efficiency and the effectiveness of the deployment of the organization's internal resources.

However, at some stage a need will arise to change the VMOST as a consequence of the external environment or the internal capabilities changing.

Mapping the system

By way of introduction to understanding the need for change it is useful to map the organizational system at a high level.

The external environment for any organization can be conceptualized by a number of concentric circles. Its immediate environment would be the part of the market it is in – which itself will be within the larger map of the industry. This would include its competitors, suppliers and any partnerships it has. Beyond this would appear the general political, social and economic framework at both national and international levels. Public sector institutions would populate a slightly different terrain, with less competition, no shareholders but many more interest groups.

An organization's internal environment would be all the things that go to make up the organization – its structure, its systems, its processes, its people, its financial resources, its culture, for example.

We could look at the external environment and at the internal environment to assess the need for change. However, looking at stakeholders as a separate dimension can aid the assessment process. A stakeholder is a person, group or entity that has an interest in or will be impacted by the activities of the organization either directly or indirectly.

As a change agent you may wish to take a long hard look at your organization and ask what shape it's in and what it's capable of doing and then look at the environment it finds itself in. Alternatively you may want to scan the external environment to assess what is happening out there and then look to see what needs to change in here. Of course in reality this is an iterative process and perhaps one of the essential skills of the change agent – the alchemy of internal and external transformation.

External environment

PESTLE

By understanding the wider context or bigger picture of political, economic, social, technological, legal and environmental (PESTLE) forces you will be able to see what possible future scenarios might be facing your organization. What this external analysis does is to scan the current and future environment to see what trends might impact on the strategic decision-making process. Under the various headings below are listed the sorts of questions that a leader or senior management team might care to ask.

Political

- What are the key policy directions of the current government (European, central and local) as it relates to our operating environment?
- What are the possible and likely alternative policy directions on the horizon (of this and any future government)?
- What are the effects of the wider global political environment?

Economic

- What are the current trends in the economy and how might they impact (favourably or adversely) on our organization, market and industry?
- What are the trends in individuals' prosperity and how will this impact on our current and future offering?

Social

- What are the social trends that will affect our customers and markets?
- In what ways will demographics, changes in purchasing patterns, families and community cohesion influence our strategy?

Technological

- How will new technologies help us get our products and services to market?
- What challenges and opportunities will technology present in the future?

Legal

- Given current and emerging trends in national and international legislation, what do we see as the most significant factors?
- What are the internal and external requirements of future legislation?

Environmental

- What environmental factors are likely to influence or require us to adjust our strategy?
- How are the unfolding environmental crises (potential oil shortages, climate change, etc) likely to impede our direction and what opportunities might arise?

The purpose of doing the PESTLE analysis is twofold: identification of general external trends or events that will influence the organization's ability to deliver; and identification of the key factors that will either enhance or impede any current or future strategy of the organization.

Having collected and sifted the data, you need to draw some conclusions as to the likely impact and the depth of impact. Similarly, if opportunities present themselves one has to assess the importance and possibility of grasping them.

Table 2.1 takes a snapshot in time of the PESTLE environment and applies it to three different industries. As you will see, different factors loom larger in the different industries.

Table 2.1 PESTLE snapshot

	Financial	**Pharmaceutical**	**Social housing**
Political	Looming pensions crisis Regulatory regime Security issues	Low-cost drugs for developing countries High cost of drugs for hospitals Security issues	Uncertainty around Government's ability to tackle housing crisis
Economic	Increasing household debt House prices continue to rise	More money to purchase life style	House prices continue to rise Lack of affordable housing
Social	Increased public sophistication Family breakdowns Student debts	Shift towards alternative medicine Movement towards food as a channel for taking medicine	Ageing population requiring more residential care
Technological	Greater ease of access to online accounts Greater potential for fraud	Continuing development of efficient and effective production methods	Systems improvements to allow for internal efficiencies and better customer service
Legal	Increased regulatory framework	Increased regulatory framework Rise in compensation culture	Increased regulatory framework
Environmental	Ethical investment	Ethical issues around drug testing	Greener house building

Key questions to ask in each case would be:

- What is the meaning of this?
- What is the probability of this?
- What is the likely impact of this?
- What are the implications of this, on revenue and/or on costs?
- How might we respond to this?

Industry, competitor and market analysis

The next part of the jigsaw is to look at the immediate operating environment. By this I mean the industry you are in and the competitors that are there or may well be there in the future. As an aside, managers within the public sector or not-for-profit organizations would still benefit from doing this analysis, though they may prefer to use different terminology. Increasingly the boundaries between public and private are being eroded and for better or worse managers need to be able to operate across these boundaries.

What we are looking at in terms of change are a number of things. First how the macro-environment might impact the industry; second how the different constituent parts within the picture might be acting and reacting now and into the future; and third how the overall structure of the industry might change.

You may also wish to conduct a market analysis to ascertain where you should be focusing your efforts. Principally, in any given situation you will have a number of options:

- to focus on current products and services in current markets;
- to expand your current products and services into new markets;
- to develop new products and services for current markets; and
- to develop new products and services in new markets.

Responding to any and all of these options will mean adapting something in your organization. Indeed, only if in the first option there were no changes in customer expectations or buying patterns; there were no changes in competitor activity; there was a stable economic environment; and there was a stable equilibrium within the organization, would you not need to make any changes.

Scenario planning

As we scan the environment and scrutinize our particular operating environment for what might happen in the future we'll note that there are some things that we're pretty sure will happen while other things might have some chance of happening. With others, they may or may not happen – we don't know the probability. Each will have different meanings when viewed within the overall context of the future. Rather than take a view on just one set of circumstances coming about and planning for that, it can be useful to construct a number of different future scenarios and see how well placed the organization is to meet and master those.

Conclusion

An external analysis looks at the macro and micro factors that may or may not impact on your organization and its performance in the short, medium and long term. Having done the initial analysis you can then generate a number of possible futures that would suggest some of the scenarios that you may wish to plan for and exploit. Each of the factors that might impact your organization can be seen as a potential threat or a potential opportunity.

Internal analysis

We now need to turn our focus inside the organization to assess its current capabilities and to see whether it is fit for the purpose for which we want it to be.

There are a number of ways to look at an organization's efficiency and effectiveness:

- track and map the value chain and identify areas of misalignment or under-performance;
- assess the level of resources that the organization has in terms of its financial, physical, intellectual capital, human, customer and social capital; or
- identify the organization's core competences.

In *Making Sense of Change Management* (Cameron and Green, 2004) we suggested that:

> the McKinsey 7S model is a rounded starting point for those facing organizational change. This model of organizations uses the same metaphor, representing the organization as a set of interconnected and interdependent subsystems. Again, this model acts as a good checklist for those setting out to make organizational change, laying out which parts of the system need to adapt, and the knock-on effects of these changes in other parts of the system.

The 7S categories are:

1. Staff – important categories of people within the organization, the mix, the diversity, retention, the development and the maximizing of their potential.
2. Skills – distinctive capabilities, knowledge and experience of key people.
3. Systems – processes, IT systems, HR systems, knowledge management systems.
4. Style – management style and culture.
5. Shared values – guiding principles that make the organization what it is.
6. Strategy – organizational goals and plan, use of resources.
7. Structure – the organization chart and how roles, responsibilities and accountabilities are distributed in furtherance of the strategy.

In looking at what core competence and distinctive capabilities the organization has, the 7Ss are a useful way of assessing the infrastructure of the organization as it is now and what it needs to be like in the future in order to maintain or attain a competitive advantage or sustained effective performance.

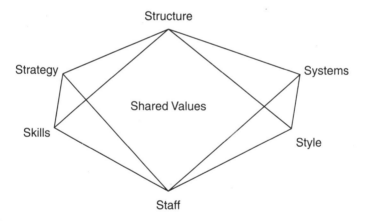

Figure 2.1 McKinsey's 7S model

Strategy, structure and systems are more tangible and are sometimes the ones that people concentrate on when managing change. If there are problems managers often want to change the strategy, or upgrade the system or restructure. The beauty of this model is of course the inter-connectedness – if you change one thing it affects all of the others, and then in turn they interact with the external environment.

The internal analysis is the mirror side of the external analysis. It looks at where the organization is currently, either in its capability of maintaining or improving performance in relationship to furthering its strategy, or where there is malfunction or unease. In the same way that the external analysis reveals opportunities and threats the internal analysis reveals strengths and weaknesses.

Stakeholder mapping and analysis

In our assessment we have been looking at forces, situations, scenarios, competencies, structures and the like. This can be a heady mix, but what they all have in common is people. People will overlay or underpin all of these elements. Whether they are politicians or the general public; the executives or the sales force of the competitors; your staff or your management; the shareholders or the customer; the sponsors or end user – each of these will have a stake in your organization's future. They will have an interest, they may have a voice, they will have some needs and some wants. One of Lewin's (1951) insights was that in human systems there are forces at play, and generally these forces can be identified when you begin to look at where the various stakeholders are sitting in relationship to the changes envisaged.

The purpose of stakeholder mapping and analysis is to bring these often disparate interests into focus and establish what they want from any change, how they may be affected by the change and how they may be managed through the change.

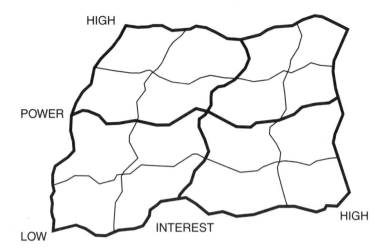

Figure 2.2 Power and interest matrix

At this stage identifying and then placing stakeholders on a matrix as shown in Figure 2.2 is a useful exercise. It is really establishing the levels of interest and importance in any situation, or their general feelings and behaviours towards the organization. One axis has the degree of positive attitude or interest from very positive to very negative; the other axis charts the level of power and influence. There are three important considerations when you undertake the mapping:

1. Segmenting everyone into stakeholders can be an inexact science. When it comes to change you might want to differentiate some staff from others, indeed some managers from others.
2. In order to place stakeholders on the matrix you need to establish where they are – what their attitudes really are, rather than just surmising.
3. Remember that those stakeholders with little current interest or power may well still be important, either because you have social or corporate responsibilities to address the needs of those without a voice, or they will emerge as people who find some power and some interest when you start to make your changes.

SWOT analysis

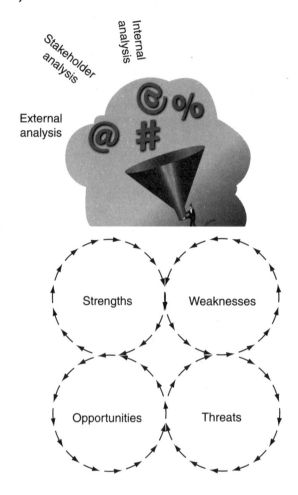

Figure 2.3 SWOT analysis

Looking at the external and internal analyses, you will have generated a set of potential opportunities in and threats from the environment, and some strengths and weaknesses in the organization. You will have discussed the attitudes of your stakeholders and therefore know their views on the current situation and the future. You will have identified various future scenarios which necessitate changes to the organization.

The point of a SWOT analysis is to ensure that key strengths and weaknesses within the organization, and key opportunities and threats from without, are considered, prioritized and addressed. One of the main aims is to identify whether or not there is an imbalance between an organization's current capabilities and future needs.

The strengths and weaknesses will relate to the internal aspects of the organization. They are those aspects that your organization has more ability to influence. In contrast, the opportunities and threats are those aspects in the external environment over which you might have a limited degree of influence, you cannot control but which will have an impact on your organization. Once the points have been entered into the matrix the organization's position and potential may be analysed.

The principal idea, in terms of strategy formulation and strategic positioning for the future, is to maximize the strengths of the organization in relation to potential opportunities, whilst minimizing the weaknesses and threats. It is important to remember, however, that strengths, weaknesses, opportunities and threats are relative concepts, relative, that is, to the whole organization's efficiency and effectiveness.

You should by now have a clearer idea of where the organization is in relation to its internal performance and its ability to operate in its external environment, and you will have a good understanding of future challenges and possible scenarios. This in turn will lead to your reviewing your VMOST and creating an agenda for change.

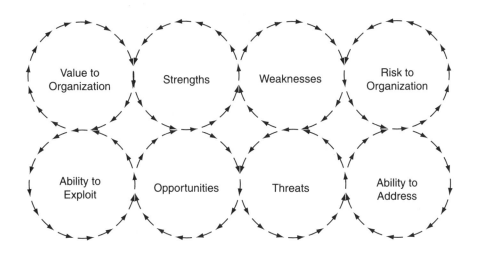

Figure 2.4 SWOT assessed

It is important to re-emphasize just why we've done the analysis in the first place. It identifies:

- the ways in which your external operating environment will change;
- possible areas that can help profitability and areas that will hinder;
- what you're good at now and what you're capable of developing; and
- areas where you either need to improve or mitigate the effects of poor performance.

In summary, it gives you the baseline from which you need to change and gives you a wealth of ideas on what to change and in which direction to go.

Change formula

Beckhard and Harris (1987) developed a change formula which identified the factors that need to be in place for change to occur:

$$C = [D \times V \times FS] > R$$

where:
C is the change that will occur;
D is the level of dissatisfaction with the status quo;
V is the desirability of the proposed change, the end state or vision;
FS is the first practical steps of the change; and
R is the resistance to change.

Although very simple, the formula does capture the essence of many a change project. Indeed if ever your change initiative is stalling, a quick check of the status of the factors will reveal where the potential problems lie. As in any such equation the basic premise is that factors D, V and FS must be greater than the resistance or cost of the change for progress to occur.

The multiplication signs imply that if any one factor is not present (ie zero) then the change effort itself will definitely be faltering as the product of the equation will also be zero. So if there is very little dissatisfaction with the status quo, or if there is no compelling vision, or if there is no clearly under-standable plan then momentum is unlikely to build.

Beckhard and Pritchard (1992) later added a further factor of believability (credibility that there's something wrong with the status quo, that the new vision is realistic and there are cogent plans in place) and De Woot (1996) added the concept of capability (the organization has the means to make the

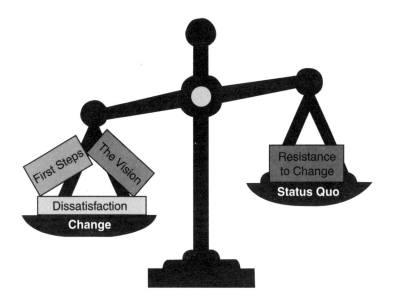

Figure 2.5 Balancing the equation

change). From my own work with organizations going through rapid change, I would also add capacity (the resources available).

Dissatisfaction with the status quo

 When we look at the organizational case studies in Chapter 3, we see that they all had significant internal or external drivers for change, or that the change emerged from a continuous process of engagement and dialogue with stakeholders (principally customers/end users and staff).

Each had taken the chance to formally or informally review the changing nature of their operating environments and assess their internal capability to maintain momentum or change direction. Typical questions which were explicitly or implicitly asked were:

- What are the significant trends in the PESTLE environment and how do we factor them in to our worldview?
- What are the short to long term challenges emerging in our immediate operating environment and how shall we respond?
- What are our customers or clients telling us they want and what do we need to do to meet these requests?

- What are our key stakeholders telling us and how can we respond?
- What are our core competencies and how can we improve on them?
- Where are the areas of internal risk and what are we going to do about them?
- Are we on purpose, both externally (mission) and internally (values)?

In Beckhard's terms we are looking at a felt need to change, either because something right now is causing discomfort, or something looming will. There may be a preferred way of doing things that has been spotted or an opportunity emerging. Our stakeholders may well have said they are dissatisfied or want something better. All these in effect are saying we are motivated to move from where we are. It is not necessarily saying that we definitely know where we want to go.

Vision, mission and direction towards the end state

Each of the case study organizations wanted to create or continue to create something that was 'fit for purpose' and was motivating and exciting to be part of. What they all had in different degrees was a real sense of where they were in terms of immediate strengths and possible weaknesses. They also had a clear understanding of some of the internal and external forces that were either shaping the way they were thinking or needed to in the future. They had an emerging sense of where they needed to be. For some this formed into a clear vision, for some a sense of direction. Some, as we shall see in the next chapter, had a specific plan of how to move the organization, others set off without this detail. But what each organization did have was a set of values they wanted to adhere to in the process of getting from here to there:

> We started the journey armed with two essentials – a route map and a compass. The map showed the point of departure and the destination, with all the stops in between and the nature of the tasks to be performed at each stop. Our compass kept us on track.

Once you've decided on a specific change that has a clearly defined outcome (for example, a systems change or a restructure) then you are more likely to be able to use the analogy of needing a route map that can specify different inputs which will result in specific outputs. A compass on the other hand is useful when you have the general direction but aren't necessarily sure on the exact nature of the end state. You just know that it's over that particular mountain range and in the direction of, for example, 'world class customer satisfaction'.

The importance of mission and vision

When I became Director of Strategy for IBM, the communications department came to see me almost immediately and said, 'We need a mission and vision statement for publication in the annual report. Will you help us?' Being new in the senior planning job, I said 'Ok, let's work on it.' And we worked and worked and finally produced a statement that was printed in the 1990 annual report. It's absolute trivia. Why? Because there was no involvement of the CEO. There was no involvement of top management. There was no involvement of people in the company...

We changed CEOs in early 1993. The new CEO, Lou Gerstner, called me up on his first day and said, 'Let's talk about strategy.' I went to see him with a long list of strategic issues that had to be dealt with, headed by the topic of vision. He responded, 'Let's not worry about vision for now, let's get right down to the issues – the problems that are making this company a poor performer. Let's get to profitability, our software and our hardware architecture, and the guts of our distribution system.' And so vision got scratched off the list.

I think you know what happened next. Last July, Lou Gerstner told the press, 'the last thing the IBM Corporation needs now is a vision'.

(Pete Schavoir, Director of Strategy, IBM)

(Of course, he changed his mind three years later: 'What IBM needs most right now is a vision.' March 1996, Louis V Gerstner)

What is the purpose of a mission and a vision? Well, on a simple level they tell everyone inside and outside of the company where you want to be; what your ultimate aim is. The organization's mission or purpose is to state what business you are in, and the values state what's important to you. The vision is the overarching direction and ultimate goal you are heading for. In that sense it's an excellent tool for orientating the organization and starting the process of change. But what we will see in the case studies is that generally 'the vision thing' came after the change process had started. It was only one component of the package, and for some it acted as a summary of what had been agreed beforehand and for others it acted as an inspiration for what the organization could be.

Although most organizations now have mission and vision statements, often combined, there has been little research into the effect they have on organizational performance. Certainly those involved in developing the statement report back a sense of purpose and motivation from the process. In the case studies, where a statement was produced it certainly had the effect of engaging stakeholders.

Sidhu (2003) found in the Netherlands that mission statements can lead to superior performance. Bart *et al* (2001) had previously found similar results in that mission statements are correlated positively with:

performance and make a positive contribution towards it. Thus mission statements matter! However, for a mission to be successful there are several provisos. Ultimately, it must have the proper rationale, contain sound content, have organizational alignment and bring about sufficient behavioural change in the right direction. To get the maximum effect out of a firm's mission requires that a number of intermediary variables be properly managed. Only when employees feel the heat of the mission or have a sense of mission, will they be in a position to execute and implement it with profound passion and resolve.

Force field analysis

As part of Lewin's model of organizational change in which he said you needed to unfreeze the current situation, make the changes and then refreeze the organization, he highlighted the importance of spotting and working with the forces at play. In order to do this he devised his force field analysis. Starting from the premise that any given present situation represents equilibrium between forces driving change and forces resisting change, which are in tension (ie, a force field) the point is to identify those forces, their direction, nature and strength, and how they can be modified. This is an effective tool in change situations as it helps picture 'the whole' system at play. One of the key aspects is that you work on both sides – the driving forces, yes, but also those restraining forces.

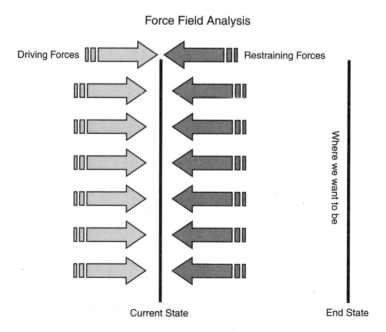

Figure 2.6 Force field analysis

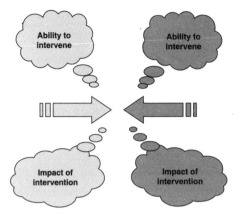

What we can see appearing is the desire to move away from the current situation and the need to have an understanding of the end state to which you have to be moving. When you start taking the first steps to increase the driving forces and reduce the restraining forces you will get movement towards the end state.

There are a number of stages to the process:

1. Make a clear statement about where you want to be or your outcome.
2. Identify and list all those elements that are driving forces, and restraining forces. These are likely to include personal, interpersonal, group, inter-group, cultural, administrative, technological and environmental forces. (Make sure you include yourself!)
3. Analyse each of the forces. How influential/strong are they and have you any control over them? What are the connections between the forces, eg if you influenced one would it affect another? Rank those that you can influence in order of importance. Identify practical actions that you could take which will build on driving forces, and reduce resisting forces. It is important to note that building the driving forces alone will generally have the effect of increasing the resisting forces. A classic example of this is increasing management force in an industrial dispute, which will normally have the effect of increasing union/staff resistance. A government taking an intransigent line during a fuel shortage crisis will increase resistance! At this stage it is often the case that managers discover that the outcome identified at the beginning is too large scale and complex to deal with in one analysis, and the individual 'forces' have their own force fields to be identified.
4. Develop a detailed action plan with target dates. Remember that making small steps on a number of fronts is usually more effective in the long run than trying to achieve too much in a short space of time.

From > To analysis

From > to analysis is a technique designed to help bring into focus the possible consequences and actions resulting from adopting one strategy rather than another. It helps to simplify strategic choices in the change process to enable clear business decisions to be evaluated and taken.

It primarily contrasts existing and potential future characteristics of the organization and encourages evaluation of the consequences of alternative actions. It is particularly useful when sketching out the intended future state to get a clearer picture of that state, and also to ensure that there's shared understanding between the initiators of the change. It is also a way of engaging with stakeholders either to start the mobilization and engagement process or to involve them in deciding what the future will look like. Finally, it is an important tool in beginning to flesh out a set of objectives and supporting activities necessary for the change to happen.

At this stage a preliminary exercise is useful to ensure that the orientation is correct by defining what the current situation and the preferred future state are. The level of detail of this analysis will vary according to the type of change. A business process change may have to define exactly the nature of the end process so that software can be written to deliver the process. A restructuring may be detailed to an outline level – perhaps the top two tiers – so that people know in general what the new departments are, but the actual working through of the finer detail of job roles and accountabilities may be best left to local line managers. In culture change, where the new culture is defined as primarily one of enhanced customer service, this may well start with a statement of guiding principles but these will need to be interpreted very differently in different parts of the organization with different segmented customers.

Table 2.2 Developing more autonomous business units designed to deliver enhanced customer service

From	>	To	Consequences	Actions
Functional structure	>	Business unit structure	More results focus Recruitment of business managers Changes in reporting systems	1. Cost centre management 2. Decentralized HR or shared services? 3. Balanced scorecard 4. …
Poor customer service	>	Outstanding customer service	Customer service revolution Training budget Greater consultation	1. Training programme 2. CRM system 3. Account managers 4. …
Internally focused	>	Market focused	Reorientation of services Joint planning Outcome focus	1. Re-engineering 2. Market segmentation 3. Sales force training 4. …

Approaching change

If we look at our approaches to change from Chapter 1 we see that the different approaches will have different things to say about orientating for change.

The machine metaphor assumes that those in charge will design the process that will have a clear direction and be able to formulate a plan that will simply get us from A to Z, the final destination. The design process will probably follow straightforward analytic lines – external and internal analysis, assessing strengths and weaknesses and generating strategic options through a rational problem-solving decision-making process. Once the direction or end state has been decided then it really is just a problem to be solved as to how to carry it out. Any hurdles in the way can be resolved in technical terms and the human side of change doesn't figure too much in the thinking.

The political metaphor will involve considerably more discussion and negotiating a way through the various stakeholder groups and communities of interest. It will be no use in setting out in a particular direction unless there is a real sense that the key players are 'on board' with the idea. The more you can factor their ideas into the final direction then the more confident you can be of a successful change process. The change is not seen so much as a technical problem to be solved as a coalition of the willing.

 The organism approach to change would suggest a more ongoing responsiveness to external conditions, emerging needs and internal dysfunction, so a final destination might not be fully envisaged, although various organizational imperatives might emerge as the key issues that need to be worked on. Given that the health of the organization is at a premium, a lot of effort would be made in ensuring there was healthy functioning across the organization as a whole and especially at its boundaries. The direction could well be in making the organization better, more responsive, more effective, maximizing its potential in the now rather than a theoretical end state.

Like the organism metaphor, an organization immersed in the flux and transformation mindset is more likely to be focusing on themes emerging within the present rather than the future. Effort would be put into building capability and capacity and enabling the organization to respond to and harness environmental changes and to spot areas of movement, improvement, creative tensions and innovation hot spots and blow on those particular emerging embers.

In terms of de Caluwé and Vermaak's paradigms of change, we can see that the orientation process would take different paths depending on which paradigm you were operating from. So the blue (change through design) would follow similar lines as the machine metaphor in using strategic analysis and a project and programme management mindset and toolkit. The yellow (change through addressing interests) would be similar to the political metaphor in bringing together different interests groups and power-broking agreement. The white (change through emergence) would involve a greater collaboration with perhaps future search conferences, open space meetings and self-organized task groups looking into areas of special interest:

> *Open Space* technology is 'a whole system participative work approach... enabling participants to define their own agendas and focus on the issues they consider most important. It relies on four basic principles: Whoever comes is the right person; whatever happens is the only thing that could have; whenever it starts is the right time; and when it is over, it is over.'
>
> *Future Search* is a 'large-group intervention method developed by Weisbord and Janoff which aims to create a vision of a desired future for a department, company or community. It explores possible agreements between people with divergent views and interests, and helps them to search for common ground and plan consensually. This approach is particularly suited to addressing complex problems within large systems.
>
> (Huczynski, 2001)

Red (change through people) would probably use a variety of techniques depending on the industry and the prevailing company culture. Typically organizations operating out of this metaphor would have well developed HR processes and as such might well have processes of engagement to involve staff at critical stages of the change process. Early participatory workshops and employee reference groups could be a feature of the orientation process.

The green (change through learning) may well have previously invested in knowledge management processes tapping into the explicit and tacit knowledge within the organization, have installed feedback loops to monitor organizational performance and have ways of changing course as a result.

Summary

Before any change is undertaken it makes complete sense to undertake an appraisal of the organization and its operating environment. This would comprise an external and internal analysis together with a stakeholder mapping and analysis. The resulting highlighting of internal strengths and weaknesses, with external threats and opportunities, and understanding the needs and wants of stakeholders, should combine into an understanding of what needs to change in the vision, mission, and strategy.

Beckhard and Harris's change formula is a simple but practical tool to evaluate where you are stand in the change process:

$$C = [D \times V \times FS] > R$$

Where C is the change that will occur; D is the level of dissatisfaction with the status quo; V is the desirability of the proposed change, the end state or vision; FS is the first practical steps of the change; and R is the resistance to change.

Undertaking a rigorous analysis of both the external and internal operating environments will help you decide on the need for change but also help you articulate the level of dissatisfaction with the status quo.

Creating a clear vision and mission of where you want to go linked to rectifying the causes of the dissatisfaction is a crucial early stage in the change process.

Developing clarity of from where and to where you are moving (from > to analysis) coupled with a force field analysis will help set your direction.

Remember, the different approaches to change will dictate the degree to which you focus on a planned or emergent approach and the style you take: machine, political, organism, and flux and transformation metaphors; change through design; addressing interests; emergence; people; and learning paradigms.

Part II

3. Organizational Case Studies

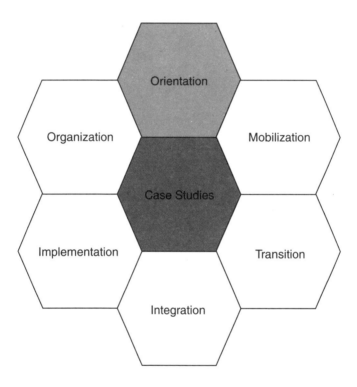

Introduction

Over the course of the last two years I tracked the management of change in seven organizations:

- the organizations were managing change relatively well;
- there was a mixture of large and small organizations;
- there was a mixture of public and private sector and some in between;
- there was a variety of changes being managed including a large scale global information system rollout, a Europe-wide restructure, a merger, a culture change, a start up and operational performance improvement;

- there was a variety of leadership styles; and
- there was a variety of change approaches adopted.

The organizations and their orientations

- Aster Group is a registered social landlord, very successful and expanding fast.
- The Institute of Public Health in Ireland was set up as a result of the Good Friday Agreement to foster better cross-border working on health matters.
- Biogen Idec is a global biotechnology company.
- The British Council has a worldwide presence in over 100 countries promoting education, development and the fostering of relationships between the UK and the rest of the world.
- The County of Aarhus is the largest county in Denmark, serving over 600,000 people, and has an innovative approach to managing change.
- A small entrepreneurial kitchenware company that has doubled turnover and increased profitability six-fold in six years.
- A primary school that has transformed itself into a highly effective school.
- A medium-sized financial services organization seeking internal realignment through restructuring.

Drawing in on ideas from the last chapter there follows a brief summary of how each organization oriented itself.

Aster Group

For Aster there were a number of internal and external drivers for change which shaped the future orientation. There was the move away from the local government culture and mindset towards a more entrepreneurial one; the untimely death of the Chief Executive; the significantly increasing competition in the sector; a continuing housing crisis in the UK with not enough new and affordable houses; and the Housing Corporation's decision to restrict the number of housing associations it did business with.

These factors led Aster to appoint a new chief executive who would meet these challenges and develop a strategy based on growth, building houses and securing efficiencies of service and economies of scale as it went. This was all underpinned by the need to create a culture that would underpin the delivery of this.

A number of growth strategies were considered but two stood out – organic growth through the acquisition of land to build new homes, and the possibility of partnering, merging or acquisition. Both needed to produce economies of scale and synergies across the organization.

This was later encapsulated in its vision – 'passion for excellence, pride in performance' – and its values: to be customer responsive; honest; open and true to their word; and fair to all.

Although quite clear about the direction, it realizes that sensitivity to the external environment is one of the key factors affecting its change process. In many senses it is operating under the organism metaphor.

The Institute of Public Health in Ireland (IoPH)

The IoPH was set up as a result of the Good Friday Agreement to foster better cross-border working on health matters. The new Chief Executive had the authority to develop the Institute within quite broad parameters. Through careful and constant networking with a multitude of stakeholders the Institute developed a vision for tackling inequalities in health across Northern Ireland and the Republic of Ireland. This vision has been a critical factor in its success, and the many innovative programmes it has set up to do this suggest that its primary approach has been one of change through learning.

Biogen Idec

A key aspect for Biogen Idec in its orientation was its ongoing commitment to constantly reviewing and refreshing its global development, manufacturing and commercial capabilities in pursuit of its vision of making advances in human healthcare. It was uncompromising in its challenge of existing processes and practices and therefore didn't shirk from asking the tough questions of whether or not its European structure and way of doing business was fit for purpose. If it was challenging in this respect it was also very clear in adhering to its core values in making those challenges and subsequent decisions – quality, integrity, honesty and team as a source of strength being paramount. So the combination of having a clear vision about excellence in its field coupled with an emerging dissatisfaction with the status quo led it to start a review process into its European structure, which was the first practical step on the road to change. The approach that Biogen Idec took was a relatively planned one, given that the nature of the change was one of restructuring, which had a number of employment law implications. Having said that, the process was well planned and structured, but the solutions (moving its European HQ and the setting up of a number of centres of excellence) emerged from the process.

The British Council

The British Council's change originated from a strategic review. The review revealed the need to design and install a new information system throughout the UK and the rest of its global operations. This review had identified a number of internal and external drivers for change which impacted on the Council and moved the thinking towards an integrated system that would reduce costs, enable open data flow across all parts of the organization and allow decisions to be made at a local level in a competitive environment around the world. There was also a felt need within the organization for these changes to happen as staff wanted to provide a service to clients and customers without relying on old systems that didn't communicate. Culturally the Council also tried to engender openness of communication, customer service and a learning environment. There was dissatisfaction with the way the systems created a feeling of separate businesses and functional silos. In addition to these changes linking directly to the new vision and strategy there were clear outcomes required:

- total organizational information and communication integration;
- the breaking down of functional and departmental barriers;
- the same consistent real time information for all areas; and
- the capability to analyse data in a variety of critical ways, for example, budgets could be viewed at any sector, unit, country or regional level.

The County of Aarhus

In Aarhus the organizational change was contained within the county's organizational model. The model created a common language and frame of reference; it established the links between different parts of the organization and the decision-making process; and it clearly articulated the county's political goals. The model laid out very clearly the underpinning values and their behavioural indicators that any management of change needed to abide by, namely dialogue, openness, respect, willingness to develop, commitment and credibility. So, change in Aarhus was driven by a negotiation through dialogue between the citizens, their political representatives, the end users and the professional staff. Change management would be done through a process involving openness, transparency, mutual respect and dialogue.

The vision translated into providing a high level of professional care in a coherent and integrated fashion. The main driver for change was the mismatch between a structure based on professional lines and one which had the end user in mind.

The kitchenware company

The kitchenware company, which was purchased by two entrepreneurs, wasn't punching its weight in the market. It had poor product lines, a bad customer fulfilment reputation, high central overheads and demotivated staff. These drivers coupled with the enthusiasm of the new owners led to radical changes within the company. Focusing primarily on customers the company recognized it needed to refresh its product lines, change its fulfilment practices, but above all focus on the customers and their needs. The change approach was one of top down but emergent as different opportunities presented themselves over the course of a number of years.

The primary school

The primary school had clear internal and external drivers for change in that, although performing satisfactorily, there was a real danger of becoming complacent and performance easing off. These drivers for change, the appointment of a new head with new ideas and the parents' successful campaign to get a new school all helped shape the nature and the direction of change.

The head began to address the current state of the school as part of the health of the whole community system. By seeing the school as one subsystem of the community she realized that all stakeholders needed to contribute towards its overarching vision and development.

The orientation of the school therefore was conducted with strong visionary leadership from the head but tapping into the communities of interest; a vision and values-making process involving all stakeholders; and continuing to focus on business as usual as well.

The financial services company

Through a process of diversifying some of its saving and lending functions and through the acquisition of a number of smaller businesses, the financial services company had developed a transition vision that it would 'transform itself from a traditional bank into a group of confident, successful and specialist financial services businesses'.

The increases in the scope, scale and complexity of its activities had led to the need to restructure into a clearly defined group of businesses.

It was envisaged that the new group structure would better enable the bank to achieve its strategic aims in three key ways:

1. The new group structure would facilitate the management of an expanding group of distinctive businesses. It would enable the acquisition and management of a number of separate business units with minimal disruption to other parts of the group.
2. The development of distinctive business units within new group structure would enhance individual business unit competitiveness. This would result from increased focus and commitment from all business unit management and staff to the delivery of the business unit customer propositions and achievement of competitive advantage.
3. In addition to improving the effectiveness of the management of the group business activities, the new group structure would facilitate the effective management by the group CEO of the relationship with its overseas parent and other relevant external relationships (Bank of England, the City, etc).

Aster Group

Introduction

The Aster Group is a thriving group of companies providing homes and housing-related services in central Southern and South West England. The Group has assets of over £420 million, annual turnover of over £65 million and employs over 680 staff. The operating companies own and manage over 15,000 homes and provide services to over 40,000 people.

Aster Group is one of the Housing Corporation's Lead Investors and provides development agency services to other organizations and the New Futures partnership of regional and specialist housing associations.

Aster Group operating companies have a substantial degree of operational independence but work closely together to gain maximum benefit from their combined strength and resources.

Residents and other clients play a strong role in influencing the operation, and surveys show that Aster enjoys high rates of satisfaction with the services it delivers, with around 90 per cent of tenants saying that they are very or fairly satisfied with their landlord.

 The strong growth over the last three years was recognized in 2006 when Aster Group was given the 'Beacon Company' award by the South West Regional Development Agency. It is the first housing association, and one of just a few not-for-profit organizations, to have been given this award, which 'brings together some of the South West's most forward thinking and ambitious companies to promote success and spearhead the growth of the region'. This status is given to companies that can demonstrate outstanding achievement across a range of criteria. In Aster's case the rapid growth and influence of the Group was a factor in its nomination. Other companies can turn to Beacon Companies for examples of leadership and business performance.

Housing Corporation Assessment for Aster Group

Viable

The Group meets the expectations set out in the Regulatory Code in terms of financial viability.

Properly governed

The governing body gives effective leadership and control, has a wide range of skills and experience and, supported by appropriate governance and executive arrangements, is improving its own performance and that of the organization.

Properly managed

The Group generally meets the standard expected given the context in which it works and the available resources.

Development

The association demonstrates a good performance by achieving or exceeding its annual targets, maintaining good progress against targets during the year and delivering quality housing that meets our standards.

(Housing Corporation's assessment, June 2006, http://www.housingcorp .gov.uk/)

History, culture, orientation

The Aster Group's history can be traced back over a decade when Sarsen Housing Association was born out of a housing stock transfer from the Local Authority. The Local Authority Director of Housing became the new Chief Executive and a board was set up comprising four tenants, three representatives from the Council and eight independent people from the business and community.

For five years the Association focused on delivering on its original promise of improving homes to modern standards whilst keeping rents stable. Sarsen was efficient and effective in its operation. As a result it was able to begin to generate revenue surpluses in 2004, three years earlier than envisaged in the original plan. Both the board and the management then realized that they needed to develop their strategy further.

The board and the Chief Executive quickly became more entrepreneurial and began to seek out opportunities for growth and development. So, for example, during 1997 they began new initiatives – 'care and repair' for elderly people, developing new homes outside their original base and putting their toe in the water of market renting being just three. This was evolutionary change but they were beginning to be more confident of their capabilities and began to ask the more strategic question of where they might go from here.

Aster was 110th in the league table of housing associations, with 5,000 housing units. A relatively medium-sized association, to be in the top 50 it would have to grow to 10,000 units.

Sadly the Chief Executive died suddenly in November 2001, sending a shockwave through the organization. The new Chair, John Heffer, had been in place just a week. Appointing an interim Chief Executive from in-house Aster began to look for someone to lead it who was entrepreneurial, pace-setting, had a track record but who would work with its values and its staff.

One of those short-listed – Richard Kitson – wanted to know from his side whether Sarsen was ambitious, keen, prepared to take calculated risks and adventurous. A match had been made.

Richard had experience within the public sector – leading and growing a local authority housing service, and within the housing association world – managing the fastest-growing region of a well respected national association with a long history of success, including managing large numbers of staff in an operation that was noted for its efficiency and its substantial development. He also had prior industry credibility as the President of the Chartered Institute of Housing.

Sarsen entered its second transition period as it moved further away from the local authority world, shedding a rather bureaucratic culture. One of the first tasks was to create a group structure to facilitate the growth that was the emerging strategic theme. One or two senior people left, of their own accord, and this provided the opportunity to recruit senior people with an ethos of not only delivering a stable high quality housing service but also those with an eye on proactivity, seizing development opportunities and the continuous improvement of existing services together with a move towards creating innovative new products and services.

The organization turned more outward, making connections, using its networks to get business, establishing a reputation with its stakeholders and attracting new blood into the organization.

A formal new group structure was created in the autumn of 2003 and a new top team was formed with new teams underneath them. Silbury Group had been launched.

An important focus was to increase the capacity and capability across the organization. This required shifting the culture away from the traditional local government mindset. New members were recruited to the Group board, which became a blend of the old and the new, and a management development programme was launched for the top 30 managers. Individual managers and groups of staff were asked what the key organizational issues were and this in turn informed the design of the development programme.

A theme throughout this period was the relative stability of the board. There was a clear demarcation between executive management functions (the management team) and the governance (the board) and working relationships were always excellent. The board did change over time as the Group grew. It had to cope with governance issues over an ever increasing range of activities – hence one of the reasons to adopt a group structure, which enabled the different companies to be managed and have effective governance. And of course the board sought to get the requisite variety of people onto it with a mix of skills appropriate to the businesses being overseen. Interestingly the board was not committed to growth for growth's sake. In John's words, 'We are not bothered about being big but about being the best, and if growth can add to economies of scale and synergies then so much the better.'

Drivers for change

There were a number of internal and external drivers for change:

- the continuing shift away from a local authority culture to one of an autonomous not-for-profit business;
- the untimely death of the Chief Executive and consequential re-evaluation of strategy and need to appoint a new chief executive;
- the Housing Association world continuing to grow with the creation of organizations receiving the housing stock of local authorities, a particular feature of South East and South West England. This change was significantly increasing competition in the sector;
- a continuing housing crisis in the UK with house prices increasing dramatically year on year and not enough new homes being built to satisfy demand;
- migration of older people to the South and South West of the country looking to retire with affordable housing but also the necessary services for their population group; and

- a pivotal event was the Housing Corporation's decision to restrict the number of associations it did business with.

Rather than invest in over 350 separate organizations it decided to restrict itself to investing in around 70. Silbury had been 110th in the league so therefore needed to redouble its efforts to grow. A number of growth strategies were considered but two seemed to be paramount – the development team had been acquiring land and building new homes and was continuing to prove successful at that. But the board also began to think in terms of partnering, mergers or acquisition. They considered a number of associations informally but there were obvious reasons for not moving ahead – too different geographies, unaligned systems and processes and strategies, and different world views. However they became a preferred partner in their own right, scraping in at number 69 out of 71.

The Role of the Housing Corporation

The Housing Corporation is responsible for investing public money in housing associations which are registered with the Corporation (legally known as Registered Social Landlords) to provide homes that meet the needs set out in local and regional strategies and, through regulation, for protecting that investment and ensuring that it provides decent homes and services for residents... to encourage innovation and good practice and to promote improved performance.

The growth agenda had been set and they started actively to seek out potential partners. They already had links with one similar sized organization and both Chief Executives, Board Chairs and Vice-Chairs had a number of informal meetings to see if there was a match. All were keen on exploring each other's philosophies and the degree of compatibility. This wasn't just six people, it was who they represented. The informal meetings became formal and then there was widespread consultation with all stakeholders – especially tenants' representatives and staff. Testway – the other association – set 20 criteria for the selection of a merger partner.

The two Chief Executives realized they needed to acknowledge that there would be winners and losers from individuals' and different teams' perspectives. This led to some tricky but open discussions – 'let's think about this and come up with an acceptable formula'.

They also agreed that a group structure would work best with a continuing fair degree of autonomy for individual businesses. All key players were involved and those people most likely affected were engaged.

As the grouping became more and more likely the meetings of necessity became more formal, but from the inception of the idea staff in both organizations were given full updates and asked to contribute their views. Managers recognized the need to disseminate information and build confidence throughout the new Group. So, when in April 2005 the grouping happened it seemed that no one really noticed – it was effected with the minimal degree of disruption. The Aster Group had taken off.

Following the successful grouping the board were becoming more and more comfortable with the decisions of the Chief Executive and fully supported him when, for example, he formed a working partnership with a black and minority ethnic housing association in an urban area – away from Aster's heartland. He also pushed for becoming one of the four strategic partners in an important sub-regional configuration of urban local authorities. Aster was bidding against national and established competition but was short-listed and successful, being described as coming with 'A fresh approach and a good team'. Currently it is a major player in the region and another housing association has since joined the Group.

Leadership

Although the previous Chief Executive had led the Association out of local authority control to being a stable housing association in its own right, he had done this with a rather autocratic management style. Richard Kitson was determined to move the organization away from that. A rather coercive style – useful in some situations – can lead to a risk-averse culture and create dependency upon its leader. Creativity and innovation can also be stifled. There were elements of all of these in the previous culture.

Richard managed this transition carefully. On the one hand he relied on voices from outside to feed back to staff and managers inside what sort of leader he was; and on the other hand he engaged in regular and open conversations with staff and all managers. Naturally they were apprehensive at first but, through staff briefings, conferences, small group and individual discussions, they saw that here was a man they could trust and follow, and who was open to ways in which they could contribute to the future.

His initial style can be described as pace setting – knowing where he wants to go, having the intellectual firepower to argue his corner, encouraging people around him to participate in creating the future, leading from the front and by example and taking people with him. What was interesting was how the culture as a result shifted from one of, 'We don't normally do this' or, 'I'm not sure we can do that' to one of, 'Let's try' and, 'I think we can win this contract.'

In the longer term Richard is aware that he needs to spread the leadership across the senior management more and down into the organization. His challenge is to sustain the success by becoming a leader who is primarily a facilitator or enabler and also to continue to build the leadership capacity throughout all parts of the Group. The relationship between CEO and Chairman has been a critical success factor. They share similar viewpoints and both operate on the basis of no surprises for each other. Once convinced of the other's arguments they are both willing to promote the arguments. The board seeks to challenge and test the ideas and suggestion from the management team and once satisfied that the thinking has been rigorous enough they tend to be happy for the managers to proceed.

The Aster Board mirrors the Aster GMT in that they are focused on longer term strategic issues rather than this year's bottom line. And as such the operating businesses have considerable autonomy in terms of day-to-day operations.

No shotgun wedding

Testway had a somewhat different route to the grouping. John Spens as Chief Executive had steered the association out of local authority control just four years before, delivery of a premier housing service to its tenants being a primary aim.

For Testway the first three years after the housing stock transfer was one of finding its feet, establishing its reputation and credibility and also, in a sense, discovering its new identity. By the spring of 2003 there was some pressure for change – managers and board members were beginning to ask what was next in the strategic picture. They recognized their vulnerability due to their size. The initial impetus of the transfer had made them fully aware that they hadn't transferred out of local authority control just to stand still. They spent some time with an external adviser working out strategic options for the future. Their deliberations started by taking a long hard look at their internal capabilities and assessing the current and future market and external environment.

Through a combination of an ongoing working party and a series of board away days they developed the following options:

1. Stay as we are.
2. Stay as we are plus increased development activity.
3. Stay as we are plus increased development activity plus acquiring other local authority stock.
4. Growth through merger.

They concluded that if they could find the right partner then the fourth option was the best.

It was at this time that the Housing Corporation announced its intention to limit the number of its strategic partners (external driver) and also, following a number of performance issues, it was decided to replace its development team (internal driver). Informal links were made with the neighbouring Silbury, which offered help resourcing the development function. Continuing in that vein of cooperation, the two Chief Executives started to seriously discuss the possibility of closer working between the two associations.

The grouping criteria were agreed and both parties looked at whether there was indeed a match. The other partner needed to be:

- of equal size (and equal partners);
- an active developer;
- high performing:
  - upper quartile
  - meeting Housing Corporation Key Performance Indicators
  - low rent arrears
  - efficient turn around of vacant properties
  - good repairs record
  - good rent collection;
- reputable (eg with the Housing Corporation);
- with a geography that would be different enough to avoid overlap but close enough to produce synergies;
- financially strong;
- with a natural synergy when it came to attributes such as stability, being a charity and having similar values.

The Testway board went through a rigorous process of analysis and assessment of the 35 or so associations within the distance specified and filtered them down to 10. A series of meetings and further appraisal reduced the possibilities down to just three or four. However, there was one clear front runner. The board were already witnessing the two CEOs working well together and trusting one another and they recognized that there was most likely a good cultural fit.

Staff and tenants were kept updated with open communication and consulted about all of the options. The grouping proposal went through the usual due diligence processes – assessing the financial, cultural, commercial and legal risks; the two Annual General Meetings; and a number of board meetings. The difficult issues were put on top of the table (not under the table!) and discussed, with a clear challenge on the tricky issues – 'What's best for the business?' The grouping was ratified. As a symbol of the beginning of the new organization and to demonstrate that it was a merger of equals a new name was given and Aster was born.

The transition period – one year on

Aster Group is now beyond the honeymoon period. At a high level there was a cultural fit – and indeed the set of espoused values are very much values in practice – but the devil will always be in the detail and differences have emerged. This is not surprising, given the somewhat different backgrounds, some different attitudes and different sets of competencies. So a period of learning how to live together was experienced. But, continuing the wedding metaphor, they decided against an exit clause or pre-nuptial agreement.

The glue in the first few months was the two Chief Executives (or rather the new Chief Executive and his Deputy Chief Executive). They kept the dialogue going as and when differences or issues emerged.

Aster's vision of 'passion for excellence, pride in performance' is encapsulated in its mission to be a leading provider of high quality affordable homes and services and to help create thriving and successful communities. Its business objectives for 2006–2009 are:

1. Achieving excellent customer and community focused services.
2. Delivering more new homes.
3. Strengthening the foundations.
4. Maintaining robust businesses.
5. Developing our people.

The Group has adopted a set of values that underpins how it operates. These are to be customer responsive, honest, open and true to their word and fair to all. Within this there is a strong emphasis in involving and responding to the needs of customers.

(Housing Corporation's assessment, June 2006, http://www.housingcorp.gov.uk/)

On a detail level the cultures, although similar, had different emphases. There were many more similarities than differences, but where there were differences they needed to be identified and discussed and worked through to reach a common understanding and an appropriate way of working together. There were good and bad aspects to each of the cultures, but there was enough openness for people to say, 'Hang on a minute, let's talk about this'.

Also there was a difference in life stage – one had been autonomous for almost a decade, the other until quite recently had still been wrestling control away from the local authority (which found it hard to relinquish control).

A number of binding and bonding interventions have helped the different companies operate alongside each other, managing the 'what's tight – what's loose' tension between each other and the centre. An expanded management development programme has brought the senior managers together on a number of occasions and there are clear signs that a new Aster culture is emerging.

Many staff – often the managers – have embraced the change whole-heartedly and have been focused on making things happen by just doing it. Others further away from the decision-making process felt it was more like the proverbial emotional roller-coaster. The pace of change was such that on an emotional level there were a lot of feelings to deal with and on a task level there were quite a number of things that needed doing or clarifying.

Whenever a new structure is implemented there are always issues around the difficulties of managing and control – where are decisions made, where the power and authority lie, who has clarity about roles and responsibilities.

What helped people during this time was the development and communication of a clear strategy, the reflection back of a core set of values that were role-modelled by senior mangers, a sequence of staff briefings and cascades and the establishment of an annual staff conference to celebrate success, involve and engage staff in the future direction and test out ideas.

It seems that there has been no period of consolidation – the Group grows, other partners seek to join and change continues at a similar fast pace.

Project management

Both the technical and psychological aspects of the project management of the grouping process were conducted with openness and no hidden agendas. A key question all parties returned to when there were difficult decisions to be made was, 'What's good for the business?' Staff were asked for their views and ideas about what form the partnering should take.

An external project manager was appointed who had the sponsorship of the two Chief Executives. The project manager was called in from outside for a number of reasons:

• the project seemed too big for anyone to take ownership of and do their business as usual as well;

- they wanted an experienced credible project manager for such a high-profile initiative; and
- both associations welcomed an objective third party.

The project itself was run along effective best practice project management guidelines with a detailed plan of activities, all tasks having a responsible person owning it and clear reporting procedures.

A key wish was for there to be limited staff upheaval, certainly no redundancies, and indeed with the growth agenda, promotion of cross-organization staff opportunities.

Terms and conditions differed in the different parts of the Group and whilst some integration has taken place many of the differences are actually down to the varied levels of maturity and development of the businesses and the fact that the same set of policies and procedures wouldn't necessarily fit across the whole. There no doubt will be convergence over time if appropriate. Part of the process is defining what is tight and what is loose – movement towards one integrated IT system makes sense; a coordinating HR function with semi-autonomous units in the businesses might also evolve. Financial control systems and diversity and equality policies emanate out of the centre – but financial management is left with individual businesses. A central tenet is to give as much autonomy as possible to individual businesses provided they perform against business plan and budget. Where there is scope for efficiencies and synergies, grab them.

Organizational development

During the initial period of change prior to the grouping, external consultants were brought in to help Silbury manage organizational change. As part of the mobilization process all managers and a cross-section of all staff were invited to give feedback as to how they saw the organization, what the key issues were and what some of the solutions might be. The following were the main themes to emerge from the discussion groups and interviews with managers.

Developing common purpose, values and shared understanding of objectives

Some managers and staff were very clear about what the Group's vision and values were. Others were not so sure. People needed more clarity about what the new organization would look and feel like in the future.

Developing a shared understanding of what sort of organization we need to build for the future

People saw the need to further develop the vision and values for the organization through greater communication and engagement, both vertically and across the organization.

Managing for growth

Balancing the drive for growth whilst maintaining and improving the level of current service emerged as quite a creative tension. Ways had to be found to increase management capacity and capability.

Balancing between managing and leading

Managers needed to shift the balance from managing the increasing complexity of the Group (planning, organizing, controlling and problem solving) to demonstrating leadership and strategic thought (through setting a direction, aligning people, motivating and inspiring).

Where do we need to innovate as managers/management team?

More creative and innovative ways of doing things were needed to get to grips with the challenges. That included creating an environment where some risk taking was more acceptable and mistakes were inevitable but could be learnt from.

Individual and collective energy

Managers needed to be able to match their efficiency (doing things right) with their effectiveness (doing the right things). As roles, responsibilities and structures change the challenge on an organizational level seemed to be, 'Where should managers' time best be deployed and how much can they empower their staff?'

Personal responsibility

Managers acknowledged the shifting culture and are generally and genuinely signed up to developing it and taking their part in shaping it. However, it might be difficult to step fully into the new role of manager and leader and even more difficult to develop staff to play their part.

Developing management and leadership capacity and capability

A series of workshops were designed to address these issues:

- to help managers share knowledge and understanding across the whole Group;

- to develop skills to better manage change;
- for managers to understand their management style and the impact it has on others; and
- to address the important and pressing issues arising from a dynamic and changing organization.

In addition three working groups were set up to:

- develop practical ways in which people will 'buy-in', own and act out the values;
- develop ways for managers to keep their 'finger on the pulse' – know the key issues emerging for staff and the organization to take action on; and
- generate ideas as to how people can take on responsibility and grasp opportunities.

Managers and staff were involved, in a variety of ways, with developing the ongoing agenda for change. In addition to the workshops there were staff briefings, staff discussion groups and a staff conference (which now continues annually) where the forward agenda was communicated, ideas generated, and potential obstacles highlighted and worked on collaboratively.

A key component of the grouping was the bringing together of all the managers from both organizations. They spent time together over two days addressing the following challenges:

- meeting and getting to know one another's organizations and ways of working;
- developing a shared view of Aster's strategic opportunities;
- identifying some of the practical synergies for individuals and constituent businesses; and
- agreeing key lines of ongoing organizational development.

As a result of the workshop three working parties were set up, initially with managers from across the Group and then involving staff. The key themes to be addressed were:

- *Direction* – guided by Aster's vision and values and taking account of the strengths and weaknesses of the Group, where would you want Aster to be in five years' time?
- *Improvement* – examine current service improvement practices to confirm, a) whether they are appropriate for Aster Group and, b) how they can better engage and be made more meaningful to staff and customers.

- *People* – taking account of the staff surveys across Testway and former Silbury Group, examine and made recommendations of what we need to do to make the Aster Group a better place to work.

At the time of writing a further housing association has joined and once again managers and staff have been enfolded into the Group. Roles and responsibilities, synergies and business opportunities were all discussed openly and frankly. Whilst still embedding the previous grouping, Mendip Housing Association approached Aster as it was desperately seeking a partner. It needed support, protection, guidance and advice. Aster GMT recognized the resource implication and recruited a dedicated person to deal with these aspects of the Group's development. The joining criteria were different for Mendip. Whereas Testway had a reputation for award-winning community development and Silbury had a reputation for development, Mendip had expertise in care and support and the elderly. The process was the same as for Testway/Silbury but was concertinaed into a much shorter timeframe.

A key creation has been the concept of the Aster Group Manager – someone who not only exhibits good management and leadership within his or her own area of the business but who has rights and responsibilities across the Group both at an operational level (for example, spotting and sharing best practice, efficiencies and economies of scale) and a strategic level (for example, shaping and responding to the external environment and key partners, contributing to leadership thinking and development of strategy across the whole organization).

The challenge for the Aster Group going forward is how to maintain momentum in its growth strategy whilst embedding the changes that have already been made; and how to manage change fast enough for the senior management but at the right pace for staff to continue to perform effectively and provide an excellent service to their customers. Of course, since Aster is now the largest in the South West the relationship with the Housing Corporation has changed from one where it was needing to seek attention and probably had very limited influence, to one where it plays an important part in the Corporation's plans and as such could always pose a risk if it doesn't perform. Aster very much sees itself as a true partner with the Corporation – the challenges now being to continue the growth strategy, staying on the preferred list of partners and having to make year-on-year efficiency savings as laid down by the regulatory authorities.

The Institute of Public Health in Ireland

The Institute of Public Health (IoPH) in Ireland, funded by the respective Departments of Health in Northern Ireland and the Republic of Ireland, was established in 1999 to promote cooperation for public health in the whole of Ireland. It was a major cross-border initiative, which emerged at the same time as the Belfast Agreement intended to end the centuries-old conflict.

At a high level the Institute's remit includes providing public health information and surveillance; strengthening public health capacity; and advising on health policy. In reality it has made its major focus the tackling of inequalities in health across Northern Ireland and the Republic.

> The Belfast Agreement was signed on 10 April 1998, a Good Friday, hence its unofficial title of the 'Good Friday Agreement'. Former US Senator George Mitchell, Canadian General John de Chastelain, and the Finnish ex-Prime Minister Harri Holkeri chaired the multi-party talks that led to the historic Agreement. The participants included the governments of the Republic of Ireland and the UK, and 10 political parties representing unionist, loyalist, nationalist, republican and cross-community constituencies in Northern Ireland. The US President Bill Clinton provided political support and encouragement.

The work of the Institute

The Institute of Public Health has been engaged in the development of information, policy and practice relating to poverty and health as part of the organization's overall commitment to combating health inequalities in Ireland.

The Institute uses the World Health Organization's definition of health as 'a state of complete physical, mental and social well-being and not merely the absence of disease or infirmity'.

 It also has developed an all-Ireland Population Health Observatory that supports those working to improve health and reduce health inequalities by producing and disseminating health intelligence, and strengthening the research and information infrastructure in Ireland.

The Institute firmly believes that the development of strong multi-sector partnerships is a crucial step in tackling inequalities in health. As a result it has developed a framework for partnerships in health and organized the first all-Ireland conference on partnerships for health.

It has developed an all-Ireland Leadership Programme to create a network of leaders from different sectors who will work collaboratively and creatively for a healthy society. Over the last five years it has produced publications and reports, held numerous seminars and conferences on key issues in public health, developed innovative and effective programmes and contributed to significant policy developments in Ireland and Northern Ireland. It has worked with a range of partners to bring people and organizations from across Ireland together to promote collective action for sustained improvements in health.

Beginnings

The original idea for an all-Ireland health body came from the Chief Medical Officer in Northern Ireland who began conversations with his counterpart in the Republic. He identified the need for greater cooperation on health. There was an exploratory small group set up by him and his counterpart. They discussed the idea and its potential for success with a whole range of people across the field, from universities to environmental health. One of the key observations was that people clearly didn't want any duplication, though something with a low resource and probably with an emphasis on things uncontroversial (ie, not political) such as focusing in on specifics like a register of diseases. The political context was delicate and so the focus at this early stage could only really be about information exchange.

Through careful networking and discussions, the civil service and some politicians were eventually won over. The Good Friday Agreement provided the necessary momentum to crystallize the idea and the Institute of Public Health for all Ireland was established – the germ of an idea with the starting point of employing just six people from different health professions and seeing what happened.

The Director's job was advertised later that year. The Institute actively sought someone who would develop the original ideas and move the health agenda forward proactively with limited resource, which was highly credible in the health field but politically astute concerning all the North–South sensitivities. Jane Wilde was appointed as Director of the Institute in the autumn of 1998. She had been active politically in the Northern Ireland Women's Coalition and professionally as Director of the Health Promotion Agency. She had been a consultant in public health and on a health board, having trained both in the UK and the United States.

Initial challenges

Immediately a number of challenges arose for the Institute. One key issue was where it was to be located – in the system, more than geographically. The Republic and Northern Ireland had different jurisdictions, different cultures, different health structures organizationally, different budgetary regimes and time periods and clearly different political institutions.

The Institute was to be housed literally and metaphorically within the Royal College of Physicians in Dublin. It was a beautiful building with porticos and marble. However, the Institute hadn't been allocated any space – it had to work from what amounted to a broom cupboard with no windows and a redundant PC.

One possibility was to be further absorbed into the Royal College but the College was focused on standards, training and exams. It was steeped in history, some might say rather archaic. Jane conceived of the Institute as being modern, transparent and permeable, facilitative and enabling rather than imposing and laying down the law.

For the first six months she went out meeting people all over the island, initially those in the more obvious public health roles. She saw her job as going out and meeting, asking people what they were doing and reassuring them that the Institute was not in competition with them. Her endeavours were generally met with support and warmth. The timing was right as over 80 per cent of the Republic's population had voted for the Belfast Agreement and there was a strong feeling of wanting this North–South process to begin. Health was a relatively non-contentious issue so it had the possibility of progression.

Although the Director initially knew only a few key people in the Republic the Chief Medical Officer acted as her chief sponsor, engaging her in conversations and meetings. She had had a credible track record and indeed, first by listening to people and then explaining what they were willing and able to do, people became interested and wanted to be involved.

Concurrently the organization's infrastructure was developed. Technology, web and internet, e-mail and other lines of communication were established. Recruitment processes were set in motion, and budgetary, purchasing and financial systems established. It became clear that the future of the Institute required independence to set its own direction.

During this initial time people were recruited based on what they could contribute and deliver on certain things, rather than from what profession they came. It was during this period also that the Director and her emerging team began to shift the focus away from just providing advice and information towards tackling health inequalities, though not straying from the original remit. There was a certain nervousness at having it as a main aim but the Institute was convinced that its focus should be on the wider determinants of health, highlighting the inter-connections between transport, housing, education and social networks, and how these are intimately connected with health and well-being. Initially radical, the approach is now more widely accepted. This set the scene for the Institute to be involved in areas outside the usual health arenas. It was going beyond the disease model, using systems thinking and seeing its place in the whole system.

It recognized that it had a small place in the system, with little responsibility or executive power. It had its ambitions for influencing and impacting health inequalities without becoming a gigantic bureaucratic institution.

Of course the more you start to become successful the greater the demands on your limited resources. One of the key philosophies of the IoPH was to be innovative and light many fires across the health scene. That suggested there would always be this tension between concentrating on running the successful projects and continuing to develop and implement new ideas and initiatives.

Strategy implementation

The strategy development process involved a lot of time together with the new team. It involved stakeholder mapping and brainstorming, and shaping the future possibilities within the context of understanding future needs and possible scenarios. These were then shaped up into work programmes, which were generally cross-cutting themes rather than one or two specialist areas – such as developing a diabetes register – which might have been too limiting. This was partly looking at the longer term and positioning the Institute in the context of the wider health picture – it could easily have got bogged down in just one important time-consuming initiative. It decided to operate more at a 'meta-level' and wanted to start out as it planned to continue.

Soon people were seeing the Institute as a resource that could be utilized. For example, the Department of Health in Ireland saw it as really useful in developing the National Anti-Poverty Strategy specifically to produce health targets. This in turn developed into a wonderful networking opportunity to better connect with the web of people and institutions absolutely essential for the IoPH to realize its aims.

The Institute works at a whole systems level providing some resource and expertise, supporting and influencing through facilitation via its networks. Its aims include building capacity and capability within its own organization to do the same for all organizations involved in the all-Ireland health agenda.

Vision and values

Jane Wilde had a very clear take on the importance of the vision and values to the organization and its way of working:

> The vision and values are crucial, even more important than a clear set of objectives. At the top are the vision and values, at the bottom is the infrastructure – accounting, systems, processes – both very worked out and clear and effective. In the middle is the room to juggle and be flexible – we don't need to fight for our existence, we fight for our vision.

The Institute has its work plan developed from its strategy process but it recognizes that things will come up or it'll spot things and need to decide whether to factor them into the ongoing work. It has its flagship programmes which are the core of its work, and are quite responsive at taking on additional things during the year, mobilizing resources and spending additional funding quickly and easily and in a very focused manner.

It is more interested in things being achieved than being precious about keeping ownership of things or about who controls the resources. It's not about being territorial, more about effective deployment of resources.

Vision and values come out all the time, whether it's the way the offices are furnished or how the senior management team and management board minutes are published. Keeping communication open between the Belfast and Dublin offices can sometimes be problematical though regular video conferences are organized and face-to-face 'programme' days are scheduled. It can be difficult to get people who have no reason to go to the South, say, to get to know about the South, though the ethos is to constantly reiterate the need for an all-Ireland focus.

A very cosmopolitan staff group have been recruited, drawn from many countries. They operate with a belief that says tensions are more about where they should invest their energies rather where there's conflict to be avoided. They try to do everything to a high standard, with a real attention to both the task and people process, ensuring clarity of agendas and outcomes and that all staff are supported. They support and look after each other with team days designed to allow time for creativity, reflection, de-stressing, growth and development.

Leadership style

The leadership style exhibited by the Director and her senior management team on the one hand reflect the personalities and values of the managers themselves, and on the other hand, mirror the requirements of the Institute from formation through to being a successful player in the Irish health field.

A balance was struck between being affiliative, democratic and authoritative. The Institute needed to get close to all of its stakeholders, build trust and discover what the needs and ideas were of all of these bodies and the constituencies that they represented. It then had to craft a vision and a strategy that would command respect, be authoritative and encourage engagement.

Core values which permeate the leadership are:

- being determined to stand up for what they believe (ie, tackling health inequalities in an inclusive way);
- setting out a motivating vision;
- setting consistently high standards;
- being collaborative, building relationships and fostering networks wherever and whenever it's possible; and
- building and maintaining momentum on a number of fronts with a number of initiatives.

A key leadership competency for the senior management team is being politically astute, with no game-playing whilst watching and managing the political and organizational boundaries.

In the top team the Director's style is very facilitative; occasionally she needs to remember – or be told – that she has to take the lead and make the final decision. As a matter of course there is a collaborative and consensual approach to strategy making, problem solving and decision taking.

Management board

The non-executive management board had the ultimate responsibility for directing the Institute, though in reality the process seemed to be one of collaboration and negotiation. The Director and senior team would go to them with ideas and get approval for the agenda. Initially more directive, the board evolved a way of working that is rather low key, but open, honest and transparent. The relationship between the non-executive management board and the executive senior management team has developed over the years. A lot depended on the differing states of maturity of the board as opposed to the senior management team (maturity in terms of knowledge and experience of the organization, its agenda and its place within the health arena).

The Institute tended to be senior management-led within the broad parameters laid down by the board. In some ways this reflects the confidence the board had in the senior management, though in other ways it probably needed to demonstrate greater critical challenge.

Working across the border

A key challenge was the need to work across the border with both the political sensitivities and cultural differences that implied. The line across the border proved to be a very big line indeed. The two governments had different ways of transacting and different priorities. The Institute acted as facilitators between the two in an attempt to better align the different health agendas and priorities. For example, at one stage there was restructuring in the South, another time budget cuts in the North. At both these times people outside of the Institute tended to look more inward and take their eyes off the collective agenda. It was for the Institute to hold firm to its vision and work with what and who was available. Indeed it found that rather than wait for a total agreement on any one initiative it would start things off in one area and other areas would pick it up if they saw any value in it.

Leadership programme

The leadership programme is a good case in point as its aim was to build leadership capability and capacity across all organizations working on the island. This innovative programme focused on personal development, systems change and collaborative leadership, addressing individual leadership challenges whilst promoting and developing networks. In addition to the individual and group learning there have also been two specific products created by the participants – an imaginative book, *Reflecting Leadership,* and an advocacy toolkit which is being further developed as a web-based resource. Four programmes have been run with 100 people from all health sectors nominated or self-selected to attend. These include academics, public health doctors, community health workers as well as managers from local government.

The programme didn't just focus on individual leadership development but also on the impact on their respective organizations – creating a cadre of leaders, making wider connections and operating in an all-Ireland system. The ongoing peace process has helped – creating more porous borders, being more fluid and less threatening. Likewise this increased level of communication and understanding has helped the peace process.

A key symbolic act on the Director's part was to enrol in the first leadership programme along with some of her associate directors. She recognized that full and wide participation on the leadership programme was important. By acknowledging that she was prepared to show her vulnerabilities, address her weaknesses and further develop her strengths she set a particular tone for the Institute itself and for all leaders and would-be leaders across the health arena in Ireland. This was one of the factors that ensured other high profile people attended, and the programme became something which others wanted to attend.

Learning

The key lessons from this change process are as follows.

Good sponsorship
It was imperative to have a good level of sponsorship from someone who was already respected and had power and authority in the field. The Chief Medical Officers played this role during the birth of the organization and its crucial first few months and this role has now been adopted by members of the management board.

The importance of inclusivity – looking after your stakeholders
This means identifying all of the stakeholders, discovering their needs and wants and factoring them into your strategic deliberations and demonstrating that they have been listened to.

Appropriate influencing skills
The Institute was a legitimate entity but was operating without specific powers. It adopted an influencing style based on drawing people into discussions and deliberations and offering knowledge, experience and resource as a way of gaining commitment and engagement.

Features of this style would typically be building on others' ideas, testing understanding, seeking information, being democratic and sharing power, being involved and building trust. Interestingly this works best when one has no formal power.

The importance of vision and values
The 'what' of the vision and the 'how' of the values provided a compass en route to achieving the objectives. They were used as a crucial part of the decision-making process and provided a raison d'être for the organization rather than having to concern itself with ideas of growth and acquiring and monopolizing resources.

Developing a lean, agile, responsive organization
As a consequence of clarity of vision the organization didn't need to demonstrate success by growth, assets or size but by how well it enabled the health inequalities agenda to be moved on. To do this it need to develop a lean, agile and responsive organization which it did through recruitment of the right

people (professionally and attitudinally); particularly good influencing and enabling skills; demonstrating value through building flagship projects and programmes; investing time in research and reflection; spotting the right opportunities in the myriad of issues and initiatives; and harnessing the power and influence of the networks around it.

Transformational leadership style

The senior management team adopted more of a transformation leadership style. Some of the qualities associated with this style include:

- setting out and working towards a longer-term vision;
- creation of a facilitating environment, enabling people to operate in an environment of trust, openness and empowerment;
- working towards changing the status quo and not being afraid to confront (in skilful ways) situations or people that are not committed to this process;
- recognizing that building overall capacity and capability rather than being directive and hierarchical is a means towards the end; and
- seeing and demonstrating that authority comes from the ability to influence through a network of relationships and a relationship of networks.

The use of reflection as an aid to action

Partly because the organization is involved in research and reflection, partly due to the personalities of the senior management team, there is a great emphasis placed on individual and team reflection and addressing the group process. The organization recognizes the need (as demonstrated in its leadership programme) to invest in leadership processes that pay due regard to individual and team development and dynamics as a prelude to taking action.

Non-executive board and senior management team

For an organization to be operating at full effectiveness there needs to be a stronger relationship between the non-executive board and its senior management team. Healthy relationships need to be brokered between these two groups to ensure clarity of goals and effective operating processes.

Biogen Idec

Biogen Idec Incorporated is a global biotechnology company which develops products and capabilities in oncology, neurology and immunology. Its two major drugs are used in the treatment of Non-Hodgkin's lymphomas, a type of cancer, and multiple sclerosis. Its core capabilities are drug discovery, research, development, biomanufacturing, and commercialization of its products. The company is one of just a few biotechnology companies that have biological bulk-manufacturing facilities, with one of the world's largest cell culture facilities.

Biogen Idec has headquarters in Cambridge, Massachusetts, and was formed in 2003 from the merger of two of the world's leading biotechnology companies – Biogen, founded in Switzerland in 1978, and Idec, founded in San Francisco, California, in 1985. Biogen Idec's history has been one of developing partnerships and achieving mergers with strategic fit, for example same location different drugs, different presences in different markets. In 2005 Biogen Idec invested $684 million – 31 per cent of revenues – in continued research.

The company has research centres of excellence in San Diego, California, and Cambridge, Massachusetts, and additional offices in Canada, Australia, Japan and throughout Europe, including the international commercial and administrative centre of excellence in Zug, Switzerland. In 2006, the company employed approximately 3,400 people worldwide.

For more than 25 years the company has grown through the discovery, development and commercialization of its own innovative products and through its strategic alliances.

Biogen Idec vision and values

Vision

   With passion, purpose and partnerships, we transform scientific discoveries into advances in human healthcare.

Mission

   We create new standards of care in oncology and immunology through our pioneering research, and our global development, manufacturing and commercial capabilities.

Core Values

   Courageous Innovation

   We apply our knowledge, talent and resources to yield new insights and bold ideas. We confront challenge and uncertainty with zeal, tenacity and vision and seize opportunities to excel.

> Quality, Integrity, Honesty
>
> Our products are of the highest quality. Our personal and corporate actions are rooted in mutual trust and responsibility. We are truthful, respectful and objective in conducting business and in building relationships.
>
> Team as a Source of Strength
>
> Our company is strong because our employees are diverse, skilful and collaborative. We pursue our fullest potential as individual contributors, team members and team leaders.
>
> Commitment to Those We Serve
>
> We measure our success by how well we enable people to achieve and to thrive. Patients, caregivers, shareholders and colleagues deserve our best.
>
> Growth, Transformation and Renewal
>
> Consistent with our core values, we as individuals and as a corporation are dedicated to creative and constructive growth, transformation and renewal as a source of inspiration and vitality.

Up until recently the international headquarters were based in Paris. However, following a strategic benchmarking review, the decision was made to establish a number of centres of excellence across Europe, moving from France and basing the new commercial and administrative headquarters in Zug, Switzerland, where most of the international functions reside.

What were the thought processes that led to this decision and how well was this restructuring and cultural shift managed?

The Paris headquarters had responsibility for all finance, legal, HR and commercial activities. Other international functions like regulatory affairs, drug safety and logistics were locally divided. The prevailing culture in the European operation was one of a relatively centralized controlling style with many decisions being made in the headquarters.

Due to the bureaucratic process, decision making was seen as rather slow and onerous and perhaps not totally aligned with the business culture the company wanted to live across its European operations.

While the company had direct presence in most West European countries, it operated via distributors in Latin America, Central and Eastern Europe and the Middle East. In 2003, the company was revisiting its business strategy while it was striving to launch new products and to grow its direct presence in emerging markets.

The change

A project team was appointed to conduct the reassessment of the business strategy. The key objective was to conduct a benchmarking study for the best location, in order to optimize the organizational structure and processes and develop more effective relationships with the European affiliate companies on the one hand and the corporate headquarters in the United States on the other. The head of the international business was appointed to be the project leader, supported by the directors of commercial operations, human resources and international legal affairs. The first stage was pure data gathering of internal and external information. The company was intent on following best industry practice. If, for example, staff were to be relocated or made redundant, the team needed to base its decisions on industry and regional best practices. Data gathered here related, for instance, to relocation and outplacement.

The second stage was to look at future options regarding distribution of functions and allocation of resources across Europe. In principle it was decided to create three 'centres of excellence', by moving commercial and administrative functions to Switzerland (international headquarters), regulatory affairs and drug safety to the UK, where the European Regulatory Authority is based, and logistics to Holland, where the packaging operations was based.

Part of the discussion was the role of the international headquarters as opposed to the affiliate companies. As mentioned before, there was always the possibility of tension between the two and the potential for conflict, as long as roles had not clearly been defined, in particular due to the fact that the former international headquarters and the various affiliates had grown their resources simultaneously.

As part of the move towards empowering the affiliates it was decided to redefine the role of the HQ as primarily sharing best practice, voicing local/international needs to corporate and ensuring alignment between the various operations Therefore, the affiliates had to become self-sufficient: additional resources were allocated on a local level while resources on the international level were reduced. As an example, the HR function was designed to no longer primarily report into headquarters, but into the managing directors of the affiliates, with a 'dotted line' relationship to the Vice President Human Resources. Actions such as these reflected the empowerment of the affiliates and the local managing directors. There was some resistance to change in the reporting lines but this was remedied by groups and individuals relinquishing a direct reporting line for at least a dotted line. In this manner, some connections were retained, but looser. This reinforced the notion of a move away from a largely centralized web culture to a more networked one, based on a matrix. From an early stage and to comply with employment legislation, follow best practice and to be true to the company's 'Team as a source of strength' corporate value, the team actively involved staff representatives through the representatives of the Works Council.

Data gathering and option generation

The team looked at potential sites for the new centres of excellence. Copenhagen, London, Paris, Munich, Zurich, Belgium and Amsterdam as well as the existing location in Paris were included in an in-depth analysis. These locations were looked at through various filters – biotechnology industry, healthcare and business environment, employment and recruiting, infrastructure, transport (eg direct flights to Boston) education, languages, as well as other social and cultural aspects. Data was drawn from multiple, well-accredited sources, eg the World Economic Forum and Arthur D Little's Global Headquarters Benchmarking Study European Headquarters. Finally Switzerland and the UK were short-listed.

One of the benchmarking studies taken into account was the Mercer Human Resource Consulting's Quality of Life Survey (http://www.mercerhr.com). This analysis was based on an evaluation of over 30 quality-of-life criteria for selected cities, including political, social, economic and environmental factors; health and safety; education; transport facilities; and other services. They mapped the different locations against the different criteria and with a balance between company costs and benefits and employee costs and benefits.

In the end Zug was rated high with a good multinational business environment, international schools, high quality of life, taxation and cost of living reasonable.

The legal process in France was extremely rigorous with employee rights paramount. The company involved the employee representatives completely throughout the decision-making process, consulted them on the current and future organizational structure, and provided them with a detailed analysis of how it would impact employees and what was intended to ameliorate their situation.

Local government agencies were equally involved.

Affiliates and culture change

A key aspect of the structural changes was to clearly outline key roles, responsibilities and processes in order to improve decision making and increase organizational flexibility.

The most immediate effect was on the affiliate companies. The management teams of these were given additional resources (made available from the decentralization process) and given more control related to their local organization. The ability to take more leadership was offered and taken. Business development opportunities could be seized more readily.

As with any reorganization, both the formal and informal lines of communication, authority and responsibility were shifted. There was a need to clarify responsibilities, rebuild relationships, share best practice, agree boundaries and define parameters. Once again the existing culture and values assisted this process as did the role modelling of senior change makers.

The corporate body set the overall strategy but empowered the affiliate businesses to operationalize this. Corporate defined the strategy and ensured international alignment of the strategy across the region, while operational responsibilities were assigned to local management.

Strong business results in the international markets following the restructuring, and extremely positive results of a corporate employee survey in which more than 90 per cent of all employees participated underlined the success of the reorganization.

Criteria for good change

Get the right specialist support from the beginning

Depending on the nature of the change, specific specialist functions can be crucial to success. In this case the project team recognized that external legal advice related to the complex employment matters and design of the social plan was crucial. Also, a public affairs resource was something that the company didn't have internally in International and consequently established in the Zug office.

Support from top management

A change team has more chance of success if it has unequivocal support from senior management. The project team closely cooperated with internal decision boards, external resources and local authorities.

Clarity of direction

The change team defined the objectives – to assess and review the location of the centres of excellence and put forward the recommendation on the best location and concurrently to address strategic and business requirements of its affiliates.

They went into this decision-making process with open minds but were clear that they would reach a decision and take the necessary actions to bring about any changes, if changes were indicated.

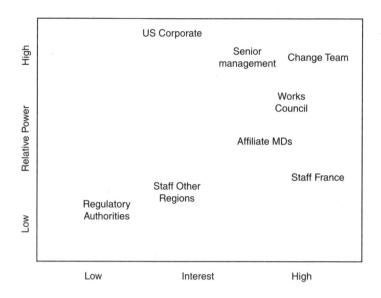

Figure 3.1 Stakeholder mapping, Biogen Idec

Clarity of decision making

They relied heavily on the prior acquisition of the necessary information to be able to make reasoned judgements and give a compelling business case to all interested parties. This also included being very clear about the criteria on which a decision would be made. Their data were comprehensive and drawn from both internal and external sources.

Leadership

They adopted an authoritative style of leadership which relied on their having clarity of direction, an understanding of the needs and wants of the various stakeholders, a certain credibility with staff and business partners but also an openness to incorporate different views and new data as they emerged, but always within predefined parameters.

Their treatment of staff was based on fairness and equity. There were no special cases or exceptions when it came to redundancies, promotions or relocations. They tried to achieve the balance between being clear, consultative and direct.

The transition

The Zug authorities turned out to be extremely supportive in their approach, reflecting their business-oriented mindset when Zug was being considered as potential location for the new commercial and administrative headquarters. The Swiss joint venture was co-located with the new office. The office is five minutes walk from the railway station which in turn is 45 minutes from Zurich airport with its direct flights to Boston.

Current employees in Paris were encouraged to conduct site visits to Zug in case they expressed interest in a potential relocation to Switzerland. At the same time tax simulations were ran for interested individuals. The project team did a risk assessment on losing key talent and decided that benefits exceeded any perceived risk.

Once it was agreed who wanted to move and who wanted to leave the company, or take up positions elsewhere round the globe, the French contracts were terminated and new Swiss contracts issued. A fair severance package and comprehensive outplacement supported those employees who decided to leave the company to find a new job. New staff was recruited in Switzerland, the UK and the Netherlands to fill the gaps and these were drawn from more than 17 different nationalities.

Centres of excellence were established across Europe. For example to the west of London, UK and close to the EMEA (European Medicines Agency, the drugs regulator), the company established its international regulatory, clinical research, data management and pharmaco-vigilance centre.

The British Council

Founded in 1934, the British Council is a non-departmental public body (NDPB) and public corporation with charitable status, receiving grant-in-aid from its sponsoring department, the Foreign and Commonwealth Office (FCO), of £185 million per annum (2005/06). It has a presence in over 110 countries and its overall turnover is currently £502 million per annum including partnership funding, revenue from teaching, administration of exams and development contracts. The Council's purpose is to build mutually beneficial relationships between the UK and other countries and to increase awareness of the UK's creative ideas and achievements overseas.

During a strategic review in 2003 the senior management team developed a vision for the British Council.

Given the British Council needs information systems that underpin the stated objectives within the vision, allied to the strategy-making process, a review of the internal information systems was undertaken. This revealed the need to design and install a new system throughout the UK and the rest of its global operations.

By 2010:

We will be a world authority on cultural relations, English language teaching, and the international dimensions of education and the arts.

We will understand the needs and aspirations of those we are seeking to reach much better.

We will be using our expertise and knowledge to help millions of people reach their goals and make a difference.

We will have built many lasting relationships between people in the UK and other countries and strengthened trust and understanding between our different cultures.

We will be welcomed as an effective and sensitive partner for societies wanting to bring about a fairer and more prosperous world.

We will be connecting millions of people with creative ideas from all over the UK and with each other, both face to face and with innovative online and broadcast communications.

We will be broadening the UK's world view, particularly how young people in the UK understand and value other cultures and traditions.

And everyone who works for the British Council will feel valued and will enjoy opportunities to be creative and realize their potential.

The first stage was the implementation of the new system across the UK, particularly within its main Manchester and London offices. This case study tracks how the project was managed and delivered on time and to budget. The UK government's National Audit Office concluded its review of the project implementation by stating that it was a 'very successful implementation'.

Drivers for change

Internal drivers

The British Council systems had evolved over a number of years and at the time of the review UK operations didn't have a particularly clear vision of where IT provision was going. It had between 25 and 70 separate systems (with a myriad of smaller localized bespoke systems), which weren't integrated with one another. There was a serious question over the Council's ability to provide an IT infrastructure for the future growth and development of the organization's business.

People at all levels within the organization identified a need for change. Indeed there were frustrations articulated from the people at the operations end who needed to provide a professional service to clients and customers but were increasingly held back by the antiquated systems. Furthermore, ideas being generated for regionalization across the world meant there was a compelling case for a standardization of systems.

External drivers

The internal drivers were further accentuated by the growing need of part-nering organizations to interface with the same system across geographies.

Governmental intervention had led to a drive for increased performance and better service. In July 2004 Sir Peter Gershon published his review of public sector efficiency, 'Releasing resources to the front line', and the British Council was being asked to show £13 million of savings, the majority of which would be realized through the successful implementation of this project.

The other important external driver was the increasingly competitive environment that the British Council was facing in some of its trading areas. So, a focus on costs and overheads was a compelling reason for these changes.

The business case

There were up to 70 bespoke systems across the British Council and its regions, from large scale investments through to tailored spreadsheets. They were all at different stages in their lifecycles. There was a complex interface leading to expensive communications which hindered the free flow of infor-mation across functions and processes. This engendered a sense of separate businesses or silos. And of course poor information hindered managerial decision making. A less fragmented system would allow for centralization, or decentralization or regionalization. It would allow for the organization to become more flexible and responsive. Partner organizations were at the same time decentralizing and empowering operatives in the field to bid and manage development projects locally.

The software solution which emerged was Enterprise Resource Planning (ERP), which is the technical term for the range of activities supported by multi-module application software that assist the organization to manage and administer the important parts of its business. It does this by integrating and automating many aspects of these business operations.

After considered and considerable debate, an off the shelf solution was agreed which would provide the whole British Council with a consistent solution. Allied and aligned to this would be the creation of 10 core business processes across the world. Key benefits of the system would be:

- total organizational information and communication integration;
- the breaking down of functional and departmental barriers;
- the same consistent real time information for all areas; and
- the capability to analyse data in a variety of critical ways, for example, budgets could be viewed at any sector, unit, country or regional level.

All these benefits had links with and indeed underpinned the 2010 strategy and were aligned with creating a cohesive business direction. It was to be the biggest change project in the British Council's history. It was a radical response and would affect every single department across the organization, with 360 global job losses, and 80 reductions planned in the UK central finance department in the first year of implementation.

Key players and stakeholders

Key stakeholders included the following.

Senior management

Senior management took a very close interest in the project as it was so intimately tied in as an enabling strategy for the 2010 vision. At implementation stage the Deputy Director General was appointed as the senior responsible owner (SRO), which sent a clear message to the whole organization of making this a top priority.

The programme board

The programme board was set up as the senior sponsoring and monitoring group, with representatives of all the major stakeholders on board and chaired by the Deputy Director General. It provided informed challenge and stakeholder management. A support office was set up to ensure a uniform approach to change management and tracking and monitoring of delivery and efficiencies gained.

The business

All parts of the business were consulted and involved at each stage of the process.

Consultants

The consultants' consortium was an important and critical part of the project. There was one large consultancy and a number of smaller specialist consultancies. The decision was to have a representative of the consortium on the programme board in the interests of open transparent communication and good partnership working.

Finance and IT

The finance and IT departments were most directly affected, partly with both having important roles to play in the design and implementation, but also with the finance department requiring restructuring as a direct result of the changes, with a reduced headcount and a decentralization process.

Staff

All staff were affected to an extent. Their involvement and interest in the project was in direct proportion to the degree of change which they would undergo and the timescale in which it was to occur. The British Council ethos was one of openness and consultation and this was embodied in the way that people were involved, communicated with and consulted.

Union

The trade union was an important stakeholder to work with, address inevitable staff issues related to the change and to negotiate a way through them. The union was also an important communication tool and thermometer for taking the emotional temperature of the organization.

Other stakeholders

The FOC, the government's stakeholder, was content to be at arm's length and, although with considerable power, would only get interested if major issues were highlighted.

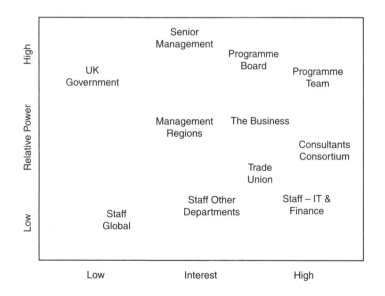

Figure 3.2 Stakeholder mapping, The British Council

Although the first phase was a UK rollout, managers and staff from other countries were interested, mainly for three reasons to ensure:

1. business continuity;
2. difficulties in implementation were resolved before the overseas rollout; and
3. full understanding of the impact of this large integrated solution on both UK and overseas operations.

Programme team

The programme team comprised people drawn from finance, technical and operational sides of the business, the change training team and members from the consortium. The programme team demonstrated their credibility by being recruited not just from the finance and IT departments (though of course they were fully represented) but through selection on the basis of their operational track record, experience in the business and change management expertise.

Richard, the programme manager, had been a director for the British Council in Indonesia, with experience in change management and process re-engineering. Paul, the Change Communications Manager, had had 10 years' experience teaching and teacher training in Hong Kong and had been involved in overseas business development.

Design stage

The programme team followed the programme guidelines and terminology as laid out by the Office of Government Commerce (OGC). The programme support section became a centre of excellence (in OGC terminology), followed the managing successful programmes methodology and aligned the various project management methodologies which had grown up across the Council.

OGC works with public sector organizations to help them improve their efficiency, gain better value for money from their commercial activities and deliver improved success from programmes and projects. Our priorities are to support the delivery of:

- the public sector's £21.5 billion annual efficiency gains by 2007/08;
- £3 billion saving by 2007/08 in central Government procurement;
- improvement in the success rate of mission critical projects.

At an early design stage a significant decision was taken. The systems review had reached a decision on what was needed but the 2010 strategy process had not been completed. One of the first acts of Robin, the Deputy Director General, on becoming SRO was to declare that 'Strategy leads the system not vice versa.' As a result the project, now called Finance and Business System (FABS), was held back for six months to allow completion of the strategy work. A key aim was to keep the strategy and the system development together. So, for example, a decision was made to restructure and downsize the finance department at the same time as changing the finance system. Although challenging and in some ways doubling the amount of change during a specific time period, the alternative was to do them sequentially, and having the wrong structure and the wrong people operating a new system or having a new way of working with new people but not the system to deliver the new objectives. In some quarters this was seen as brave, in others seen as potentially foolhardy.

A series of senior management workshops was held to engage managers from across the Council in the strategy-making process; to involve them in looking at the consequences and implications of developing the new system; and to elicit their support for the change process and the turbulence it might cause. This resulted in a document outlining the new strategic direction, the challenges ahead, and clear outputs and outcomes.

The prevailing culture at the British Council was one of a collegiate decision-making process. This produced a 'dynamic tension' in different stakeholder relationships:

- the design team were keen to move forward at a rapid pace;
- the consortium consultants tended to come from a culture of proactivity and focused action; whilst
- British Council operational staff were immersed in their usual way of doing things.

Various dynamics were at work in that many staff, as previously mentioned, were keen to update the systems and develop more responsive ways of working. However, they also needed to be listened to and asked for input.

There were different levels of engagement in different parts of the business which needed spotting and managing. Inevitably there were some winners and some losers. One aspect was that some areas, previously benefiting from bespoke systems, were now being asked to give up those systems for the greater organizational good. Overall 100 staff participated in the design stage, which included, in addition to the finance and IT functions, both the UK business and representatives from the overseas operations.

Implementation process

On the programme manager's appointment the implementation process started with a 'mobilization and visioning' event: in effect a two-day team workshop bringing together the technical people, the business people, the change training team and the consortium. This struck a balance between getting organized on the task and focusing on how that might be done – the process. This generated a commonly held and understood vision and also a set of guiding principles for team working.

The implementation process followed a normal systems project:

- configuration (done mainly by the external consortium);
- proof of concept;
- realization;
- integration;
- user training;
- user readiness; and
- go live.

Critical activities in the whole programme included the process of installing the software; getting staff to understand what the changes were for and how they would affect the way of working; and helping staff learn what to do.

Change management workshops were designed and run for all staff. Coordinators were appointed in all areas and managers were asked to complete a business readiness grid (BRG) detailing the extent to which they were prepared for the changes in their particular area.

An effective project management structure was established with a clear line into the programme management board. There was business representation for all strategic discussions whilst a business assessment group assessed the blueprint, the training and user acceptance, and reported back to the board. There was a clear governance structure with a senior responsible owner and clear responsibilities and accountabilities. An issues log and a risk management log were part of the everyday process.

One key point in the implementation process was the decision in the summer of 2004, following a Gateway Review, to delay the go live date. There were previously agreed criteria, evidence based, to assess whether both the system and the business were ready for implementation.

A business assurance group (BAG), drawn from both the business and the project, had been set up for this very purpose. It was a critical part of the change process. Delaying go live was a difficult decision, though the BAG was empowered to take that decision. There was pressure from many quarters (the consortium, some senior management and the programme team) to press ahead.

The OGC Gateway Process examines a programme or project at critical stages in its lifecycle to provide assurance that it can progress successfully to the next stage. Purposes of the review:

- Confirm that the business case is robust.
- Confirm that appropriate expert advice has been obtained as necessary.
- Establish that the feasibility study has been completed satisfactorily.
- Ensure that there is internal and external authority, if required, and support for the project.
- Ensure that the major risks have been identified and outline risk management plans have been developed.
- Establish that the project is likely to deliver its business goals and that it supports wider business change, where applicable.
- Confirm that the scope and requirements specifications are realistic, clear and unambiguous.
- Ensure that the full scale, intended outcomes, timescales and impact of relevant external issues have been considered.
- Ensure that there are plans for the next stage.
- Confirm planning assumptions and that the project team can deliver the next stage.
- Confirm that overarching and internal business and technical strategies have been taken into account.
- Establish that quality plans for the project and its deliverables are in place.

(Office of Government Commerce, http://www.ogc.gov.uk/)

There were some tensions around this decision, it being an admission that the project wasn't ready. Though there was the potential for some negative consequences in terms of the project and people's perceptions, all agreed with the overarching aims to deliver a successful implementation. It was a dramatic decision to delay the go live, but it was felt that the British Council was a healthy enough and robust enough organization to withstand this.

The programme board took the decision to delay go live but regained the lost time by merging that implementation phase with the next one.

Everyone agreed that the business readiness grid had been an extremely useful tool as it highlighted the extent to which the whole business was ready and the areas in which the change team needed to prepare some more. Generally, though, all managers were somewhat overly optimistic and thought they were more ready than indeed they were.

Although a productivity dip had been planned, the extent of it hadn't been fully predicted. Many affected areas were operating in competitive environments with clear contractual obligations to existing clients and ongoing work projects – the idea of turning inward and putting resource into assisting the change process at the expense of the operational imperatives was not particularly welcomed.

In each area, staff who were acquainted with the changes and had the necessary specialist skills were appointed as 'power users' or FABS coaches to help others familiarize themselves with the new system.

Communication

Communication was seen as a critical success factor, due to the prevailing culture of openness and transparency within the Council and because the change team knew that communication is one of the keys to success. Indeed there is a considerable overlap between what change management is meant to do and the function of a good communication strategy. As early as January 2003 Paul, the Communications Manager, had organized a global 'web chat' on the company intranet to provide a forum for information dissemination and addressing any queries or concerns. Only a few people were needed for the blueprint, design and user testing stages, which lead to the interesting question of 'How do you keep people informed when they don't actually need to do anything?' If you start too early people will feel disinclined to show an interest, or their interest will wane; if you start too late then you run the risk of rumours, gossip and disinformation taking the place of the intended knowledge transfer.

Communication with the trade union continued throughout the design and implementation phases. The management stance was to always be open and always attempt to gain agreement through discussion. Therefore management was generally consultative with a negotiated agreement on how to deal with the various job losses – through redeployment and voluntary redundancy. Given the legal nature of the consultation, though open, it was formal and through HR channels.

At some stages there was criticism that people were consulted but there were no changes as a result of that consultation, which left some wondering why bother with the consultation. This is often a criticism of consultation, and the change team and those consulted needed to be clear what is open for discussion, consultation and consequent change, and what is just information. Additionally, if ideas were taken on board there needed to be a mechanism for letting people know that changes had been made and that they were seen to be made.

During the implementation process a network of 80 FABS coordinators was set up, acting as a formal communication conduit between the programme team and the affected areas. They had a key communications role in being the eyes and ears for the programme team and, having their fingers on the pulse, could be an integral two-way communication channel. It was through them that it became apparent which departments were having difficulties coming on board and therefore highlighted where more communication effort was needed. The coordinators also had a role in ensuring that the relationships between business and project were managed effectively.

The programme team invested heavily in the coordinators and ensured there were monthly meetings, regular updates, teleconferences and workshops.

Training

The programme team didn't see communication as one distinct area and training as another – for example, there's an overlap between communicating something to someone and explaining how to do something.

There were one or two things that were not aligned and the training in some instances missed the mark. Training was seen (after the event) as being too generic. The initial evaluations were positive, but once people had a chance to work on the new system the evaluations dropped.

Training could have been more contextual, and more specific for particular groups. The potential of the new system was hinted at but it was left to individual departments to work out how this might be engineered. There could have been more partnering with the business to understand what was needed. One of the challenges was the level at which to pitch the training – how specific can you get when the imperative is to communicate generally with all staff? Resources didn't allow for bespoke training across the organization and yet it was felt that some training needed to be given before the system went live. As the go live deadline approached there were still changes occurring in what the operators would see when they viewed the system on their PC, so what the operators saw in their training sessions was not what they saw on their screens on day one of go live. This investment in upfront training – for many people there were five days of training – could, perhaps, have been better spread over training and coaching post-implementation.

A further difficulty was the interplay between the outside consultants who knew the system intimately, the staff who knew the British Council workings intimately and the programme team who knew how the original off the shelf system had been tailored to British Council needs. Each group was coming with a different knowledge base and different understanding, and sometimes transfer of knowledge was lost in translation.

The ERP system, although meeting all the criteria from a business and systems perspective, was counter-intuitive and so, in order to acclimatize oneself to the system there was an element of learning by rote. This then had a knock-on effect on the training, because however you designed a familiarization package, unless there was enough resource for tailored training for each section, department and person, there was always going to be a sense of the training not being truly fit for purpose.

Lessons were learnt for the overseas rollout and corporate finance trainers were located in specific departments before the changes were implemented, during the go live process. Most important, they stayed on site after go live until local managers and staff were capable and confident in operating the system.

Leadership

The leadership style of the key players involved in the change process was characterized by an outwardly calm attitude with a focus on balancing the different aspects and demands of the programme, involving all stakeholders every step of the way, including the consultants' consortium.

At crucial decision points – when to delay implementation or merge two go live dates – they had to hold their nerve and balance the need to be authoritative with the need to be both democratic and affiliative.

The programme manager at times had to focus more on the people than the task; for example, on the morale of his team when getting stuck and getting stick during the immediate post-implementation phase.

Likewise the DDG as senior responsible owner needed to network with all senior and key people. Generally hands-off when it came to project implementation, he was available if there was a need to escalate any concerns. A communication structure was set up between the consortium and the programme board and team to ensure that there was direct and regular contact between the opposite numbers within each organization.

During key points in the change process the SRO took the lead. For example, when assessing business readiness he held meetings with each area of the business to establish, through frank and open discussion, whether or not each area was confident enough to go live.

Leadership throughout the project was variously described as 'firm but responsive' and 'honest but robust'. Getting the appropriate style for the different situations within the change cycle was important. Before the go live decision was made the DDG had one-to-ones with all the managers to ascertain whether or not their area was ready. This was leadership by asking the difficult questions and demonstrating that a) this was a business critical decision, b) that the line managers were jointly responsible for the decision, and c) there was a collective confidence in going live.

When the organization was facing changes that it had never managed before, an overly directive style would not work. Accessing the shared wisdom of all the key players was crucial. As time went on people became more competent and confident in this change process and were more able to take the lead in their own specific areas.

The Deputy Director General didn't know enough about the intricacies of the ERP system to make individual executive decisions. He built on the consensus within the programme board. Ultimately responsible for decisions, invariably it was always after consultation and reflection. That didn't stop decision making – he recognized that it was better to make a decision and be sensitive to the impact of that decision than not make a decision at all.

The leadership style was based on the context, on the level of complexity of the project and the levels of shared knowledge and wisdom. For example the Deputy Director General felt quite able to make decisions based on his widespread knowledge of the security situation in Saudi Arabia without reference to a programme board, whereas the ERP was a different arena.

He also recognized the capacity of people, when in high risk situations, not to accept responsibility for their actions, and as such was keen to instil an ethos of no blame, no retribution within the board and programme team.

Working in partnership

This systems implementation was the British Council's biggest ever commercial contact. The risks were huge if it were to go awry, given the history of failed and costly government IT initiatives. At each level within the organization there was a suitably credible and competent individual to interact with the equivalent manager within the consortium. For example, the Director General met the CEO of the main firm of consultants on a regular basis, the programme team had a good commercial manager who formed a good working relationship with his opposite number, and at least 90 per cent of all issues were easily resolved. There were monthly meetings and all potentially big issues were discussed openly and frankly.

The programme team always had a clear plan of the outcomes they wanted and as a consequence were never browbeaten into agreeing something they later regretted. They were also aware of needing to manage the relationships both with the main consultant and the various sub-contractors.

One of the main areas of potential tension was the differing cultures of the various organizations. For example, from the consultants' side, the British Council was perceived to have a culture of 'consultation about everything at the rate of the slowest' whereas they saw themselves at the opposite end with the project management ethos of one accountable person who would get on and do what they needed to do – make a decision and tell people what it was.

Another tension was the pool of knowledge between the consultants, the programme team and staff throughout the business. There was the need to translate ERP technical language into an understandable form for staff operating an ERP system with their own unique processes.

The dynamic between consultant and client organization is often understandably taut, with in-house people wondering whether the consultants really understand the client organization, and questioning whether the consultants were willing to learn and adapt from the client rather than impose a system on them.

Post-implementation

From the programme teams' point of view go live happened on time and relatively smoothly. It was up and working when it was meant to be and the team felt justifiably satisfied with their achievements.

The major issue on go live was the effect of not having had enough bespoke training. Although users had access to desktop learning support, a central helpdesk and power users to coach and support within each department, the fact that individuals didn't quite know what to do meant that for each seemingly trivial question, the user would not be able to use the system until their query had been answered.

People saw their small part of the process but hadn't really been shown where it fitted into the whole process and so were looking at how to do their bit well rather than leveraging the capability and potential of the whole end-to-end process.

Calls to the business support centre (helpdesk) increased dramatically as did requests for assistance to the power users. Both support mechanisms were overloaded for a number of days.

In retrospect it became clear that the power users were the ideal people to have done the training. They were very familiar with the British Council operation, were from the departments and involved from the beginning (from user acceptance and testing). They would know what it was that people needed and also what the system could provide and in what ways.

A few software design faults and systems interface issues emerged. There were also some legacy system problems which hadn't previously been spotted.

A key change management issue was ensuring that the support and assistance post-implementation were available. Investment in the original training could have been reduced and reallocated to either more bespoke training prior to implementation, or coaching and supporting around the time of implementation. For a different sort of change, the logistics might have prevented it (geography, health and safety, time constraints, etc). It was, perhaps something that either the consultants' consortium might have better advised on or the programme team in terms of their research on implementation of similar systems elsewhere.

The prevailing culture and focus on the customer ensured that staff were immensely tolerant and worked hard to achieve their goals during this period – a reflection on the strength of the British Council culture and core values.

The programme team quickly set about looking at remedial action for the support levels and the glitches that had appeared. Monthly monitoring reports led to setting up of specific projects to tackle outstanding issues and a variety of workshops were organized to address the issues.

Stabilization and embedding

The programme office had created stabilization criteria for each part of the process and used a traffic light system to track progress. From the implementers' point of view an important tension then emerged between, on the one hand, the programme team focusing on the next phase – rolling the system out overseas – and on the other addressing the stabilization issues in the UK.

From the users' perspective a tension arose between accepting the new system with limited knowledge and creating 'workarounds' on the one hand and on the other hand gaining the necessary expertise to fully exploit the system.

Business process ownership resided within the business, within the process itself. This idea fitted with ensuring empowerment and indeed ownership where it belonged, but it did require specific responsible managers being appointed and enough resources attached to those roles. As often happens within organizations, managers with a full load of duties and responsibilities are asked to take on the additional responsibilities. Unless the role is reconfigured around the process the role might be either too large or cumbersome, or deflect from giving the process adequate focus.

The programme support office established a set of key performance indicators (KPIs) to have a reasonably objective measure of how things were going and which were used to:

- decide on areas that needed following up;
- decide which areas that were a priority for action;
- illustrate and illuminate where things were going well; and
- manage expectations of the stakeholders.

Managing expectations helped at this stage in introducing the new system as it addressed the following key questions:

- Does each part of the system function – yes or no?
- Are we able to process sufficient volumes at sufficient quality?
- Are we operating more efficiently than before?
- Are we demonstrating best practice?

The reviews of KPIs themselves formed the basis of an understanding of what had worked well and what needed to change.

Next steps

The next, overseas rollout, phase is now in full flow with various technical and business functions fused into one business support centre. A global implementation team has been appointed with the necessary technical expertise and a programme management office set up. Training needs have been identified and change teams set up across the regions. A process of consultation and stakeholder involvement has begun. For the overseas rollout, people won't be exposed to anything unfamiliar to the programme team and staff will this time have specific training. So, for example, all the processes are now well documented, there is revised, high quality training material and the 'sandpit' practice, play areas are identical to what users will see on their desktops.

All this in turn feeds into a larger vision for the future of IT within the business – an integration of corporate IT with other business applications into a single commercial management function, perhaps even outsourcing to a leading provider.

Likewise the project itself has gone through a lifecycle for staff as the introduction of the new system with all the resource and attention generated the idea of a 'process is king' mentality. Having come to the foreground it is now subsiding as people start to use the technology and the new processes to deliver better customer service.

County of Aarhus, Denmark

The County of Aarhus is the largest of the 14 counties on which the local government system in Denmark is based. It serves over 600,000 people, employs over 22,000 staff and has a budget of £1.25 billion. Services provided include a complex and comprehensive network of hospitals, schools, institutions for the disabled, housing, the road network, environment and bus system.

In 2004 the County of Aarhus was awarded a prize by the Bertelsmann Stiftung Foundation of Germany for being the most effective public organization in Europe.

The management board has developed an organizational model which has a number of objectives:

- to generate a common language and a common frame of reference;
- to create integrated analysis and documentation of endeavour and results;
- to give a collective description of the County of Aarhus' political goals.

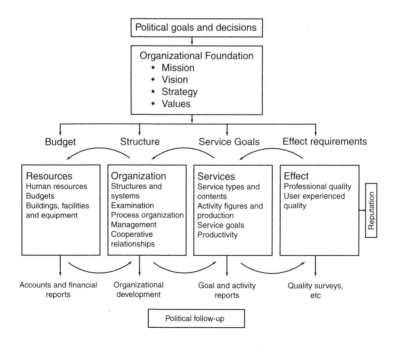

Figure 3.3 Organizational model, County of Aarhus

The model has been developed to allow the efficient and effective running of the County with clear direction and accountability from the politicians and translated into meaningful objectives for the management to operationalize.

The outcome of an enhanced reputation should produce positive answers to the following questions:

- Is the County known for providing high quality services?
- Is it financially well run?
- Are the employees satisfied with what they deliver and how they are managed?
- Is the County's infrastructure and environment well looked after and attended to?

There is a rolling review of the effect of the County's services and therefore on the services themselves. Consequently the organization is reviewed and the deployment of resources across its divisions and geography.

The model is underpinned by the County's five fundamental values which in turn contribute to the maintenance and development of an enabling culture in which staff work and deliver the services. The county's five values are:

1. Dialogue.
2. Openness.
3. Respect.
4. Willingness to develop.
5. Commitment.

In any organizational change there is reference back to this set of values to ensure the changes are being managed properly.

Dialogue. Expressed as a willingness to enter into fruitful dialogues with citizens, end users, employees and other partners and stakeholders

Openness. Expressed by the development of a transparent process of decision making whilst holding client confidentiality as sacrosanct.

Respect. An important focus for all interactions is the aim to understand and respect users' needs and desires and maintain an equity and equality of service. This is also demonstrated by the valuing and capitalizing positively on the difference and diversity found in the community and the workforce.

Willingness to develop. Developing the ability to adapt and improve services to better meet the needs of the user goes hand-in-hand with the need to develop the capacity and capability of the organization and its human resources.

Commitment. Staff are recruited for their professionalism, skills and their commitment to their work and there is a requirement on staff to take responsibility to carry out their work to the best of their ability.

A further value of *Credibility* was added in 2004 which was concerned with ensuring that statements and actions would be believed and build confidence and provide quality to the customer.

At the beginning of 2002, as part of the rolling review looking at service improvements, it was decided to restructure the psychiatric service in the County, merging local and social facilities with the hospital services. The final decision about this change was a political one, though the pre-planning had been worked on by managers for a couple of years. This work was headed by the Directory of Psychiatry in the County of Aarhus, assisted by a group of consultants.

Jørgen's organizational development unit was called in to help facilitate the restructuring in one of the four general psychiatric units of the County. In effect a new organization was created. In this unit there were 300 employees, a top team of four reducing to three and a management population of 25.

As you might imagine in an environment providing psychiatric services, second only to the care and treatment of patients, the health and well-being of staff are a prime concern. Any change within the organization can be quite disturbing for clients. This then creates additional stresses on the staff providing the service. In turn the management population have to manage the changes and support staff through the changes.

Jørgen's task was to work with the management group to create and move everyone into the new organization. He called this stage of the development process the 'founding and grounding of the new organization'.

The idea was to work with the top team to develop new organizational mission, vision, strategies and values. The mission is to ensure psychiatric treatment to the population of the region, and the vision translates as: everyone who needs psychiatric treatment, from whatever the sector – social, local or hospital – is assured of a high level of professional care which is given in a coherent and integrated fashion.

The process was started with a two-day workshop which adopted a slightly different approach than some more conventional interventions. The accent was on developing dialogue, understanding and insight. As Jørgen described it:

> dialogue means to discuss with the intention to implement. That is, a situation or problem exists which demands new ideas in order to proceed... ideas, attitudes and opinions are exchanged, and a common insight arises... a common space is established in which everyone can participate without consideration of organizational position, professional or scientific experience.

Martin Buber used the term 'dialogue' to 'describe a mode of exchange among human beings in which there is a true turning to one another, and a full appreciation of another not as an object in a social function, but as a genuine being'.
Physicist David Bohm saw that:

> Dialogue would kindle a new mode of paying attention, to perceive... the assumptions taken for granted, the polarization of opinions, the rules for acceptable and unacceptable conversation, and the methods for managing differences... the group would have to learn to watch or experience its own tacit processes in action. Dialogue's purpose... would be to create a setting where conscious collective mindfulness could be maintained.

(Senge, P *et al*, 1999)

In addition, over a six-month period there were monthly facilitated meetings with the three senior managers. The outcomes from this process were a well defined vision, mission and strategy to lead the unit into the future. This was underpinned by the adoption of a set of values which were aligned with and also informed the corporate values.

In this approach there are two crucial underlying assumptions. The first is *open systems*. The organizational system that the managers and staff found themselves in cannot be taken in isolation. Every system is to some degree connected to other systems. These systems are therefore in some ways interrelated, in some dependent, in some influencing – always therefore having an impact. The change agents themselves were also part of this wider system.

The second is *the unconscious*. In Jørgen's words again:

> we have an assumption that human beings have thoughts, ideas, fantasies, emotions, reactions, actions, and many other things, which are both rational and irrational. As individuals we do not always act consciously or rationally. Our actions are controlled also by the unconscious and irrational, values and valencies... and unconscious actions can though, to some extent, be investigated. Groups and organizations are the result of the conscious and unconscious actions of human beings.

Of course the idea of open systems and the unconscious, if true in this setting, is also true in all organizational settings. However, in Aarhus this was deepened by the knowledge that the decisions made by the management would not only be affecting staff but would clearly be affecting the end user, the psychiatric patients, with their myriad vulnerabilities and anxieties. This in turn would impact on staff and management who are required to create an environment 'good enough' to allow the healing process to take place.

Organizing in the units – development of leadership (2003–4)

Having put down the foundations of the new direction the task was now to create an organizational structure that would be 'fit for purpose' – the purpose of delivering the new strategy. The two key elements here were to develop a workable formal organizational structure, and to ensure that the structure was supported by the necessary lines of two-way communication, which in turn were based on a common understanding of roles and responsibilities and a healthy engagement vertically, horizontally and externally within the new structure.

So, working with the management group, Jørgen and his change team planned further developmental interventions focusing on the leadership, the organization and collaboration across the organization. In parallel managers reflected upon, discussed and planned their own personal development needs.

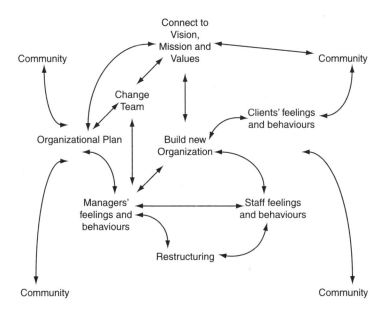

Figure 3.4 Map of the system/causal effects

A two-day working seminar for all 30 or so leaders was arranged with the primary task of establishing the necessary structures, communication and information protocols, and formulating leadership development activities. This was once again based upon a working model of iteration between dialogue, construction (or application) and reflection. The working seminar was designed in a way that made it possible to work on this double task: formulating drafts and ideas to make the organization more effective while simultaneously investigating and interpreting attitudes and values among the leaders present at the seminar.

The following year saw a period when both the structure and the people within it 'settled' in. There were new jobs, new roles and responsibilities and different reporting structures. There was cross-disciplinary working and collaboration – something that had not been a particularly common feature before. Issues were surfaced and dealt with in a number of ways: regular leadership meetings; supervision/coaching sessions for individual managers; and a programme of leadership development activities.

Further development of leadership (2004–5)

Interestingly, although both the structure and staff interactions were proceeding relatively well, there was a shared feeling that something was missing in the system. It was something that was not particularly obvious, that is, not conspicuous by its absence, but something that, on reflection wasn't there.

There was quite some thought given to and dialogue around this. It was acknowledged that there had been different speeds of development of both the new service structures and the managers themselves. There had also been different levels of engagement – or 'buy-in' – to the process of change, and there had been tensions between those in professional roles and those in managerial or leadership roles. These tensions were also a challenge within some individuals themselves. How much focus do I have on the professional, specialist part of my job and how much focus do I have on the managerial, leadership part of my job? At the same time managers had stepped into their roles perhaps as traditional leaders, or leaders with a traditional notion of leadership. Through continued reflection and dialogue what became apparent was that within the new structure there needed to be the notion of shared joint leadership.

Again a two-day working seminar was run with the theme of shared joint leadership, and with a double task as in the former working seminar. In the local psychiatric units there were instances where two leaders would have a real responsibility for a department or work area. Across the organization as a whole there was the need to establish a common understanding of leadership and enact it. You could call this 'strategic leadership', but it was more than that. In the example of the individual who had tensions between his or her professional role and his or her operational (hierarchical) leadership role, there is the added dimension of what responsibilities that individual has for managing and leading across the organization as a whole and what responsibilities for co-creating the future direction of the organization. Typical questions arising were:

- How do two people take shared leadership for an area of work, or more likely an agreed organizational objective?
- How do they agree on systems, policies and processes across the organization whilst being an advocate for their own areas?
- How do they allocate scarce resources equitably across the organization whilst arguing for more for their own areas?
- How do they spot and transfer best practice across the organization?
- How do they create an enabling environment where shared joint leadership can become a living reality?

The structure of the working seminar was designed in some ways to simulate, mirror or replicate the organization in the minds of the participants. Consequently the very issues that the management group were grappling with in Aarhus emerged within the workshop setting itself. These issues could then be confronted in the here and now – issues related to leadership, shared understanding, relationships, communication, and the like. Indeed the stated aim of the workshop was:

> Starting from the existing organization of management, the primary task is to investigate, develop, discuss and formulate activities, which aim at developing and making more efficient the leadership in the units, through the implementation and utilization of shared joint leadership.

All participants were asked to use the workshop as an opportunity to fully experience the organization (temporary though it might be), reflect, engage in dialogue, collaborate, learn and construct appropriate actions. The imperative involved:

> Listening to other participants' experiences and opening both these and their own experiences to investigation, in order to try to understand why things happen as they do. The individual must himself, or herself, decide how many of these experiences to open to investigation, by the way the individual decides to manage his or her role.

New Challenges, 2005–06

So, following the laying of the foundations of the new organization (in terms of its vision, mission, values and strategy) Aarhus spent a considerable time organizing the way that that should be done. This time was well spent. It afforded the agents of change the time and the space to set a course while organizing and orientating themselves and their staff. They highlighted the areas of tension, spotting the examples of best practice and continuously monitored the organization as it emerged.

The day-to-day reflections were supplemented by frequent leadership supervision and coaching sessions and the regular workshops or working seminars, which created an environment where both task and process could be confronted in the spirit of trust, openness and a willingness to collaboratively tackle issues which got in the way of the organization fulfilling its purpose for the people of Aarhus. This period amongst other things was one of 'grounding' or embedding the changes and the way of working together. At the same time of course, there were further changes made and even more radical ones were on the horizon.

At the time of going to press a new challenge has emerged. From 1 January 2007 following a governmental review there will be a wholesale restructuring of public services generally in Denmark, consequently breaking up the current organization, established in 2002. The 14 counties will be reorganized into five large regions.

The County of Aarhus will merge with two other counties, precipitating the biggest change in history of the public sector in Denmark. The recently planned workshop has therefore to take this on board and ask some searching questions:

- What do the managers feel about this and how are they going to react?
- How will they factor in these new changes into their other strategies or will these new changes supersede all that's gone before?
- How will they manage the current changes, prepare for the new changes and still focus on the patients and the delivery of services to the patients?
- How might they support, enable, motivate and sustain staff throughout this coming period?

Figure 3.5 summarizes the changes during the period 2002–06.

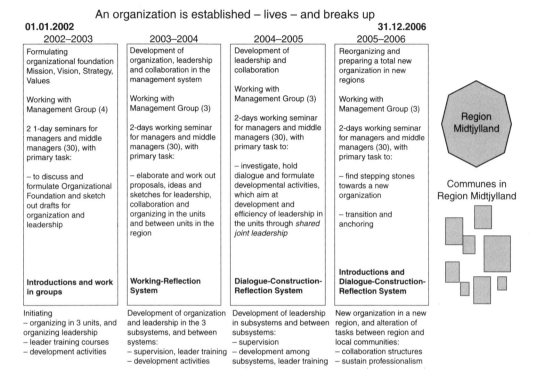

An organization is established – lives – and breaks up

01.01.2002			31.12.2006
2002–2003	2003–2004	2004–2005	2005–2006
Formulating organizational foundation Mission, Vision, Strategy, Values	Development of organization, leadership and collaboration in the management system	Development of leadership and collaboration	Reorganizing and preparing a total new organization in new regions
Working with Management Group (4)	Working with Management Group (3)	Working with Management Group (3)	Working with Management Group (3)
2 1-day seminars for managers and middle managers (30), with primary task:	2-days working seminar for managers and middle managers (30), with primary task:	2-days working seminar for managers and middle managers (30), with primary task to:	2-days working seminar for managers and middle managers (30), with primary task to:
– to discuss and formulate Organizational Foundation and sketch out drafts for organization and leadership	– elaborate and work out proposals, ideas and sketches for leadership, collaboration and organizing in the units and between units in the region	– investigate, hold dialogue and formulate developmental activities, which aim at development and efficiency of leadership in the units through *shared joint leadership*	– find stepping stones towards a new organization – transition and anchoring
			Introductions and Dialogue-Construction-Reflection System
Introductions and work in groups	**Working-Reflection System**	**Dialogue-Construction-Reflection System**	
Initiating – organizing in 3 units, and organizing leadership – leader training courses – development activities	Development of organization and leadership in the 3 subsystems, and between systems: – supervision, leader training – development activities	Development of leadership in subsystems and between subsystems: – supervision – development among subsystems, leader training	New organization in a new region, and alteration of tasks between region and local communities: – collaboration structures – sustain professionalism

Region Midtjylland

Communes in Region Midtjylland

Figure 3.5 The changes, 2002–06

Leadership

We can look at different types of leadership through this change – the three senior managers and the role of the change agent. The three managers were quite different personality types with a consequential variation in leadership styles. One was a quiet thinking type of person who had quite a few ideas but also always allowed time for reflection before a decision. The second also thought things through but was more outgoing and translated ideas into creative possibilities. Interaction with others was important for him as through his questioning approach he was able to discover new avenues of thought and action. To complement the first two, the third manager was much more focused on the here and now, had an eye for detail and required proper ways of doing things. Rules-driven might be one description; another would be attention to the quality of the process and the procedures. He had a handle on the resources and allocation of those resources.

The internal consultants/change agents applied their model of organizational change quite strictly early on, to allow participants to, a) familiarize themselves with the process, and b) to ensure that everyone felt 'safe enough' to be able to enter fully into the realm of dialogue. Once trust had been established such rigid boundaries were, to a degree, softened.

The consultants on their part, as interveners in the system, inevitably picked up emotions from different people and groupings within the system. As part of their working practice the team underwent its own supervision in which it in turn could reflect upon their experiences, enter into dialogue with one another, and further ideas for action could be generated and then fed back into the system.

Key features of this approach

Key features of the approach adopted by Jørgen and his team were:

- Always have the end user in mind, and refer back to them when deciding on what changes to make.
- Hold the organizational values in mind and refer to them as a 'touchstone' in both what you do and how you do it.
- Address both the task issues (project implementation) and the process issues (the group/team dynamic) as an imperative.
- Entering into real dialogue with key stakeholders takes longer but ultimately enhances the chances of successful outcomes.
- Taking the time upfront to create a 'facilitating environment' that will enable you to allow tensions and potential conflicts to be raised and addressed reduces the possibility of those conflicts being 'acted out' negatively during the change process itself.
- Creating dialogue means everyone's voice is heard, thus increasing the possibility of 'buy-in' and engagement in the change process.
- Having complementary leadership styles in the top team creates a broader spectrum of leadership capability.
- Providing coaching, supervision and development for the management population – linked to strategic objectives and operational realities – enhances management capability and provides emotional support (and challenge) during times of change.
- Creating the time and space for the change team itself to address (ie, confront and work through) the 'emotional baggage' they may have picked up during the change process.

Jørgen Jørgensen was the organizational consultant working on this change. He can be contacted via jj@udd.aaa.dk.

The kitchenware company

It was almost 15 years ago when Dennis and Nick, two young sales executives, were chatting together as they were driving to see one of their clients. The topic was careers and what they really wanted to do with their lives. Like many people they dreamt of running their own business. But unlike most people they held onto their vision and commitment and drive over many years to make it a reality.

From that initial conversation, it took another seven years for them to refine their vision, decide on the nature of their business, spot their opportunity and get the finances agreed and then to step into their new lives.

They were kindred spirits, with a mutual affinity for sales, and they alighted on the fast-moving homeware business as the one where they had knowledge, competence and skills enough to make an impact.

During this gestation period they set about acquiring more skills and contacts in their chosen field and also putting money away to finance their potential loss of earnings through the period of transition. Nick was working as a sales director in the homeware industry for a household name. Although extremely successful he was frustrated at being constrained in his ability to shape the · future of the brand and the business. He was the guardian of the brand – getting customers to accept what the brand was like, not taking feedback from the customer to improve the product and the brand. That was decided not by customers, not by employees, but by the senior management. Dennis was in a similar position, again in the UK homeware industry.

They bought a very small company where they had a remit for sales but subcontracted the existing warehousing and logistics to a long established company. Dennis took over the running of this operation whilst Nick continued in his employment for a further year. The business grew to a £1 million turnover and they decided to separate from the warehousing company. However, the larger company's owner wanted to sell his company to them.

They approached the acquisition with optimism and although their research suggested this was a viable company, they based their decision more on a sense of their own competence, their knowledge of the market and their abilities in sales, marketing and managing a sales force. The acquisition was completed with the managing director of the homeware company taking a one-third stake.

The company turned out to be more problematic than they first thought. It had poor quality products, a large slow-shifting stock, a sales force and a strategy that targeted wholesale outlets rather than key retailers, and the warehouse itself was 200 kilometres away from the head office. They had a small number of key customers and the majority of their purchases from the Far East were paid in US dollars. The economic environment had been relatively stable for the previous five years and there were no indications of a downturn. The company was purchased. The deal was financed by their borrowing £1.5 million to refinance the business and agreeing a scheduled purchase of all shares owned by the previous management over a period of 10 years. With more attention to detail and less of a gung-ho attitude they probably could have negotiated a better finance deal.

Drivers for change

In the first 12 months, four of the company's main clients were lost – two accelerated their pre-existing, but unbeknown, plans to withdraw, one went into receivership, one into administration. At the same time the exchange rate for the dollar against the pound moved from around $1.70 down to $1.40. The more the new owners met their customers the more they realized how bad their customer relationships actually were. Fulfilment was perhaps the single highest irritant from their customers' perspective.

Internally they began to realize that the stock that was moving was the stock that was newly bought. There was a considerable amount of old stock which was not being moved at all and hadn't for some considerable time.

It wasn't long before Dennis and Nick realized that the managing director they had inherited was out of his depth. He suffered from a lack of ability to establish meaningful relationships with key customers, an unresponsiveness to market demands and a poor buying and stock management capability. His sales force management skills were also lacking.

Nick went out to meet one of the longer-term customers who had decided to move his business elsewhere. He was met by the owner-manager who's first comment was, 'You're the worst f***ing supplier I've ever had. The only reason I'm still with you is your sales agent has always done the best he could, in bloody difficult circumstances.'

Nick, as part of his preparation for the meeting, had visited various outlets and realized that there were a number of lines that were missing. He talked straight: 'This is unacceptable and we'll do something about it starting today.' The customer stayed with the business and sales have increased six-fold!

Taking the bull by the horns

On entering the business they had decided to take six months to understand it before trying to change it. They agreed that you don't change something until you understand it. One of their two core product ranges was described generally as something that was a little grubby, poorly perceived, and an undervalued secondary brand. For many people this would have been an ideal opportunity to ditch the product and concentrate on the other, higher value brand that they had. Their analysis, after evaluating the product and seeking customer views, was that it could be turned into a cash cow and today it is one of the most widely distributed in the industry, well known and recognized everywhere, 'from wholesalers to Harrods' as Nick likes to put it.

After six months they realized they needed to concentrate on the front end of the business:

1. Marketing became the main focus, developing one product line into a bolder brighter brand. It had exceptional distribution, was quite well known but had appalling packaging. By radically re-branding this they could set their business apart from similar suppliers and make a huge impact on the store shelves. With the second product line a new award-winning product was launched – a better quality, innovative ergonomic range of kitchen tools, designed to be comfortable and functional for both left- and right-handed users.
2. They extended the spread of distribution by saying 'yes' to anything – whether the customer wanted the company brand, their own brand, or a modification. Their aim was to consolidate the customer base, by understanding all their customer requirements.
3. They shifted the emphasis from predominantly wholesale distribution to include retail.
4. They invested heavily in wooing the buyers from the range of super-markets and stores just under the main supermarket chains – the buyers, more personable, had greater decision-making power and also were able to respond much quicker. This was a key business decision. The decision-making process for the larger players was often cumbersome and drawn out. With the many smaller players there was immediacy in the contact and both parties could agree to tailor their needs and responsibilities according to what the relationship demanded.

Whilst developing a number of strategies to make this happen they also had to address some other key issues within the organization.

The sales force were suspicious of the new owners who wanted a new sales process quickly implemented. As Sales and Marketing Director, Nick actively set about upgrading the sales aids for the sales force – quality literature was produced (rather than the shabby dog-eared photocopied brochures that they were used to). A national accounts manager was recruited from the industry to manage the key accounts tightly.

The nucleus of back office staff in the HQ were entrenched in their own culture and uncaring of the downtrodden warehouse staff. A tough decision was made – to close down the head office and relocate it in to the warehouse. Those who wanted to move could, but the reality was that a whole new tranche of people would be recruited and subsequently were employed locally. The huge overhead cost of the previous offices stopped; the prevailing culture was disbanded at a stroke; and the warehouse staff felt that something significant was occurring which made them realize the new value that was being put on them. Having been largely ignored for a number of years they had developed into a relatively undisciplined and at times rather disrespectful group. Dennis and Nick from early on had demonstrated that the relationship needed to change. They had moved the HQ there, they showed drive, energy and commitment to the business and also a real interest in the staff and what they were capable of.

This was reinforced the first time Dennis and Nick visited the warehouse. They were met with a whiteboard on the wall which read, 'Problem Customers' and had a large list of customers who wanted something different in terms of product specification, price, delivery or relationship. Rather than fulfilling the different customer needs the warehouse staff saw these needs as problems. Dennis and Nick had the whiteboard removed.

They also created an ethos of promoting from within unless there wasn't the capacity or the capability. The old stock was got rid of – sold at knock-down prices or dumped. It had merely been keeping the warehouse full and using up valuable space.

Leadership

The company strategy was all about getting close to the customer and delivering what they wanted. Their vision became 'Grow our business stronger and better.' In Nick they had a front person who was the customer's advocate – committed and passionate about the products and satisfying the needs of the customer.

War stories soon became commonplace as the new owners worked tirelessly on reorientating the company, developing better customer relations and supporting and challenging the sales, warehouse and back office staff.

For example, at Europe's biggest trade fair they spent the day and evening wooing customers and suppliers, and galvanizing the sales force and then returning late at night to their hotel rooms to work on the business (or battle) plan. Dennis and Nick's personalities and roles complemented one another. Dennis, very affable and focused on relationship-building dealt primarily with suppliers and with employees. Nick was very focused on the task of engaging with customers and galvanizing the sales force.

Moving forward

Given that they were in a market with lots of competition, low-cost goods and little margin, all the players were relatively indistinguishable with very little points of difference. They were being squeezed on cost by the supermarkets on one side and price increases on new stock from the other.

Where the company seemed to stand out was through its poor and inconsistent stock fulfilment! The move towards a sales driven/customer needs culture, however, was under way. They relied heavily on their customer feedback, which they actively sought and then responded to wholeheartedly. They invested in the stock that was wanted and gave continuity with guaranteed supply. It wasn't about price, it was about availability.

It took nine months for customers to understand and embrace this approach but over that time customer orders rose 40 per cent and this provided some room to move prices up 17 per cent.

However, there were unintended consequences. With orders starting to flood in there were more and more strains put on the warehousing and procurement staff. Dennis and Nick had put the majority of their efforts into the customer-facing front end. When orders flooded in, the back end collapsed. The sales effort had created real success and orders were climbing month on month. However, the warehouse was falling behind in its fulfilment. Indeed events came to a head and Nick one day dramatically took his whole sales force off the road and brought them into the warehouse to pick orders.

They had inherited a nightmare in the warehouse – there were 36,000 square feet and 2,000 active stock lines but no stock management system. They had tried appointing a stock manager from within but there was no real expertise in the company so they externally recruited a capable operations manager, but it still took 18 months to produce an efficient and effective system.

Taking stock

They had doubled the turnover, increased profitability six-fold, created a stable workforce and were beginning to get a reputation in the industry for fulfilment and customer responsiveness.

They had learnt from initial enthusiasm to be more disciplined, to hold regular strategic reviews and to be extremely responsive to customer needs on the one hand and adding to the product ranges on the other. They needed to be incredibly fleet of foot.

On the product side, although there was a wide range of products which, overall, were selling, there was a real need to improve. They were in a market where it was hard to differentiate one company's offerings from another, and small improvements in terms of product enhancement or new product lines would, at least for a little while, provide an advantage.

Their attentiveness to their customers' needs was matched only by their attentiveness to their suppliers. So not only did they convey what was needed from their customers, they also listened to what the suppliers believed would be good ideas. This listening and engagement led to suppliers, over the course of time, becoming less intransigent and more flexible in their responsiveness.

Stakeholders

Staff were treated as colleagues with an open door policy and ability to contact managers at any time. Significant policy changes were communicated early and discussions were held about significant company issues and any customers needs.

The sales force are involved with setting the sales plan. The plan is agreed using a bottom-up process with all the sales force engaged in agreeing their targets with their managers and the final sales plan is endorsed by them.

Other staff ownership is connected into the customer supply chain developing a teamwork ethic where there is no divide or barriers between sales force, warehouse staff and administration. As one of the staff said, 'It's not just about moving boxes, it's about making our customers feel they've chosen the right company to supply them.'

The small number of private investors are clearly a crucial stakeholder group, with most dealings and the bulk of communication through the major shareholder who heads the group of investors. As Chairman and non-executive director, Paul takes the role as the fulcrum. He is highly credible, financially minded and trusted by both the managers and the other shareholders. Whilst Dennis and Nick take full responsibility for day-to-day operations, the

Chairman is fully consulted at critical stages in the yearly cycle. Although primarily 'hands off', the Chairman, as the major investor, is clearly very interested in how the business has been running and was able to identify certain key issues which needed rectifying. The static stock lines were a case in point. He was clear that all that was being done with these lines was they were being housed and heated and dusted from time to time. Whatever their book value they needed to be sold, whatever the price.

Likewise he identified the poor product literature as something which just shouldn't be put up with. Although funds were short the message was clear – invest in new marketing literature and it will repay the investment.

One of the things the Chairman brought was the role-modelling of identifying key business issues, assessing the risk between taking or not taking action, and then making the decision and getting on with it. Business is about taking risks and both Dennis and Nick began to see that it's better to take a qualified risk, make a decision and live with the consequences, rather than letting things continue in a sub-optimal state.

'If you're not growing then you're dying,' Paul would say. Having chosen to invest in the company he was focused on making it profitable in the short term and a viable business in the medium to long term. He worked at arm's length with Dennis and Nick, believing that they were there to manage suppliers, customers and all the operations in between, seeing one of his key roles as being to question and challenge.

Coming from a finance and banking background he was focused on getting a good return on sales and establishing a higher profitability relatively quickly. That did not necessarily mean increasing sales, but stabilizing them whilst developing excellent customer relationships and good products, and ensuring that operations were cost-effective. Working on the business plan with Dennis and Nick they decided on a few key performance indicators, set realistic but stretching targets, and then established good monitoring processes.

Paul wanted to 'give the work back to the people' – enabling them to do the job they're best at, matching people and their skills to the roles critical for business success. He played to people's strengths by giving them the leeway and headroom to get on with the job whilst mitigating their weaknesses by getting others to take on those aspects of the job.

Paul's entrepreneurial style was encapsulated by the desire to make decisions, take action, review progress and, if necessary, take remedial action. Although reviews and reflection were built into the process, Paul believed that the company needed to capitalize on opportunities when they came along. Mistakes were perhaps inevitable, but if you create an open culture and if everyone learns from the mistakes then this will lead to better performance.

Paul believed more in evolutionary change than coming in to a business and causing maximum upheaval and distress. Focusing on performance, reducing blockages, those people who felt they had a contribution to make would stay and they would contribute; those who didn't fit the culture would leave.

Paul also believed in more emergent change rather than overly planned change. Yes, there was a business plan, which was monitored and questions asked if there were deviations. But there was also a culture established which sought opportunities when they arose. The failure of a competing business led the very same day to establishing contact to buy them out.

Paul was concerned to maintain the momentum for growth within the company, whilst at the same time not wishing to lose the entrepreneurial culture that Dennis and Nick had established. One of the ways that this was maintained was by having the organizational infrastructure lag somewhat behind the sales – as demonstrated by probably employing $n-1$ people rather $n+1$ when n is the current level required in an expanding situation.

Many customers, employees and suppliers through the changes have required deliberate focus and energy. Changes to product, product lines, structures within the company, acquisition of other companies, taking on other companies' accounts, all impact on stakeholders' perceptions, create instability and can generate anxiety. Dennis and Nick seek to engage customers and suppliers alike in these changes through a combination of nurturing the relationships and straight talking.

Next steps

The strategy continues to work well, with customer orders continuing to grow. The UK kitchenware market, however, is declining so standing still is not an option. They need to grow organically or through acquisition, and this growth can be through existing or new products. They had demonstrated they could grow organically through greater customer relationship management and fulfilment; they had responded to customers' needs and suppliers' ideas and enhanced the brands and developed the product range. They were also alert to their competitors and the possibility of acquisition as and when they fell on hard times.

In the last 20 months they have made two acquisitions of companies with similar product, low-value, high-volume profiles covering similar accounts. The advantages to the customer was having to deal with a smaller number of suppliers, the advantage to them was a greater product range, new ongoing accounts and expanded existing accounts. The company has itself attracted the attention of a larger European company keen on expanding into the UK market. The challenge for Dennis and Nick is how to embed the current success into a sustainable growing business.

Indeed there are challenging plans for expansion by doubling turnover to £25 million over the next three years. One of the ways to achieve this will be to establish more product lines. Given this in itself can take up to three years to become profitable, they are currently investigating partnering with a large Dutch firm with whom there is a strategic fit. The Dutch have the product lines already established, and they have the territory covered in the UK.

However, as the company grows there is probably the need for more formal training and development, more formal soft management skills and perhaps more attention paid to sustaining an entrepreneurial culture. Such a large expansion will require different skills and capabilities across the organization; issues both of organizational capacity and capability will have to be addressed.

The primary school

This particular case looks at a small primary school in the South West UK. Situated in a rural community, it has 150 pupils between the ages of 4 and 11, with 26 full- and part-time staff of whom 8 are teachers.

In 2001 a new headteacher was appointed. The previous head had moved the school from one that had been in decline to one which the Government Inspection Agency (Ofsted) had described as 'satisfactory'.

Ofsted Scale

Very Good
Good
Satisfactory
Unsatisfactory

(http://www.ofsted.gov.uk/)

Nicky, the new headteacher, inherited a school that had somehow plateaued and was now facing a number of challenges:

- the previous head had been in post for 10 years and was suffering declining health;
- the chair of governors had also been there for many years and was himself approaching retirement;

- the governing body had traditionally looked to these two figures for direction;
- a further Ofsted inspection was looming;
- the school's financial situation was tight but manageable;
- the school itself was overcrowded and was a classic mixture of an outdated Victorian building and a number of 'temporary' Portakabins which had been there for several years, together with outside lavatories for the pupils; and
- the school could be characterized by falling morale and a rather controlling and dependent prevailing culture.

On the positive side, as a result of a principally parent-led campaign, the school had secured new premises and the children and staff were due to move into the new building in September that year.

Although Nicky had previously worked at the school some years before, this was her first job as a headteacher. She saw her immediate tasks were to:

- familiarize herself with pupils, teaching and non-teaching staff;
- manage the day-to-day duties of being a head;
- begin to think about the current health of the organization; and
- prepare for the wholesale move to new premises.

Nicky realized that there had been quite a lot of management – very often micro-management – at the school but very little leadership. Indeed the only real leadership exhibited had been by the parents' action group in their campaign for securing a new school.

Nicky set in train a number of things that would result in developing a shared vision of the future and also an increase in distributed leadership across the organization. She formed a leadership team consisting of the two senior teachers and herself and she began conversations with each subject head to shift them away from seeing their role as merely ordering mathematics books, for example, to developing a vision and strategy for that particular subject.

She invited all staff and all governors to an initial vision-creation workshop where they focused on different aspects of what the school could be. This was the beginning of a process that gradually became more and more familiar to the participants. Initially starting off with perhaps an air of cynicism and certainly a feeling that they would prefer the head to set the direction, participants soon realized that they had a genuine stake in the future of the school and the creation of a specific future for the school.

Her rationale for developing a vision was:

- that the process itself was inclusive and might engage many of the very people she needed to rely upon;
- it would highlight both the areas of agreement and those areas where there was some tension;
- it would bring people together around a common purpose;
- it would 'start the ball rolling' by creating some momentum and hopefully some remotivation;
- it would create the backdrop for developing a coherent strategy and agreement on choice of priorities given scarce resources; and
- it would allow all the school's stakeholders to see themselves and their interests represented.

Of course many of the outcomes of the process would be dependent on, a) the visioning process itself, and b) the components of the vision. The process modelled one of the school's core values, which was to generate the spirit of collaborative inquiry. The components that were generated covered all aspects of the school's work and life.

At this early stage Nicky had already involved the pupils. Although aged just 4 to 11 years old, they were asked their views on what sort of school they would like.

Children who...

Are happy	Are sensible
Help each other	Don't smack or fight
Are kind	Are friendly
Help	Share
Listen and learn	Pray

Teachers who...

Explain things well	Are kind
Listen	Are nice
Help us learn	Make work fun
Help you when you're stuck	Like you
Work hard	

A playground where...

There's lots to do	Children are careful
There's a big area to play in	Children play nicely
Children cooperate	There's lots of air
Children chat and shout	Children aren't naughty
Children look after each other	Children are safe
There are brilliant colours	

The final school vision was:

> The children in our care will be high achieving, self-confident learners who have respect for themselves and others.
>
> Individual talents, interests and needs will be recognized through the provision of an imaginatively structured curriculum that promotes the all-round development of children and prepares them for citizenship in today's world.

Along with the vision creation process the head conducted one-to-one discussions with all staff to understand their current role and also how they saw their role in the future of the school and to share with them how she saw the school's culture developing. It was also an opportunity to have frank discussions as to what is expected of staff in terms of performance, and clarification of what was expected of them and what they could expect from the head in terms of support.

What makes an excellent school?

Children who…	Teachers who…
Support staff who…	Parents who…
Governors who…	A head who…
A community which…	An environment where…
A Local Education Authority that…	

The head was perhaps fortunate in needing to appoint teachers to two vacancies so she could demonstrate what sort of co-workers she would like to see employed.

There was also the need to build the relationship with the governing body. Here again there was room for improvement. By this time the Chair had also retired, which allowed for a new, more motivated and energetic person to take over. The Chairs of the relevant sub-committees were also newly appointed and over the coming months it became apparent that the governing structure needed a rethink. Governors reviewed their effectiveness and realized that what they needed was a more streamlined, less bureaucratic body, with the Chairs taking on more responsibilities and the sub-committees being delegated more responsibility and authority. Consequently the number of full governors meetings could be reduced.

Leadership style

The head's leadership style was very much symbolized by three pictures that had struck her as encapsulating the task ahead: one of a woman having to juggle many things of different shapes and sizes; one of someone trying to get a flock of penguins to move in the same direction; and one of her on a high diving board ready to take the plunge!

These three pictures symbolized to her the need to be very clear about what she was embarking upon (in terms of vision and strategy); to be aware of all the different, and sometimes competing, interests amongst the stakeholders; and to recognize that going through change oneself and leading others through change can be a scary, anxious but exciting experience.

How did she approach this? Initially by constructing a mental roadmap of where she was headed with the process and then by investing time and energy in the individuals and teams that made up the teaching and support staff. Underpinning this was the need to hold onto a sense of the important when crises came and went. This was why it was so important for her to ask herself at regular intervals what the leadership task now was; to differentiate between when she was managing and when she was leading; and to step into an appropriate leadership style for the current situation, whilst not being too distracted from the overarching objectives.

A key aspect of this was forming the leadership team and also for all members of staff not only to take a lead on something but to demonstrably link that into pursuit of the vision and the strategy. So it wasn't just about ordering a new set of geography books but about how to make what was happening across the world relevant for pupils in a way that would engage them, concern them and lead them towards being more able and understanding citizens.

The initial visioning process was more purposefully led by the head and over time this control was gradually relinquished. Staff had a greater say, as did the parents who, through a newly revitalized Parents' Forum, were also included. The pupils were encouraged to set up a School's Council and also become 'Associate governors'. Of course this wasn't just a way of tapping into the wisdom of the children: it was also a way of promoting ideas of citizenship and representing others in the community. Building on this the school began to see the pupils as researchers – tapping into their ideas and insights as the basis for future curriculum development. For example, the children wanted more time devoted to foreign languages and certain elements of science (astronomy!). It was also from the pupils that the idea of a peer mentoring scheme was set up – children from the higher years were then encouraged to buddy with the younger children on a one-to-one basis, resulting in the younger children being supported academically and emotionally whilst the older children learnt some teaching skills and also how to take on responsibility. As one of the teachers said, 'It's so powerful when you hear a five-year-old speak their mind, tell you what is wrong and what could be different!'

Building capacity involved developing all groups of stakeholders, for example, Pupil Voice (the children's representatives), the leadership team, the development teams and focused parents' working groups.

In terms of the school's wider set of stakeholders – primarily the Local Education Authority and the geographically clustered schools – discussions were had and decisions were made as to what the nature of the relationship should be. Given the school's high standing the Education Authority's attention and budgets were focused on the less well performing schools. This enabled the primary school a certain degree of independence. Likewise, with the cluster group of similar schools it was found that their needs didn't fit with the school's needs. As a result of these two things links were made with a newly funded group of networked schools which were drawn together through their desire to experiment with both an action inquiry approach to learning and a desire to expand the international dimension of the learning environment. This was linked to the UK's National College for School Leadership. Its Leadership Network, launched in 2002, consisted of over 250 heads who were engaged in innovation and reform in their schools and committed to collaborating in stimulating national debate and informing policy development. A key plank of this initiative was determining how schools move forward and had at its core the idea of the head as a researcher.

Culture change

There were a number of shifts intended in the culture. Some were quite well defined earlier on, whilst some developed later as the head and the school became more confident with the changes:

- From a culture of dependency to one of distributed leadership where the roles and responsibilities of the different stakeholders within the school community were redefined. This process engendered a stronger sense of participation and interest in the development of the school and created the basis for an ongoing model of consultative leadership.
- From head as heroic leader to head as co-researcher – this provided a model of headteacher as head learner. By engaging in school-based research and enquiry, the headteacher was able to model the behaviours of a reflective and analytical practitioner. This gave rise to rich professional dialogue regarding a strategy for change management and within a short space of time teachers were keen to engage in lines of collaborative enquiry to develop practice in their curriculum subject areas.
- From curriculum-centred to pupil-centred, moving away from the 'one size fits all' philosophy to understanding the development needs of each pupil.

- From rural community to citizenship in the world, expanding the number of perspectives with which we can view the world.

Leadership and personality

It was interesting to see the interplay between the head's personality and her leadership style, and it was important for her to assess her strengths, develop her other areas and engage with others to leverage their strengths. Organizationally she:

- provided insights and design skills for the future;
- translated and organized ideas into structured action plans;
- identified and worked to remove obstacles along the way to the stated objectives; and
- had strong ideas of what the school could become.

Therefore she could lead by making use of these strong ideas and convictions; by enabling the team to define, decide upon and begin to action its strategy; and also keeping the team on course by emphasizing the boundaries.

Her strengths were the ability to drive both herself and others towards their goals; to act strongly and forcefully; to be pretty tough minded (again both with herself and her team); and to be able to step back and conceptualize what was going on and generate new models and ways of working for the whole system.

Of course there were downsides to this way of working. Taken to extremes she could appear unyielding, might work out on her own the 'best way of doing something' and may come across as too task focused and somewhat uncaring of others' contributions and efforts.

A tale of two schools

A windswept evening the lone parent struggles up the dark street to find the school gate closed. She looks at the piece of paper she clutched in her hand. The governors' meeting was open to the parents and it was on tonight. She stood on tiptoe to see over the gate. There was a light on around one side, and she followed the fencing until she found a side entrance, unmarked but unlocked. She headed for the light, entered the building and hear the sound of muffled voices. She paused for just a moment and summoned up enough courage to knock. A few moments more and a voice says, 'Come in.' She pokes her head around the door and asks if this is the school governors' meeting. A person at the head of the table says, 'Yes it is and who may you be?'

'A parent' she says. 'A parent?' is the reply.

A cold Thursday evening two weeks before Christmas, over 60 parents repre-senting a majority of the children at the school gratefully accept a warm mulled wine and hot mince pie as they are welcomed into the new school hall. They have come for the annual governors' report – a meeting which the school has to have by law but only used to attract a handful of parents. Now, because of the increased partic-ipation and inclusion of parents in setting the direction of the school, people turn up in droves to hear not just what has happened but to have a say in what will happen. Tonight they are also blessed with the presence of the Ofsted inspector who, by special request, has been asked to present his initial findings. They are that:

> the School is a highly effective school where pupils achieve very well and have very good attitudes to their learning. The headteacher provides outstanding leadership and the school is well managed. Teachers are very enthusiastic and knowledgeable, and work well as a team. They have very high expectations of what pupils can achieve and give lots of praise to encourage them to do well. The school provides a very rich and varied curriculum, which contributes significantly to the high quality of pupils' education. There are excellent links with parents and no significant issues for improvement.

Conclusion

Nicky saw her role as headteacher as focusing on a number of areas:

- Making sense of headship.
- Manageability.
- Streamlining systems.
- Clarifying roles and responsibilities.
- Quality assurance.
- Development of an 'Excellence model' providing a guiding visionary framework.

She saw her leadership challenge as:

- Developing leadership.
- Building capacity.
- Distributed leadership.
- Researching informed practice.
- International learning.

And what it meant for the children:

- Children valued as stakeholders in the learning process.
- Student Council.
- Pupil Voice.
- Pupils leading their own learning.
- Personalized learning.
- Pupils as 'Associate governors'.

Looking ahead:

- Futures thinking.
- Revisiting vision, values and purposes.
- Embedding consultative processes.
- Considering 'remodelling'.
- Working collaboratively.
- Building capacity for continuous improvement.

Finally, Ofsted reported that the school is:

> a highly effective school. Pupils achieve very well and have very good attitudes to their learning, relate extremely well to each other and are very well taught.
>
> The headteacher provides outstanding leadership. The school has made a considerable improvement in the standards it achieves and in the quality of education it provides for its pupils since the last inspection. The school offers very good value for money...
>
> ...it helps pupils of all abilities to make very good progress and to achieve results that are very high...
>
> ...it provides high standards of teaching. Teachers are very enthusiastic and knowledgeable, and work well as a team. They have very high expectations of what pupils can achieve and give lots of praise to encourage them to do well.
>
> The school provides a very rich and varied curriculum, which contributes significantly to the high quality of pupils' education.
>
> The headteacher provides outstanding leadership and the school is very well managed.
>
> There are excellent links with parents.
>
> There are no significant issues for improvement.

EXCELLENCE MODEL

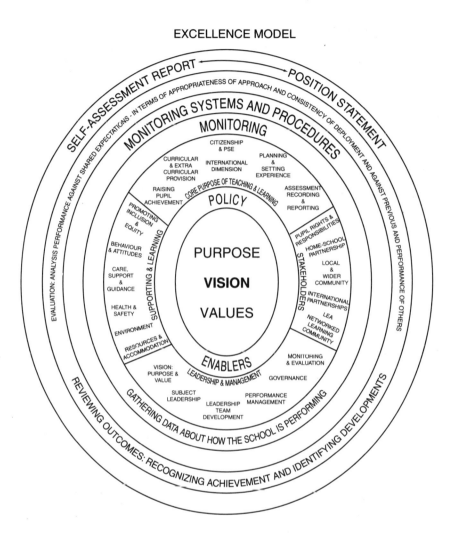

Figure 3.6 Application of the excellence model to the school

The financial services company

This case study takes the form of a review into the effectiveness of an organizational realignment of a medium-sized financial institution. It focuses especially on the leadership role of the top team and the areas for further learning. It specifically highlights the planning, objectives, risks and executive team working prior to the realignment; the task and people processes; the executive team working; and leadership during implementation.

Planning

The top team spent many months planning the realignment. Although the nature of the proposals introduced by the CEO and his deputy varied little from the final structure, all the executive team were involved in testing its validity, and at times forcefully arguing for one way or the other. The executive went through a facilitated process of ensuring the 'integrity' of the structure, assessing the risks and reaching a common understanding of the reasons for the realignment.

The executive also began to look at how the realignment might work in practice through:

- finalizing the top level structure;
- clarifying the composition of regulatory committees;
- drawing out the various decision-making processes; and
- agreeing a 'high level' split between business units, shared services and group functions.

Although the logic of the structure was understood and accepted, the motivation for supporting or challenging it were never really addressed. The proposed realignment was no doubt a *fait accompli* and this led to an inevitable demotivation and marginalization of some of the team.

Although the realignment decision-making process was well planned and well implemented, the degree of planning of the actual changes by the executive as a whole did not stand up to the rigours of implementation, as we shall see. Specifically:

- there was no executive team discussion and agreement on the organization structure one level down;
- people who could have contributed meaningfully to developing the best structures lower down were excluded;
- there was not anywhere near the 100 per cent clarity on the split between business units, shared services and group functions;
- there was no plan to involve the next level down in the process; and
- there were unrealistic timescales jointly agreed.

Objectives

The proposed vision was that the organization would 'transform itself from a traditional bank into a group of confident, successful and specialist financial services businesses'.

Reasons given to realign in support of this new vision was that it already had started successfully to implement this strategy, for example through a process of diversifying some of its saving and lending functions and through the acquisition of a number of smaller businesses. The increases in the scope, scale and complexity of its activities had led to the need to restructure into a clearly defined group of businesses.

It was envisaged that the new group structure would better enable the bank to achieve its strategic aims in three key ways:

1. The new group structure would facilitate the management of an expanding group of distinctive businesses. It would enable the acquisition and management of a number of separate business units with minimal disruption to other parts of the group.
2. The development of distinctive business units within new group structure would enhance individual business unit competitiveness. This would result from increased focus and commitment from all business unit management and staff to the delivery of the business unit customer propositions and achievement of competitive advantage.
3. In addition to improving the effectiveness of the management of the group business activities, the new group structure would facilitate the effective management by the group CEO of the relationship with its overseas parent and other relevant external relationships (Bank of England, the City, etc).

This was a transition vision – setting out the broad changes that the group was seeking to achieve. Whereas previous visions had the ability to motivate internally and describe a core aspect of customer strategy externally (eg, world class customer satisfaction, world class company) this vision did not seek to do that.

What was important therefore was to ensure that both staff and customers were able to feel included in the primary purpose of the organization. For the business units this might be somewhat easier than the other parts of the organization.

A greater business focus has got to be good for the company.

(Employee)

In terms of the rationale for the realignment the first key point, of facilitating the expanding group of distinctive businesses, was overwhelmingly accepted by managers and staff as sensible and logical. However, there was no mention of the customer in this greater business focus and no articulation of what greater business focus actually meant.

The second key point of increased focus and commitment from all business unit management and staff to the delivery of the business unit customer propositions and achievement of competitive advantage, was to be one of the key indicators of strategic success over the coming months. Comments with varying degrees of frequency had been made that questioned whether there was enough impetus for this to really make an impact on organizational effectiveness and the bottom line.

The third key point of sustained business unit focus required certain behaviours to occur, namely that:

- the chief operating officer would spend more time with the business units and less time with Group-wide issues;
- the business units heads would not get involved with overseas parent or Group 'bureaucracy';
- reporting lines through to the CEO and directors at the centre had been rationalized.

Additionally, the realignment could have addressed the challenges and issues that were not being addressed previously – in terms of, for example, further developing the organization's core competences and overcoming organization dysfunctional behaviours, etc.

Potential risks

The executive also assessed the potential risks in implementing structural change and identified some issues as potential risks in the implementation of the new organizational structure. The risks broadly split into risks inherent in the new structure itself, and risks inherent in the process of change. A subjective assessment, by the executive, of the perceived level of risk was undertaken. (Risks inherent in the new structure are shown in Table 3.1; risks inherent in managing change in Table 3.2.) It was suggested that the organizational structure change management plan should include solutions/contingencies to mitigate all these risks.

Table 3.1 Risks inherent in the new structure

Risk	Perceived level of risk
Costs may increase if we move to devolved support functions. Cost inefficiency is a risk – the structure may lead to some duplication of costs across the business units	High
Inadequate clarity of role and responsibility between the central services, shared services and business units	High
Inadequate motivation of those in the centre re: their relationship with the business units ('policeman' role) and central management	High
Inadequate business unit control and consistency to enable adequate servicing from the centre	Medium
Loss of integrity of the strategic group marketing function (product/market matrix) which may result in a lack of clarity about the boundaries of the businesses	Low
Centre and shared services may remain under existing constraints	Low
Risk that shared and central services may not be closely aligned culturally and process-wise with the business units that they interact with	Low
Devolution of shared services may impact effectiveness and efficiency	Low
Core group identity may be dissipated	Low
In some areas staff's 'affinity' with the group may be significantly diminished	Low
Throwing the baby out with the bathwater – possibility of getting rid of what is good as well as bad	Low
Group-wide synergies may be harder to exploit	Low
Loss of knowledge – inadequate capture and transfer of knowledge, eg strategy formulation and implementation	Low
Inadequate transfer of best practice and innovation across the group	Low
Risk of 'unilateral declaration of independence' by business units and not fully engaging with central services and group issues	Low
Change at the macro level will not necessarily provoke change at business unit level	Low
Business unit management may feel 'un-empowered'	Low

Table 3.2 Risks inherent in managing change

Risk	Perceived level of risk
Staff as a whole may feel that the organization is returning to functional or business silos with inconsistent values across the organization	High
Not keeping the people we want to keep	High
During the change process the organization may spend 6 months to a year with its 'eye off the ball'	High
Lack of change/implementation expertise and skills	Medium
The executive tends to get 'bored with the detail' quickly and therefore may lose interest and impetus	Medium
Staff may 'misread' the implications of the new structure	Medium
An inadequate change programme will be developed	Low
Reputation as 'poor managers of change' may inhibit change process	Low
Staff may see this as 'yet another restructure' not tackling the 'real problems', and therefore become demotivated	Low
Not having the best people possible for each job	Low
Managers not having the necessary capabilities to run their part of the business and manage the transformation	Low

All the perceived risks rated at medium to high either materialized or were kept on the 'at risk' register. All require active management of the risk involved.

The one possible exception was the short-term retention of key staff. Due to factors such as individual managerial interventions, the majority of senior management staff were retained. However, there was an ongoing major risk that over the following year the turnover of middle managers and staff would rise as a direct result of the management of these changes.

All the perceived risks rated as low still required attention and management with varying degrees of focus.

Executive team working

Prior to the full planning process the executive commissioned a 'health check' to assess the degree to which they were being effective as a team. Key observations were:

- There were uncertain priorities.
- The organization's key indicators of strategic success (KISS) did not drive the agenda.

- There needed to be greater clarity of purpose and roles.
- There was confusion as to who was progressing the agenda.
- Too much time was spent on the trivial.
- Some felt there was not enough meaningful time together.
- Collectively the executive was not good at planning.
- Some cliques were seen to unduly influence decisions.
- There was not enough of a culture of challenge.
- There was little mutual support in times of change.
- There was a need to translate strategy into action.
- Everyone agreed there was a need to manage change better.

Implementation

The observations and conclusions below are a summary of the one-to-one discussions held with the majority of senior and middle managers during the process of realignment, together with updates from individual directors, focus groups of staff and a further survey of the management population.

The broad conclusion is that the executive collectively failed to manage and lead the realignment process and consequently demonstrated to the organization the way not to manage change and as a result lessened the chances of true transformation. The risks inherent in managing change highlighted above either came true or are likely to be proved true without further positive executive action.

> I honestly cannot provide thoughts on any aspect that was well managed. It was the most poorly managed restructure I have ever known!
>
> (A recipient of change)

Clearly, individual directors have sought to fulfil their responsibilities as best they can – collectively they did not manage this.

From a project, ie task perspective, some things were managed well:

- The process of cascading the restructure from the top down was in theory right.
- Initial communication to everyone on the strategy, the structure and the rationale.
- Initially there was documented and formal communication.
- Initial communication was good, briefings arranged, etc.
- Updates via the intranet were useful to a point.

From a project perspective some things could have been managed differently:

- The message that only a few, that is 5 per cent, of people, all managers, would be affected came to be seen either as a deliberate attempt to downplay the traumas ahead or a gross miscalculation of the affect.
- The timetable slipped from day one with no detailed timetable of actions for managers to plan time in their diaries.
- It soon became clear that the appetite for communication faded once the more senior appointments had been made.
- There was an unnecessary vacuum whilst all level-one managers were appointed. This took an inordinate length of time, whilst appointments further down were generally rushed through leaving many people without sufficient time to think through their future.
- The level of work required was never fully scoped, particularly around recruitment – warnings given at the outset regarding target date of 1 April being set before the change workshops were held and the tasks identified were generally ignored.
- There was a danger that once remaining issues were left to the new business units or the functional areas to resolve they would never get addressed but lost.
- There clearly wasn't a full scoping of what had to be done before announcing a timetable.
- There has been a general feeling that there should have been more time available to complete the various stages with more thought about how the detail would work – clear timetable, plan of activities, key milestones, checklist for managers, etc.
- Once the initial communication was over there was a lull, which should have been replaced by the executive, individually and collectively communicating with staff.
- There was no contingency planning evident – some departments moved much quicker than others.
- Some managers believed that there was a lack of compliance with requirements to consult with staff.

> I am embarrassed by what has taken place here over the past few months. The loss in productivity of those staff directly affected by the changes must be huge.
>
> (A manager)

From a people perspective some things were managed well:

- Initially there was a high level commitment to communication.
- Management managed to tell people before the grapevine did.
- It was recognized that this amount of change needed to be managed into the business whereas in the past it had been less planned.

- The use of external expertise to assist the organization through the process.
- Commitment of top management in the early stages of the process and their willingness to commit key people to the programme.
- After 'the lull', internal communication was comprehensive and at the right frequency, especially the use of the intranet.
- The initial round of senior appointments divided between being completed quickly with clear and timely communication, and becoming a long drawn out affair that affected structures and appointments lower down.

From a people perspective some things could have been improved:

- There could have been more involvement and consultation.
- There should have been more honesty about the likely impact.
- There should have been a better appreciation of how the changes would feel at grassroots level.
- There could have been a clearer and consistent set of 'rules' about how structures were formed and who got what jobs; eg some senior managers were consulted, others just issued a structure; some were recruited, some just selected their direct reports.
- There was the need for more support for those affected at team leader level and below, as their line managers were often not feeling able to offer quality support at a critical time.
- The process of change management could have started earlier, indeed as soon as the executive decided on its new vision and new structure. The bottleneck in decisions throughout the business fuelled rumours, and as this early period was unmanaged from a communication point of view there was a far greater business impact and people started building up their defences.
- Overall the recruitment process was far too long and hit morale and productivity.
- Closed pool arrangements made it difficult for displaced employees to know which roles they could apply for in other parts of the business and which were not yet open to candidates from outside that area.
- There should have been some checks that line managers were doing what was expected of them in terms of communication, revised structures, job descriptions, proper selection processes, etc.
- The process for matching people to roles was not followed in each business unit, with appointments made in advance of selection processes and some selection processes failing to happen.

- There could have been more genuine two-way consultation for a closed period, with no selections made whilst collective consultation took place.
- There could have been individual consultation to establish employees' real wishes and aspirations rather than those assumed by the line managers.

It was very hard keeping a busy business area running through a very unsettled period when my boss was made redundant and I had to wait over two months to find out what was happening to me personally. I don't think anyone really appreciated the impact this had on individuals in my position either at the time, or longer term.

(Team leader)

Next steps

There are a myriad of tasks and activities that now need to be undertaken and which the executive management team are beginning to address:

- Remaining implementation actions (eg new budget processes, outstanding appointments) need to be delivered before business as usual issues take over priorities.
- Training and development of displaced people needs to be in place from now, to up-skill/re-skill employees.
- Building a sense of identity in those areas where the old identity has gone with a clear direction established as to where the business focus should be, short, medium and long term.
- A formal learning review amongst senior management, which would include the output from consultation groups of staff at different levels.

Part III

4. Organization

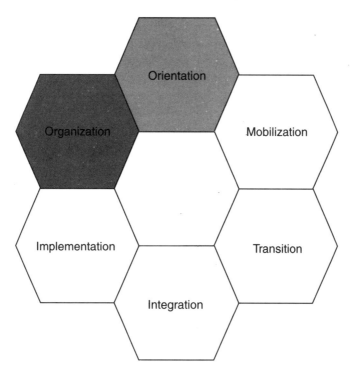

What we anticipate seldom occurs, what we least expected generally happens.
(Benjamin Disraeli)

If you can't describe what you are doing as a process, you don't know what you're doing.
(W Edwards Deming)

It is a bad plan that admits of no modifications.
(Publius Syrus)

Introduction

The aim of this chapter is to look the ways in which change can be organized. We will consider a number of ways of deciding how to address change and one or two frameworks which will assist in that process. We will cover:

- Balogun and Hailey's change kaleidoscope.
- The 7Ss.
- Johnson and Scholes' cultural web.
- Tichy's three change levers.
- Project and programme management.
- Different approaches to change.

The change kaleidoscope

Balogun and Hailey (2004) have devised what they call the 'change kaleidoscope' to help the change agent who 'faces a bewildering array of implementation decisions – the design choices – that need to be made about how change should be implemented'.

They suggest that there are a range of design choices, based upon the nature of the change – some significant aspects of the organizational change context that need to be factored into the design. They have six categories of design choices, discussed below.

Change path

Depending on the end state and how the change is to be implemented, there are four principal change paths. If you are looking for a total transformation in an incremental way then the change path will be evolutionary. If you want a transformation but with a 'big bang' approach then the change path is revolutionary. On the other hand if you are looking for realignment then you could adopt an incremental change path (adaptation), or a reconstruction approach via a big bang approach.

Depending on the approach, different levels of organization and readiness for change are necessary. Likewise different leadership styles may be called for.

Change start-point

The change start point defines where in the organization you wish to initiate the change. We touched upon the top-down or bottom-up approach in Chapter 2.

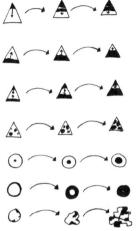

In the overwhelming majority of cases significant change in organizations is initiated or approved by a top-down process, although that is not to say that the change starting point would necessarily be at senior executive level.

A top-down approach might be driven by a strategic review which necessitates a company restructuring – say from having nine departments into having five departments. Typically this would mean recruiting five new (or old) departmental heads who would then seek to structure their new departments, beginning with the second tier and cascading all the way down the organization.

A bottom-up approach might result from the organization wishing to become 'more customer focused' and invest customer-facing staff with the task of generating ideas, and new processes and behaviours, to enact the change. Of course some organizations may well combine these two approaches. For example, a set of overarching values or operating guidelines might be generated at executive level and each functional or business unit might be empowered to translate these into appropriate behavioural imperatives. Likewise a new planning and performance system might set corporate goals, but individuals and teams might set their own target that then moves up the hierarchy until they meet the corporate objectives coming down. At the meeting point (often middle manager level) there is negotiation between the two sets of figures.

A fourth possibility, which would fit with a more emergent or flux attitude to change, is that of spotting pockets of good practice or innovative working, and fanning those particular fires. Seemingly haphazard, this can, of course, be more formalized through setting up processes – such as continuous improvement groups, knowledge cafes, away days, and the like – which would have the effect of encouraging or rewarding this type of activity.

Change style

This covers the sort of approach you wish management and the change team to adopt in their interaction with the organization during the change. Typically this could range from collaboration through to coercion. A number of Goleman's styles of leadership (see Chapter 8) might be appropriate depending on the situation. Here it is quite important to note a number of key points:

- just because the management team have an ingrained or natural style doesn't mean to say it's the best style for the change situation;
- different styles might be appropriate at different stages in the change process; and
- particular styles might be more congruent with the type of change you are bringing about.

Change target

By this Balogun and Hailey mean to what depth the change should be intending to go at an individual level. Are we trying to change the performance outputs of the organization as a whole, are we wanting to change the behaviours of people within the organization, or are we trying to fundamentally shift people's values? Different targets will take different types of intervention and need different timescales.

Change roles

These are the different roles that are needed to initiate and implement change in an organization. Different people can play different roles and indeed have multiple roles within the organization. In the organizations that we have used as case studies we found that there were different change leadership roles:

- project or change teams;
- people from the business who were either 100 per cent seconded to the change team or part time;
- people from the change team who were located within the business;
- external consultants who were located within the change team or within the business;
- people who were solely in the business who had a specific ongoing or short-term role to manage change within their area;
- groups of managers who had a collective role to play within the change;
- groups of staff who had a representative role to play within the change;
- functional disciplines that had experience or expertise related to the change;

- functional disciplines that had specialist knowledge which was needed as part of the change process;
- line managers;
- staff.

The change levers are 'the range of levers and interventions to be deployed across four subsystems – technical, political, cultural and interpersonal'. You could use a number of frameworks to assist you in this. We've already encountered McKinsey's 7Ss framework, which allows us to identify what needs to be changed in the strategy, structure, systems, management style, staff and their skills together with the organization's shared values.

7S framework

A useful way of moving from orientation to organization is by combining the From > To analysis with, say, McKinsey's 7Ss or Goffee and Jones' cultural matrix. Table 4.1 uses the 7Ss as it applies to one of the case studies (Aster Group; see Chapter 3).

Table 4.1 The 7S framework and the Aster Group

7Ss	Before	After
Strategy	To improve homes to modern standards whilst keeping rents stable through high quality maintenance work and internal cost efficiency	To be a leading provider of high quality affordable homes and services and to help create thriving and successful communities through achieving excellent customer and community focused services; delivering more new homes; and maintaining robust businesses. This mission to be achieved by focus on growth through acquisition, internal development and diversification
Structure	Classical functional structure	Group of businesses with maximum autonomy with some shared central functions and corporate governance
Systems (IT, HR, financial)	Uniform systems, policies and procedures	Enhanced systems for an expanding group of companies tailored to each company's needs, but compatible with group decision making and strategy

Table 4.1 The 7S framework and the Aster Group   *continued...*

7Ss	Before	After
Management style	Autocratic, centralist style Managerial	Authoritative, pacesetting with distributed coaching leadership at a local level
Staff	Right staff in the right part of the hierarchy	Recruitment of staff to fit with new entrepreneurial ethos
Skills	Right skills to do business as usual	Equip staff to operate in a more competitive environment which is constantly changing Greater cross-group working and sharing best practice
Shared values	Central ethos of providing a good quality service to customers with a looked-after workforce	Customer responsive, honest, open and true to their word and fair to all. Within this there is a strong emphasis on involving and responding to the needs of customers

You can extend the analysis by describing the future state of the organization in terms of each of the seven dimensions.

It is worth remembering that these factors are all interconnected. Moving from current to the intended is not just about changing the 'easier' factors like the structure but actually also about the whole system's architecture.

Using Goffee and Jones's cultural matrix you can map the current culture and the preferred culture. In the example above the current culture was best described as networked (high sociability, low solidarity) with perhaps some elements of the fragmented culture with its slightly functional and silo nature. There was cohesiveness across the organization and an emphasis on doing a good job well in a conducive atmosphere.

The new vision required a shift to the communal (high sociability, high solidarity) with perhaps a slight mercenary bent. Group cohesion was important and with more partnering and grouping taking place these was a need for people to be committed to each other, the organization and the services it provided. What were required were high levels of passion, commitment and teamwork. Goffee and Jones (2000) see a number of interventions that will assist this process:

- Regularly benchmark; compare yourself to radically different kinds of organizations.
- Build opportunities to discuss and critique credo.

- Ensure values and associated behaviours are built into the appraisals and reward systems.
- Expose to others (alliances; consultants; bring in new people).

They offer further words of advice:

- Resist the temptation to let friendship get in the way of business decisions.
- Make sure your appraisal system focuses on objective measures.
- Fight complacency by reminding everyone of the power of existing and potential competition.
- Make the mission live. Don't let it become a tablet of stone that can't be revisited.

You can now use the framework in a number of ways to help organize the change. Depending on the nature of the change, you can either, a) flesh out the desired state and begin to design a programme of work which would achieve it, or b) analyse the gap between the current reality and desired future state and design a process to bridge the gap.

For example, in looking at the shift from an autocratic, centralist managerial style to a more authoritative, pacesetting style with distributed coaching leadership at a local level, clearly you cannot wave a magic wand and have all the managers start behaving in the new way. A structured management development programme – with options ranging from formal courses through tailored on-site programmes to action learning sets and one-to-one coaching – would be more realistic and appropriate. Of course the programme can be aligned, in time, with the structural changes, which would allow and require more empowerment and distributed leadership, and some of the systems changes which would allow a greater degree of autonomy in the new business units.

The systems themselves, however, might be designed from a blank sheet of paper with business analysts looking at key processes necessary for a group of independent operating companies with shared central services.

A dual approach might be taken in terms of ensuring that staff skills fit the desired state. A training needs analysis could be undertaken which would look at the desired competencies and see in what areas there were skills gaps in the existing staff. Training interventions could be designed and developed to raise the internal capabilities of staff. In parallel the HR department may wish to use a new set of behavioural competencies in their recruitment programmes.

So we can see how the 7Ss can be used, first to diagnose the current internal state of the organization, second to articulate the desired future state and thirdly to start the process of working programmes of change.

Cultural web

Johnson and Scholes (1999) have designed what they call a 'cultural web', the elements of which go to make up the prevailing culture of an organization and which if adjusted can enable cultural change to occur in furtherance of the organizational change initiatives. At the centre of this web is what they call the 'paradigm', an underlying set of assumptions embodying what the organization is all about – where it's going, how it's going to get there and the core values to which it adheres. The organization's *control systems* monitor and evaluate its operating performance. Some organizations will have tight control systems (for example, banks or publicly accountable operations), others will be looser (for example start-ups or more entrepreneurial firms).

Organizational structures will represent the hierarchical structure, lines of accountability and responsibility, and communication and production flows.

Power structures on the other hand map out where power and authority lie in terms of decision making and mandate holding, whether power is centrally held or locally dispersed, whether leadership is located at the top of the organization or is distributed, and on what power is based – whether it's position or role, or expert power or personal charismatic power. *Symbols* would be artefacts or architecture which somehow encapsulates what the organization values. These might include designs such as the corporate logo and uniform but would also include building design and such things as office space and car parking space. *Rituals and routines* cover how the organization has come to organize and structure some of the things that it does – hence the norm for organizational meetings, how reports are written and presented, how people are enfolded into the company and how they leave. *Stories and myths* are what get chosen to be communicated formally and informally around the organization when describing significant events and personalities in its history, in its current situation or as part of its future strategy.

As the name implies, a web is very interconnected and one element will impact on others and be influenced in turn by them. Table 4.2 illustrates an old cultural web compared to the preferred new one.

Table 4.2 Old and new cultural webs compared

Element of the cultural web	Old culture	New culture
Paradigm	Trustworthy Reliable 'Steady as she goes' Marketing led	Entrepreneurial Individual responsibility Joint accountability Sales driven
Control systems	Annual review Planning committee Financial reporting Strong and tight compliance culture	Business unit profit centres Core 'tight' controls and discretionary 'loose' controls Coaching culture
Organizational structures	Functional Technical departments Pyramid	Separate business units Shared services Flatter organization
Power structures	Managing Director Credit board Director of Finance Chief auditor	Chief Operating Officer Business unit MDs
Symbols	Tower block as HQ Chauffeurs for executives Staff restaurant	New open plan building Atrium with break-out areas Riverside cafe
Rituals and routines	Board meetings Annual reports Summer party at the sports club	Quarterly reviews Business units 'doing their own thing'
Stories and myths	Historical anecdotes 'Who you know' not 'What you do' Gossip about the executive board	Sales successes 'What you achieve' not 'How long you've been there' 'Sales success' stories

Tichy's change levers

Tichy (1983) suggests that the three fundamental change levers are the technical, political and cultural systems at play within the organization, and that if you only concentrate on one of these then you risk sabotaging the change. The technical system are the arrangements whereby goods and services are produced from the various inputs; the political system is how power and resources are allocated and distributed within the organization; and the cultural system is the shared values operating within the organization.

Tichy goes on to say that mission and strategy, organizational structure and systems, and human resource management are the three management tools through which the change levers can be pulled. I have adapted a matrix from Tichy (see Table 4.3) to highlight the key questions that need to be asked and answered when effecting change across the three systems using the three management tools.

Table 4.3 Tichy's three management tools

	Mission and strategy	**Organization structure and systems**	**Human Resource management**
Technical system	Have you conducted an external and internal analysis and created a new vision and strategy to address your findings?	Have you fitted the structure to the new strategy? Are the systems in place to support both structure and strategy?	Is there clarity of role definition and allocation? Is there a performance management system in place which ties organizational objectives to individual objectives and manages performance?
Political system	Have all stakeholders been identified and key ones involved in the strategy and change process?	Is power and decision-making authority located in the correct places for the changes to be effective?	Is it clear who gets rewarded and for what?
Cultural system	Are the espoused values and culture aligned with the stated mission and strategy?	Does the management style fit with the accomplishment of the strategy and is it aligned with the desired culture?	Are we recruiting, developing, rewarding and retaining the people who fit the desired culture? Are rewards in place to support the desired culture?

Project management methodology

A project management methodology is frequently used to organize and implement change initiatives. It is not the purpose here to describe in any detail how to manage projects – there are a host of books (Boddy, 2001; Turner *et al*, 1996) and a number of methodologies (Prince 2, MSP) which will do this. It is important, however, to discuss the similarities and differences between change management and project management and why this book focuses on a somewhat different terrain than project management.

A project management method organizes, manages and controls discrete projects such as the technical aspects of installing a new system or a new structure. Managed successfully it should deliver the right changes, on time and within budget. It should help manage risk, control quality and deal with any obstacles and issues that arise during the project. Projects will be clearly defined in terms of scope, goals and objectives, with allocation of personnel, roles and responsibilities. There will be well defined and measurable business outcomes; a corresponding set of organized tasks to achieve the outcomes; an allocation of resources; and a project organization structure to manage the project.

The essential difference between project management and change management is that the project will tend to focus on the technical aspects of the change whilst change management will tend to focus on the psychological aspects of the transition from one state to the other. That is not to say that good project management will not use good leadership, interpersonal skills or focus on people, but often that is not its primary purpose. So, for example, a project might focus on the technical aspects of managing a restructure by identifying components of the new structure, generating job descriptions, developing equitable interviewing processes and designing appropriate redundancy packages. Change management will encompass managing the psychological transition from one way of working to another, dealing with the emotional aspects of change and the disturbances that can occur. Managing what is seen as resistance to the change tends to come under the remit of change management.

A project may well be deemed completed when a new information system has been successfully installed, gone live and staff trained to operate it. However, the management of change may well continue through the need for a different style of leadership, building a different type of culture and interacting with customers in a different way. It deals with embedding the changes in the organization.

Organizing for change

Project management is a process for implementing change that takes you from the process of defining the change from the business strategy through defining the project scope, understanding enablers and constraints, to developing a project strategy and plan, and then to project implementation, monitoring, control and learning.

There is also the need to cascade the objectives down to more and more detailed sets, from the overall change objectives, through the programme, project objectives to the work area, team and individual objectives.

Typically, project methodologies would cover the following areas:

- understanding the drivers for business change;
- managing the business change process;
- project and programme management team with the relevant roles and responsibilities;
- benefits management and realization;
- business case;
- identification and management of stakeholders;
- communication;
- risk management;
- issue management;
- quality management;
- programme planning and control;
- quality management strategy;
- project and programme management processes.

Two key roles in the organization and implementation of any change management project are the project manager (the person primarily responsible for running the project), and the project sponsor, or Senior Responsible Officer (SRO) in project management terminology (the person who oversees the project's successful journey, and in terms of the project's relationship with the rest of the organization has the power and authority of corporate governance). Our case studies suggest that both roles are critical to the successful outcome of the initiatives.

The project manager or change team leader needs to have an understanding not only of the task/technical side of the changes but also the ability to understand and mobilize people on a psychological/emotional level both within and beyond the change team.

The change manager must have relevant power and authority within the team (be they full-time, part-time or seconded individuals) and be able to exercise influence and impact within the pertinent areas of the business. Clearly the change manager needs to be leading and managing the team; effectively communicating to all stakeholders; be outcome focused; successful in juggling the time, budget and quality dimensions; using relevant management, change management and project management techniques and methodologies; monitoring and evaluating progress; being risk aware but not necessarily risk averse; and being able to escalate where necessary.

Different approaches to change

As we discussed in Chapter 2, different organizational paradigms will elicit different approaches to this phase of change organization.

The machine metaphor or the 'change through design' paradigm fits extremely well with a rigorous project management approach where there is a very planned and sequenced approach to change using project management methodology and a well thought out mechanistic approach– structured, organized and systematic. As we can see from the case studies, the systems changes and parts of some of the business restructuring can relatively easily begin with this approach. The initial business analysis of the systems, the design of the software and the building up of a project plan and rollout schedule improve the chances of success. Likewise the due diligence process in a merger is a systematic way of appraising the feasibility of the initiative. These types of change lend themselves to careful planning, managing, monitoring and controlling.

The political metaphor and 'change through addressing interests' suggest that the key focus in entering the change process is to ensure that you have a power base and that a careful analysis has been made of the positions of the key stakeholders – their views and their willingness to be advocates or blockers of the change. Understanding motivations and who are the likely winners and losers as a result of the change will help assess, a) the feasibility of the change, and b) where one should be putting one's energies. We saw in the majority of the case studies a greater or lesser focus on actively managing stakeholders, ensuring they were brought on board at an early stage. Some of this was formalized within the project management process; generally this was done in a relatively informal, but nonetheless proactive way. In fact we saw in all the case studies that stakeholders' interests were acknowledged, mapped and addressed – and we can see that this is perhaps an essential ingredient in why they all had successful outcomes. Each organization had a stakeholder with enough power to thwart any change (be it the Local Education Authority, the government, the shareholders, the tenants, or the staff) but they were successfully engaged and in all cases became forces for driving the change forward rather than restraining it.

The organism metaphor requires the change agent to be monitoring the environment, taking the pulse of the organization and creating an enabling ethos where people can learn to become responsive both to the environment and to the changes. Organization within this metaphor occurs around the monitoring systems in place on a strategic level (PESTLE and SWOT analyses, developing future scenarios, etc) and on an operational level (real-time feedback from customers and frontline staff, etc). Where there isn't an over-engineered project plan in place the changes can become more flexible and adapt to changing circumstances. Apart from the implicit vision of the kitchenware company ('Grow our business stronger and better') they didn't plan what needed to be done, because they didn't know what needed to be done, initially. However, they got close to the customers, the suppliers and close to the staff, and a set of possible changes emerged. Aster, having set itself up as a group focusing on growth through mergers, was constantly scanning the environment for emerging opportunities.

The flux and transformation metaphor and the 'change through emergence' paradigm assume that change cannot be explicitly managed, but rather needs to emerge. So, for example, the Institute of Public Health didn't have a thoroughly worked out plan when it was established but stayed close to its stakeholders and adapted its strategies accordingly. It watched where in the health network across Ireland there were tensions, opportunities and hot spots, then it focused its resources there and developed products and services to meet the emerging wants and needs.

The 'change through learning' paradigm, rooted in the organizational development movement, and latterly the concepts of the learning organization and knowledge management, approaches the organization stage of change by ensuring there is the building of change capacity in the organization and establishing processes for feedback and learning and transfer of knowledge. This requires thoughtfulness, itself needing time, space and reflection. The change process at Aarhus exemplifies change through learning with its structure of exploring people's feelings and emotions as an explicit and crucial part of change. Indeed, with the kitchenware company and the Institute there were deliberate attempts to capture valid data and information from the wider system. In parallel, both the Institute and Aster set up management and leadership development programmes as part of the change effort, and a key plank of both these programmes was learning about external and internal systems and the process of change.

The 'change through people' paradigm recognizes the need to include, involve and engage with all stakeholders, but principally managers and staff, in order to create solutions that address the important issues. The primary school put the children at the centre of all the changes that took place. The management and staff development processes at Aarhus, the Institute and Aster set out to develop capability on the one hand and tap into their ideas on the other. We said earlier that since change happens through people, winning the hearts and minds is clearly a key factor in this. Focus on an inclusive and engaging management style combined with setting up proper human resource management systems and focusing in on creating an enabling culture are characteristics of organizations operating within this paradigm.

Case study analysis

A key theme emerging from the case study analysis was the need to clearly define the current state of the organization along certain axes and then develop a clear, cogent and coherent description of the end state. The focus at the organization stage of the change process is being able to identify the steps it would take to bridge the gap between the two. It is often the strategy, structure and systems that are more easily defined.

Although many of the organizations took a planned approach to change the analysis suggests that actually the overall parameters were well defined but there was always room for manoeuvre within the change process itself. For example, Aster had developed a clear overarching vision with an agreed structure and an initial business plan. However, the actual working out of what was going to remain local and what was going to be centralized was open for discussion. Likewise, although there was some convergence of policies and procedures, each business unit was allowed to adopt what was best for its situation.

The Institute of Public Health on the other hand had a clear vision and set of values. It also knew who its major stakeholders were. It was only during the ongoing developing relationship with these stakeholders that an acceptable strategy could be formulated, and this strategy for change was always going to be subject to evolution.

Biogen Idec's change organization process was along project management lines, very much evidence-based – with a lot of data gathering from reputable sources and looking at best practice across the industry, across geographies and across specialisms. The decision-making process was well planned and methodical and although the initial outcome of the change – deciding on the new location – was uncertain, the next phase of negotiations with staff, restructuring plans and finding new offices and transferring old staff and recruiting new staff lent itself to be extremely well project planned.

The British Council's change initiative was organized through a programme team comprising people drawn from the affected stakeholders and the business, and with experience in change management and process re-engineering. The team also had a strong, visible sponsor in the person of the Deputy Director General. In terms of organization the team followed the programme best practice as laid out by the Office of Government Commerce using the Managing Successful Programmes methodology. It was important to note that at all times the systems change was subservient to the organization's strategy and didn't deviate from this alignment.

In developing the plan for how to restructure the department in Aarhus, the change team didn't concentrate merely on the mechanics of the change but developed a programme which addressed both task and process. They developed a workable formal organizational structure and a plan for implementing it, but they also ensured that the structure was supported by the necessary lines of two-way communication and a common understanding of new roles and responsibilities, and the healthy engagement vertically, horizontally and externally, within the new structure.

The organization of change within the kitchenware company was relatively straightforward – they listened to what their customers wanted and re-engineered their back office processes to deliver the right products on time. Everything was driven by the customer.

One of the first actions of the primary school head was to form a leadership team and then quickly extend involvement to all staff and all governors. These comprised one-to-one and small group discussions, and culminated in an initial vision-creation workshop. Through her actions the head was organizing for change, orienting the organization and mobilizing stakeholders into action.

In the financial services company case study, the company planned the high level structure very well, involving all key people in the conversations and developing an implementation and communication plan.

Summary

Whatever your approach to change it is important that you have a conceptual framework in which to operate so that you are clear how you will approach change. You need to understand what needs to be planned and what can emerge.

A useful checklist for organizing change comes from Balogun and Hailey's change kaleidoscope:

- change path;
- change start point;
- change style;
- change target;
- change levers; and
- change roles.

There are a number of useful tools and frameworks to map the current state and the preferred future state across a number of relevant organizational dimensions.

The McKinsey 7Ss – how will you organize getting from here to there on the seven dimensions of:

1. strategy;
2. structure;
3. systems;
4. styles;
5. staff;
6. skills; and
7. shared values?

Alternatively on which of the key areas of Johnson and Scholes' cultural web are you focusing:

- paradigm;
- control systems;
- organizational structures;
- power structures;
- symbols;
- rituals and routines;
- stories and myths?

How might you deploy Tichy's three management tools of mission and strategy, organizational structure and systems, and human resource management within the technical, political and cultural systems?

To what degree will you adopt a *project management* or programme management methodology and which will it be?

How will you choose what overriding approach to use (in terms of the metaphors and paradigms) given the nature of the change and the current culture?

5. Mobilization

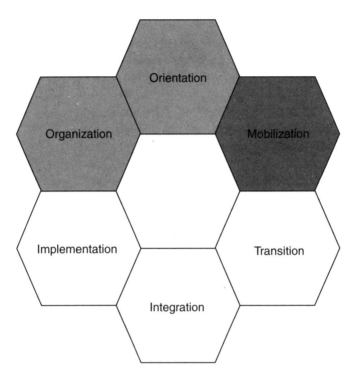

Whatever you can do, or dream you can, begin it.
Boldness has genius, power, and magic in it.
(Johann Wolfgang von Goethe)

I am personally convinced that one person can be a change catalyst, a 'transformer' in any situation, any organization. Such an individual is yeast that can leaven an entire loaf. It requires vision, initiative, patience, respect, persistence, courage, and faith to be a transforming leader.
(Stephen R Covey)

Never doubt that a small group of thoughtful, committed citizens can change the world. Indeed, it's the only thing that ever has.
(Margaret Mead)

Introduction

Mobilization is the process of involving, engaging and catalysing the stakeholders affected by the changes. The aims of this chapter are to:

- understand what will motivate and mobilize people towards change;
- provide some frameworks for understanding stakeholders involved in the change;
- look at ways to address specific groups in the change process; and
- understand the types and levels of communication required in change.

If the art and act of mobilization are the process of involving, engaging and catalysing the stakeholders affected by the intended changes then we need to address a range of issues in order for us to successfully accomplish this. We will need to understand what motivates people to be 'on board' and engaged with the change process in the first place; we will need to identify who the stakeholders are, where their interests lie and what their possible contributions to the change process will be; we will need to identify certain generic and specific groups of people who will need to be involved in the change process; and we will need to have a range of strategies to communicate with those who will be part of the change.

Motivation and mobilization

On a very basic level we can ask, 'What will motivate anyone and everyone to be positively involved in change? What gets people up in the morning?' More specifically, what will get people engaged in the changes that we want to happen? You will recall from Chapter 2 that we identified four different personality types:

1. the *thoughtful realists* who need to have a very good reason for change based on solid evidence and tangible reasons;
2. the *thoughtful innovators* who will want to know where the changes are heading and how they fit with the overall strategy;
3. the *action-oriented realists* who will want to get started on improving things but will need clarity of direction and definitely some actionable first steps; and
4. the *action -oriented innovators* who will, no doubt, embrace change, as long as they can be a part of it and as long as they are inspired to follow it.

Each of these personality types will be motivated in different ways. It may explain why some people may appear less enthusiastic or more reluctant to engage with what you say and how you say it. So, when you start planning how you might mobilize people it is worth spending some time in understanding the different types of language that will be required to get everyone on board. Successful mobilization will address these different personality needs.

Not only will different people be motivated by different things, it is indeed a good discipline for change managers to address the types of issues that different personalities see as important. So it is necessary to create an inspiring vision of the future which people can aspire to and work towards, but it is also critical that the vision – and of course the changes themselves – are grounded in reality. There does need to be an evidence-based rationale for change and some practical ways into the changes with tangible and specific objectives. This leads on to the need for a coherent business case which has an inherent logic, but this needs to be tempered with an understanding that change impacts people and can impact the core values of an organization. Some people will focus on the impact on people and values before they turn to the logic of the business case. Some people will tend to want the change to be presented (and implemented) in a structured, systematic and orderly way with little or no deviation. Others will feel hemmed in by this approach and will be better motivated to join the change journey if they believe it to be more of a voyage of discovery with options and possibilities emerging as the change progresses. In that sense it's about holding the tension between tying things down and keeping options open.

Another way of looking at mobilization is through some of the research on motivation. Porter and Lawler (1968) have tied together a number of motivation theories in an integrated model which is based on the three components of effort, performance and satisfaction. One can argue that for people to be motivated to be involved in change, those three components need to be aligned and these key questions satisfactorily answered from the individual's perspective:

● Effort – is the change worth the effort that will be involved? Will the benefits outweigh the costs?
● Performance – am I able to achieve the performance that will be required by the effort I need to put in? Indeed, am I competent to deliver the necessary changes if I get involved?
● Satisfaction – will I achieve enough satisfaction through the level of the extrinsic and intrinsic rewards on offer? What is it worth, my getting involved?

From the change manager's view the questions take on a slightly different bent, essentially becoming, 'How can we sell the benefits of change enough to enable people to make the effort to deliver the performance that we are looking for?' This in turn generates the need for the change manager to create a picture of the future that is attractive (remember, for all types!); understand and communicate what level of performance and types of behaviour will be needed; and what level of commitment and effort is realistically expected.

In *Making Sense of Change Management* (Cameron and Green, 2004) we looked at a number of motivation theories that have some relevance when it comes to mobilizing people in general and also identify areas which you as change agent may need to address directly. The behavioural school of psychology, for example, will suggest employing the possibilities of rewards if you engage with the change and punishments if you don't. Adherents of Herzberg may warn that you need to be clear that the changes that you are suggesting can have both motivating and demotivating effects, and not necessarily in the way you may have imagined. Whereas an increase in Herzberg's hygiene factors (for example: pay, working conditions, status, levels of job security) may not actually increase motivation, a decrease in these factors may well increase demotivation. Getting a car parking space may be 'nothing special'; taking it away will cause anger or annoyance. Herzberg suggests that factors such as the possibility of increased achievement, advancement and responsibility will tend to be motivating factors in any change. Though we might add... as long as the rewards are commensurate with the efforts.

Finally, it can be useful to check how the changes you are suggesting might impact on people's hierarchy of needs according to Maslow (1970).

The change equation

In Chapter 2 we introduced the change formula. Based on Beckhard and Harris' original formula, amended by De Woot (1996) and added to by me from my change practice, we can use the formula to help us establish what is necessary for the momentum for change to outweigh the costs and resistance to change:

pressure for change	x	a clear shared vision	x	capacity to change	x	capability to change	x	actionable first steps	>	resistance to change

By analysing the formula at the beginning of change and using it as a checklist during the process of change we can ensure that the maximum number of people have bought into it. Remember, different people will be motivated and mobilized by different dimensions of the change; some because of the dissatisfaction with the status quo; some by an inspiring and motivating vision of the future; some because the quantity and quantity of resources are ready for deployment; and some because there are clear, practical first steps for them to get a handle on.

Without pressure for change the change effort will never have sufficient priority: it will languish at the bottom of the 'pending' tray. In order to ensure there is pressure for change you first need to articulate the external and internal drivers for it, establishing a compelling reason for change and stating what needs to change. You need to know who has a stake in promoting change and what issues will have to be addressed through the change (for example, structure, size, staff, resources, customer organizations, roles and relationships, working methods and procedures). You may also need to establish what will happen if you do not change – the costs, benefits and likely scenarios of not changing.

Without a clear vision the change may get off to an initial start but it will quickly lose direction. You need to be clear about what will be different following the changes – what the new situation will look and feel like, how it will work and how people will be acting differently. Everyone will need to have a sense of how you will know the change has happened.

Without the organizational capacity there will be stress and frustration, so it is important to establish whether the organization is ready for change. Does the organization have the energy to make this change happen? Do you know what resources you need to apply to the change and are they available? Will this change conflict with other organizational priorities and might there be tension between delivering business as usual for today and creating the future? You may need to let people know that you are increasing the capacity for change, and this may involve stopping or postponing other initiatives.

Without the organizational capability there will be anxiety and errors. You will therefore need to establish what skills and competences are required for you to achieve your vision of the future and also how widely they are currently deployed and accessible. Part of the mobilization process is to check how great is the willingness of the workforce to change and what needs to be done to develop this. On the one hand this might link into the prevailing attitude towards risk and innovation; on the other hand it might mean investing in developing or acquiring new skills and competences.

Without actionable first steps there will be false starts, haphazard efforts and diffused thinking. In order to ensure people set off on the right track together you can build support by finding allies and other interested parties, generating interest amongst them and involvement in what needs to be done. A good start might be involving people in an audit of the present unsatisfactory situation, followed by getting ideas from people, and initiating pilot projects. It might mean the setting up of a change team or change network of interested parties whose remit is to operationalize the initial plan.

Resistance to the idea of change

Resistance to change can come in many forms and at different times during the change process. In Chapter 2 we looked briefly at Lewin's force field analysis and how, in order to ensure that the driving forces for change do indeed achieve their stated intent, the restraining forces are reduced. These restraining forces can be seen as the resistances to change, and as we have seen from the change equation they need to be less that those forces on the other side of the equation.

When dealing with resistance to change during the mobilization process it is important to at least hold the possibility that what you label 'resistance' might actually be something quite different. Remember we discussed the thoughtful realists who have as a motto, 'If it ain't broke, don't fix it' and sometimes, 'Don't throw the baby out with the bathwater.' These people value what currently is, especially if it works. Do not imagine they are resisting change because they are Luddites – they may well be making a plea not to rush headlong into change without think through all the implications.

Others, based on their knowledge and experience, may genuinely be alerting you to the fact that the proposed changes won't work. I believe a key process is to establish where you think resistance is and to discover what the views of these people are. Let them inform your choices and your designs. It may be because of some of the reasons just stated or it may be because of issues such as fear of change; lack of security; fear of conflict; reluctance of think strategically; having too narrow a perspective (job-only focus), or it might be the ownership of outdated processes. A key question to ask is, how might we use this information to reduce the restraining forces or fine tune the change plan itself?

Schein (2002) suggests that there are two fundamental anxieties that people have when facing change – the anxiety to survive set against the anxiety of whether they will be able to learn the new ways of doing things:

> Learning anxiety comes from being afraid to try something new for fear that it
> will be too difficult, that we will look stupid in the attempt, or that we will have

to part from old habits that have worked for us in the past. Learning something new can cast us as the deviant in the groups we belong to. It can threaten our self-esteem and, in extreme cases, even our identity... You can't talk people out of their learning anxieties; they're the basis for resistance to change.

Survival anxiety, however, works in creating pressure for change within the individual in relation to the consequences of not changing – being sacked, appearing incompetent or unwilling. Schein suggests that for change to occur, survival anxiety has to outweigh the learning anxiety. Of course to do this you can either raise the level of survival anxiety (for example through threats of punishment) or reduce the levels of learning anxiety.

From our understanding of force field analysis we can perhaps come to a similar conclusion to Schein in that it's best to reduce the learning anxiety by ensuring that there's an environment conducive to learning:

> The problem is that the creation of psychological safety is usually very difficult, especially when you're pushing for greater workforce productivity at the same time. Psychological safety is also dramatically missing when a company is downsizing or undergoing a major structural change, such as reorganizing into flatter networks.
>
> Most companies prefer to increase survival anxiety because that's the easier way to go. And that, I think, is where organizations have it absolutely wrong.

So we can see that on an individual level, even at this stage of mobilizing people, we need to be aware that there are different personality types with different needs, wants and anxieties, and we need to be working on a number of key dimensions (from the change equation) to ensure that the changes have a chance of getting off to a successful beginning.

Stakeholder interests

When we looked at the need for change we saw the importance of establishing who the stakeholders were and where they stood in relation to the change. In terms of mobilizing people for change it is crucial to use your stakeholder analysis to inform how you will manage and communicate with them throughout the change.

Stakeholder analysis can look at stakeholders from a number of perspectives including the level of power, energy, interest and commitment they have for the change. Or we can look at the analysis from the perspective of the impact that the change will have on them. One can sometimes assume that those with the highest interest would be those who will be most impacted. However, this isn't always the case so a separate analysis would bring additional benefits. We can also look at the levels of trust and agreement we have with them. The purpose in establishing these things is to be able to accomplish your aims of successful change whilst at the same time being mindful of the wants and needs of other communities of interest. In Chapter 2 we highlighted three important considerations:

1. Segmenting everyone into stakeholders is an inexact science. When it comes to change you might want to differentiate some staff from others, some members of the community from others, and indeed some managers from others.
2. In order to place stakeholders on the matrix you need to establish where they are – what their attitudes really are, rather than just assuming. That involves communication; it may indeed involve dialogue.
3. Remember that those stakeholders with little current interest or power may well still be important – either because you have social or corporate responsibilities to address the needs of those without a voice, or they will emerge as people who find some power and some interest when you start to make your changes. This final point is worth underscoring not least because things change as change happens. What started off as a threatening thing might turn into something positive… or vice versa.

A further important point to note is that stakeholders may well have ongoing relationships with each other, or they may form relationships because of this change. This can affect their attitudes to change – positively or negatively.

Let us look at some generic positioning of stakeholders across some of the possible axes.

Blockers (high energy/low commitment and high power/low commitment)

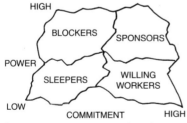

These are people who can obstruct or prevent the change happening in some way. They have an interest in the change but a low commitment to it. Given we've defined them as blockers, this implies that they have some power to impede. Alternatively it may be that they have the energy to oppose the change even though they may not have any power.

Key questions that will inform your strategy here are:

- What are their motivations?
- What is their legitimacy?

- What are their arguments?
- What is their source of power?
- What is their source of energy?

Possible strategies include winning the arguments; reducing their power and energy; circumventing their power; escalating to a higher authority; or engaging them in dialogue.

Sponsors (high power/high commitment)

These may indeed be nominated sponsors for this change project – but they may not be for two reasons. One is that the nominated project sponsor may not be totally committed to the project for whatever reason (time, interest or politics, for example) and the other is that there may not be a project management methodology operating within the organization. With those provisos we can however say that all the research suggests that the successful change management projects are the ones that have a sponsor who is committed and who has the necessary power and authority to intervene, for example, to escalate issues, to secure resources, and to open doors and such like.

The same set of questions need to be answered as for the blockers, but this is to ensure that they stay onside and are kept informed to the degree with which they are comfortable. If they are in a formal role then the governance procedures should go some way to providing a framework for this.

Champions (high energy/high commitment)

These are the people who are advocates for change and may well be active implementers of change. They may have specific power and authority; they may have a specific role within the change process; they may have a visible leading role within the business; or they may be middle managers wanting change to happen. They will naturally want to be fully involved in the change and would most likely be able to take other people along with them. A key need will be for them to have enough information and resource and also enough support to keep their momentum. Change is an exhausting business and can sap the energy and motivation of any of us. Sometimes the change champions can bear the brunt of this and so require nurturing and sustaining, even though they may not realize it.

Preachers (low energy/high commitment)

Preachers are people who are in positions of power or opinion leaders whose view counts within the organization. They are committed yet for some reason do not have the energy to make this their number one priority. Given the need for clear, visible sponsorship one may argue that someone who just preaches might have an unforeseen negative impact on perceptions about the change. If you look at the typical chief executive of a local government authority having to juggle competing demands on their time (perhaps being responsible for housing, social services, education, sport and recreation, the environment and planning) or a global leader implementing both internal and customer facing initiatives, perhaps you can understand that they may have limited time for this particular change. What is key is that the project is sponsored – perhaps by someone with access to the top person – and that the preacher is kept focused on this change, so that the limited amount of time they have available is well directed. They can either act as an ambassador for the change, or as someone who asks the right questions, or stays on message in the right forums.

Keeping them informed is important and also watching for signs of lack of interest (and the possible repercussions thereof).

Willing workers (low power/high commitment)

What I've called the 'willing workers' are those who may not have any particular power base but are nonetheless committed to the change and willing to pursue and progress it. These may be people intimately affected by the change or they may be onlookers. Your task will be to focus their energies into useful work and also to protect them from those who do have power but who may not be behind the change and may seek to disrupt it. Willing workers shouldn't ever be taken for granted: if their enthusiasm wanes you know you have a problem.

Sleepers (low energy/low commitment and low power/low commitment)

Sleepers are people who probably can't be bothered about the change. Perhaps they are just not interested, or maybe they are not aware of it. It could be that they're not interested because they've never been invited to be involved. When those leading the change are racing ahead with enthusiasm and inspiration these may be seen as the silent majority. The task here is to wake them up and ensure that they are supportive of the change. Remember the way you wake them up might determine the degree of support they give to the change!

Understanding why they are asleep might be a good place to start – change initiative fatigue; feelings of powerlessness; too much pressure in the day job; lack of awareness about the change; being comfortable as they are. Developing a communication and engagement strategy based on the change equation would be the second step.

The impact/influence matrix

The four categories in the impact/influence matrix are based on the degree to which the stakeholders are impacted by the change and the degree to which they may have some influence over the course of the change. Typically we can position the people who are driving through the change as naturally being at the high end of the influence dimension, which immediately creates issues of power and authority and how they are exercised.

Often in changes – due to time pressures, conflicting priorities and perhaps lack of interest on their part – the change agents tend to minimize the attention to those in the low impact/low influence quadrant. However, they are stakeholders, and in that sense they do have an interest even if they are not interested. At the minimum, making them aware of the changes and keeping them informed seems sensible.

Those who are in the low impact/high influence quadrant can fall into two categories: those who are in positions of power within the organization but who will not be affected personally or professionally by the change; and those who are perhaps guardians or watchdogs outside of the organization who have the potential to exercise power and influence, though normally on behalf of others. Clearly it is important to establish where these groups stand on the change (in terms of their interest, energy and commitment) and then to ensure there is some buy-in from them. This can often be done by addressing their concerns directly.

The high impact/low influence quadrant is often where the majority of the recipients of the changes can be located – be they citizens or employees. Interestingly, individuals can often have little or no influence but when they come together they can be a real force for or against the change. Just because they have little influence at the beginning of the change doesn't mean to say that they can't affect its successful outcome. Good management practice would suggest you want buy-in and engagement from this group if you want the changes to work. Some involvement is required, and communication and engagement are important.

Those people in the high impact/high influence quadrant are critical to the success of the change. You would not just be looking for approval or token support but high degrees of ownership. Clearly any concerns they may have need to be addressed but more than that, active engagement is required because of their position and their being intimately affected.

Trust/agreement matrix

Block (1991) uses the two dimensions of trust and agreement to plot stakeholder groups and individuals and to develop appropriate strategies of engagement – or disengagement.

The first step in negotiating agreement and trust is to identify the key stakeholders and any onlookers, plot them on the matrix and then develop an appropriate approach for each grouping. However, a health warning accompanies this – we will typically discover the levels of trust and agreement through dialogue, not by preconception or prejudice. We mustn't assume someone is in a particular box because we think so or someone else suggests they are, or that they were there in the previous change. It's fine to have a hypothesis and plan a strategy on that, but remain open to other possibilities. In general, to establish where people are you will need to exchange understanding about the change vision, purpose, goals and allocation of resources, affirm or negotiate agreement, and affirm or negotiate levels of trust.

High trust/high agreement

These people are onside with what you are trying to achieve. The main aim therefore is to do enough to ensure that the levels of trust and agreement remain high. Don't take these people for granted: treat them as you would any friend or valued colleague – you have to nurture and sustain the relationship.

High trust/low agreement

It's always good to have someone you can trust enough to give you critical feedback – in both senses of the word 'critical'. They may not be a friend – they could be on the other side of the political divide – but you value their opinion. One of the great things about having an honest opponent is that you can engage in dialogue with them about the change to sharpen your views; practise your arguments, unearth any faults or failures in the plan; and also have the opportunity of bringing them around to your view.

In order to do this you need to start where you both agree – on the bedrock of the trust you have with each other. You can then outline where you stand and seek to understand what views they hold. Dialogue and collaborative problem solving can then occur.

Low trust/high agreement

These 'fair-weather friends' are those people who you find are supportive of the change but who you don't have a particularly trusting relationship with, and therefore you are unsure how long they will support the change, whether they will support the next change and what their motivations are.

Naturally you are more guarded with them. They are onside and therefore should be a force for change and need to be involved in the change. Perhaps the level of openness and frankness and the degree to which you discuss any difficulties may be less than with your allies and honest opponents. There is a paradox here – the more guarded you are the less likely that trust will develop. On the other hand, if you satisfactorily develop the relationship during the course of this change, perhaps the more trust there will be in the future.

Once again you need to enter into dialogue and affirm your levels of agreement, though you may need to be quite specific about what it is that you agree and, because of the nature of the relationship, you might need this to be 'on the record'. You need to acknowledge, at least to yourself, the caution that exists and that both sides have some reservations. But there is no reason why you cannot be clear about what you want from them in terms of working together on the changes, and you can also discuss how you like to work together.

Low trust/low agreement

Some may call these people enemies. If they are an important stakeholder group they need to be brought on board if at all possible. Remember that you don't know that they are definitely against you unless you have tried to engage them and your attempts at negotiating agreement and trust have failed. By definition, because you don't trust them you are in the worst possible position to exert influence with them. Block's view is that once you've tried to move them to one of the other quadrants and failed, the answer is to let go of them! Perhaps a little more strongly than that, you may well have to marginalize them when it comes to the changes.

Block's advice is to reduce the tension and threat that exist in the relationship and this can be achieved by either eliminating contact with them or reducing the threat from them by helping them feel understood.

In summary, there are a number of things you need to develop or know in regard to mobilizing stakeholders:

- a clear identification of who they are and where they sit;
- what actual stake they have in the change;
- what their roles and responsibilities may be in the change;
- the level of engagement needed from each stakeholder;
- the level of their involvement in the planning of change;
- their potential impact on the change;
- their attitudes towards the change and any associated risks;
- the effectiveness of your relationship with the key stakeholders and how this might deepen; and
- a stakeholder management strategy.

Communication, engagement, mobilization

In discussing the identification and positioning of stakeholders we've already touched upon how we might communicate with them. Now, given the different natures of the change approaches there may or may not have been a degree of prior communication and stakeholder engagement. The notion that it is only at the stage of implementation that you'll be engaging with stakeholders would be very wrong. The evidence from the case studies suggests the need for identification and communication with stakeholders at an early stage in the change process.

Daft (1997) defines communication as: 'the process by which information is exchanged and understood by two or more people, usually with the intent to motivate or influence behaviour'. Witherspoon and Wohlert (1996) state, within the context of organizational change, that:

> Communication is the process on which the initiation and maintenance of organizational change depends... Ultimately the success of any change effort depends on how effectively the strategy for and the substance of the change is communicated to those who are the targets of change.

Both of these quotes are drawn from Frahm's paper on organizational change communication (2003), which began to look at the differences between what he calls the 'monologic' and 'dialogic' approaches. The first, giving a monologue, tends to be top-down and directed at targeted groups in, most likely, one-way communication. He suggests that currently many organizations see communication merely as part of the management function, which has a monologic approach as the default option:

> In the absence of genuine commitment and understanding of communication practices that construct new meaning and processes, the organization relies heavily on a linear communication model and ad hoc responses. Based on the findings of the first data collection, monologic communication was not improving change receptivity; rather it was decreasing it, and creating cynicism about change.

Given the importance of communication during times of change he suggests, and the initial research indicates, that a move towards the dialogic approach will aid successful change, however:

> There are times when receptivity of change will not be an issue, and then dialogic approaches are not so important… Finally, dialogic approaches are costly. They run the risk of 'too much talk and not enough action'. Further, just as it takes someone skilled enough to communicate on this level, it takes expertise in knowing how to take the dialogue into a tangible outcome, one that can be recognized for its value to the organization. However, if, as some suggest, up to 75% of popular change management programs fail (Beer *et al*, 1990), perhaps the high cost of dialogue is not as great as failed implementations and additional change consultants.

The purpose of communication is to move people from one position to another in terms of their awareness, knowledge, support or commitment to the change. In that respect we could see the process as a marketing challenge and use the AIDA(S) framework, which highlights the generic stages that someone would typically go through when experiencing a change:

- A is the need to capture their Attention and increase their Awareness of the change.
- I is the need to gain their Interest in the change usually through high-lighting the features, qualities, and benefits of the change.
- D is for Desire. Having gained their attention and interest there is the need now for them to be positively inclined to the change; the more they can want it and see the benefits of it the more they will be drawn towards it.
- A is for the Action that will then happen. Change involves changes in behaviour with people doing things differently; if the communication doesn't have this affect then it has probably failed.
- S is for the Satisfaction or realization of the benefits that the person experiences. This becomes a link into the person's propensity for further change or, if there is satisfaction arising from short-term wins, then this will encourage further commitment to this change.

Arnstein (1969) looked at the degree of participation of citizens in planning change and her 'ladder of participation', though obviously looking at community change, is nonetheless extremely relevant when thinking about engaging with stakeholders. As you work your way up the ladder, consider the level of communication within your organization and think also how some of these approaches fit with different types of change.

The first two rungs of the ladder are really about non-participation, with the goals of the initiator to direct people or 'do to' them, or 'cure' them as if something were wrong and they had no views themselves. The initiators have the best plan, the best ideas, the best way forward and the aim of this (non-participatory) participation is to acknowledge that.

The third rung is that of informing, which is probably the first step on the way to full participation and dialogue. It forms the basis of communication even if it is only one-way communication. Of course the distinction can be made between informing someone before or after the event and also informing someone before or after they have heard the news from some other source, be it television, radio or the company grapevine.

Consultation is the fourth rung and can take the form of genuine two-way information flows, or mere window-dressing with the decision already having been made.

Arnstein uses the term 'placation' for describing the use of communication as a way of placating stakeholders but not necessarily addressing the real issues. Unions or employee representatives, for example, might be invited onto advisory boards or involved in some negotiations but those in power retain the right to make their own decisions unilaterally.

The sixth rung is that of partnership. Power is redistributed from those who traditionally hold power to include those stakeholders who can contribute to the process of change with negotiations, joint planning and decision making. It seems at this level there is a genuine desire to enter into

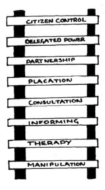

Figure 5.1 The 'ladder of participation'

dialogue with no prior decision as to what or how the change needs to be managed.

Delegated power is the seventh rung of the ladder and stakeholders are given power and responsibility to decide on some of the issues related to the change without reference back. They have a mandate to take ownership and accountability of their part of the programme.

In Arnstein's schema the final rung would be citizen control. Translated into an organizational change context, responsibility for the change would be given to the people most affected by the change.

If you were to map this ladder against the top-down/bottom-up – planned/emergent matrix in Chapter 1, then as you went up Arnstein's ladder you would notice a shift from the change being a top-down/planned approach to a bottom-up/emergent approach.

The purpose of communication at this mobilization stage is to move people up through the levels of attention and awareness, interest, desire and action. It'll be your choice as change agent as to how much engagement you want from the different stakeholders. Fundamentally you will need to decide who you want to communicate with; what you want to say or discuss; when you want the process to begin; and how you want to communicate.

- The *to who* should be generated from your stakeholder analysis in terms of those who are most affected and those who you want actively engaged in the process.
- The *what* should emerge from your understanding of the stakeholders' needs and how much you may wish to communicate with them.
- The *when* will be a mixture of the timing of the change management process; the degree of cooperation you need; and the values within which your organization is working.
- The *from whom* is defined by deciding which stakeholders need communication from whom in the organization – investors will probably need the CEO or Director of Finance; employees may need their line manager and a change sponsor.
- The *how* will be determined by the nature of the stakeholder groups; the nature and consequences of the change; once again the organizational values; and the capacity and budget of the change team.

If we return to the adapted change equation at the beginning of the chapter we can develop a communication grid (see Table 5.1) which is most appropriate for the different stakeholder groups.

Table 5.1 Communication grid

	Pressure for change	A clear shared vision	Capacity to change	Capability to change	Actionable first steps	Resistance to change
Who						
What						
When						
From whom						
How						

Depending on the stakeholders concerned, you may wish to focus on the current need to change or you may wish to focus on the vision. If you truly want a shared vision then you need to decide which group of stakeholders you wish to be part of that vision, which in turn will lead to when you need to communicate (before, during or after the vision creation!) How you might go about this will also be driven by those decisions.

Capacity and capability feed into addressing the readiness for change of the organization and the resources available for the change, the change team and line managers. Communicating actionable first steps, apart from grounding the change in reality, is a crucial way of engaging people in the actual doing of the change and eliciting some quick wins early on.

By having a column entitled 'resistance to change' in your communication grid you are immediately able to devote some time and energy to seeing where these resistances may occur and then thinking through some strategies for addressing them.

The how, that is the medium of communication, can take the form of being rich or lean. 'Rich' would involve higher personal contact (be it individual, small or larger group) and probably operate on a 'deeper' level of connecting more with people's emotions. 'Lean' would focus less on personal contact and at a more rational and superficial level.

Many organizations now invest heavily in communicating with their stakeholders, especially in times of change, but of course there are many different ways of doing this. Figure 5.2 lists a number of methods, based on the dimensions of lean to rich and monologic to dialogic. Important points to remember are to match the communication method to the type of engagement you want and to ensure the sequence enables feedback, if that is what you want or need. This will change through time.

In *Making Sense of Change Management* (Cameron and Green, 2004) we discussed communication in times of restructuring:

> Communication in any change is absolutely essential. However, communications are often variable. There is sometimes too much communication, but more often too little too late. An added problem is communication by e-mail. This is such a useful mechanism when managers need large numbers of people to receive the same information at the same time, but it is so impersonal and so heartless when delivering messages of an emotional and potentially threatening nature.
>
> The more tailored or personalized approach the better. The greater the access to people who know the answers to the important questions the better. FAQs (frequently asked questions) are useful to compile and communicate, but don't expect this to be the end of the story. Just because you think you have told

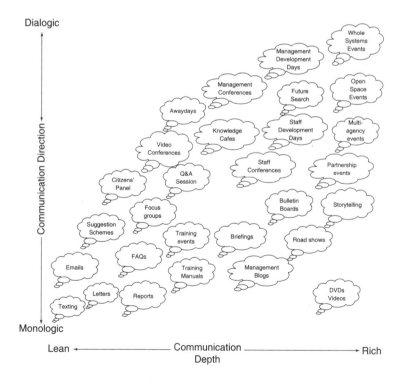

Figure 5.2 Communication methods

someone something it doesn't mean to say they have heard it or assimilated it or believed. People do strange things under stress like not listen. And they need to see the whites of your eyes when you respond!

Key questions in peoples' minds will be:

- What is the purpose of the restructure?
- How it will it operate in practice?
- Who will be affected and how?
- What are the steps along the way, including milestones and timescales?
- How will new posts be filled and people selected?
- What happens to the others?
- Where do you go to get help and how do you get involved?
- What is the new structure and what are the new roles?
- What new behaviours will be required?
- Will training and development will be provided?

Communication needs to be well planned and these plans need to be clear about how to get the right information to the right people at the right time through the right medium (for the recipient). This includes well-presented briefing notes for managers if they are to be the channel for further communication. It is also worth checking for understanding before these messengers are required to communicate the message.

Change in any form can trigger a number of emotional responses. If the messages can be personalized the recipient is more likely to receive them in a better frame of mind. Personalized messages, ie face-to-face and one-to-one communication, are especially relevant when that individual may be adversely affected by the change.

Different communities of interest have different needs when it comes to communications. Some people will need to be involved, some consulted and some told. It is important that the right people get the appropriate level of communication. It is important for them and it is important for those around them. If your manager is seen to be ignored, what does it say about the value of your work section?

Thought needs to be given to the recipients of the communication. Those responsible for communicating need to ask:

- What are their needs for information?
- What is their preferred form of communication?
- When is the best time for them to be communicated with?

For example, people in a contact centre just may not have the time to read endlessly long e-mails informing them of changes in other parts of the business. However, they would probably like to be told face-to-face of events that will involve changes to their management structure, or the introduction of a new way of working.

To prevent the rumour mill growing it is important that communication is timely and reaches each of the chosen communities at the agreed time. 'Start – Stop – Start again' communications don't help either. A continuing flow of communication will engender more confidence in the change process.

Difference and the cultural dimension

We have touched upon the concept of difference in a number of ways, primarily individual personality differences and organizational cultural differences. However, the case studies have shown a number of international dimensions:

- the reflective approach undertaken in the Danish County of Aarhus;
- the cross-border working of the Institute of Public Health in Ireland;
- the diverse cultures across Europe within Biogen Idec;
- the preparation for the global rollout of the new British Council information system; and
- the Far Eastern suppliers for the kitchenware company.

Even the small rural primary school had as one of its objectives the aspiration for all of its pupils to become citizens of the world.

Never has there been a greater opportunity or indeed a greater imperative for managers and leaders to understand the cultural dimension of business. Sadler (2003b) observes that:

> increasingly leaders find themselves in the position of leading international teams. Such teams differ from single nationality teams because of the additional complexities that stem from such factors as different languages and communication styles, different ways of looking at the world and processing information, different behavioural expectations, and different stereotypes held by team members of each other... among the key skills needed by international leaders are the following:
>
> - how to work with cultures different from one's own;
> - how to run a business that is international in scope;
> - how to lead and manage people unlike oneself;
> - how to handle a complex array of often difficult relationships;
> - how to develop the skills and attitudes necessary for effective personal behaviour.

Hofstede (1991) and more recently Trompenaars and Hampden-Turner (2001) have researched national cultural similarities and differences. Hofstede's classic study compared employees from one multinational company (IBM) across the globe. He identified four dimensions of distance:

1. *Power distance*, which focuses on the degree of equality and inequality within a nation's society. The higher the index the greater the degree to which power is distributed unequally across the organization.

2. *Individualism,* which focuses on the degree to which the society reinforces individual or collective achievement and interpersonal relationships.
3. *Masculinity,* which focuses on the degree to which the society reinforces the traditional masculine work role model of achievement, control and power.
4. *Uncertainty avoidance,* which focuses on the level of tolerance for uncertainty and ambiguity within the society. The higher the index the more likely the organization will create rules and regulations to avoid uncertainty.

Hofstede later added a fifth dimension, *long-term orientation,* which focuses on the degree to which the society embraces long-term attention to traditional or forward thinking values (source: http://www.geert-hofstede.com).

Understanding where someone (or a nation) is on these dimensions can help explain how they are behaving in any given situation. It also suggests ways in which changes should be handled. If we look at the Biogen Idec case study along national cultural lines, in Hofstede's research we can see that France has a much higher power distance index (68) to that of UK (35), Switzerland (34) and the United States (40).

Likewise on the uncertainty avoidance dimension France is high (86) when compared to UK (35), Switzerland (58) and the United States (46). We can begin to understand that perhaps an organizational cultural shift towards decentralization and a more entrepreneurial way of doing things might be more easily enabled in the UK and Switzerland than in France.

Jacob (2003) states that:

> Policy makers have to gauge when to design approaches that are global in orientation and reflect the credo, vision and corporate culture of the organization. They also have to ascertain when to use methods that are local in character and scope. Sometimes the challenge is to reconcile the two orientations. At other times the challenge is to invent approaches that are capable of adaptation despite inherent dualities. This process of invention has to be an ongoing, continuous one, given the dynamic nature of intercultural management.

Case study analysis

In mobilizing for change in Aster, the two top teams spent a considerable time discussing whether there would be a good enough cultural fit. They discussed, argued and debated, which led to greater levels of agreement and an ever increasing degree of trust. Having identified the key stakeholders –

from those most affected by the changes (tenants and staff) through to the regulatory authorities (Housing Corporation) – and incorporating open and transparent communication, they aligned all stakeholders to the new vision and ensured high levels of engagement when the grouping took place.

The Institute also put stakeholders' needs and interests high on its agenda. The vision set the scene and the direction, but it was the engagement of the stakeholders that created momentum.

Biogen Idec was faced with some winners and some losers in terms of its stakeholders and the outcome of the proposed changes. The vast majority of staff and management were brought on board by the strategy of empowering the affiliates, of establishing centres of excellence and a continued strategy of growth. The potential losers – staff in France – were treated with respect, were always communicated with and also given attractive options, of leaving or staying, which meant that no one in the company was left feeling bad about what had happened to this group of staff.

The British Council programme team managed its key stakeholders fairly well. The Deputy Director General as the senior responsible owner tied the senior management into the change, creating a sponsor for the programme with a route to the top, and signalling to the whole organization the importance of the change. In addition to having representatives on the programme board and in the change team, all parts of the business were consulted and involved at each stage of the process. Communication with the business managers and staff had begun at an early stage and continued throughout. The two departments most directly and immediately affected by the change were involved from the very beginning as part of the decision-making and design process. Managers and staff from other countries were also included as they would be impacted by the UK changes in their business operations, and they would be receiving the next wave of change.

In Aarhus the process of engagement in the change was relatively straight-forward given that the change team had set out to actively involve people right from the start. Middle management were engaged as it was seen that they are often the people who have to translate the vision and strategy into operational actions, manage business-as-usual, motivate, mobilize and coach staff through the changes *and* are often the first people whose roles are deeply affected by the changes. The way they tackled this at Aarhus was again through continued reflection and dialogue – involving the people who were experiencing the changes, the tensions and the challenges.

The kitchenware company adopted a fairly simple business model – the key stakeholders who needed to be satisfied were the suppliers, the customers, the shareholders and the staff. All had been previously dissatisfied, and the management actively seeking them out, listening to them and incorporating their ideas, needs and wants into the changes, ensured a movement towards commitment.

The school's key stakeholders were clear and their levels of interest, power, energy and commitment were quickly established through conversations. The head had a clear direction and a set of key principles of culture change as a framework for the mobilization process. The active engagement of all stakeholder groups, including the pupils, meant the vision could be made tangible and practical. It also meant that some previously disengaged parts of the school community could see that their views were valued and their input into the changes a necessary resource.

Summary

Mobilizing people in the change is one of the most critical factors in the change process. Key elements are how motivation affects mobilization, and how different people will be motivated by different aspects of the adapted change equation. You need to address each of the categories to ensure movement:

- pressure for change;
- a clear shared vision;
- capacity to change;
- capability to change;
- actionable first steps; and
- spotting resistance to change.

The importance of identifying and managing stakeholders and their interests cannot be overestimated. By mapping stakeholders on the appropriate combination of the relevant axes of energy, commitment, power, impact, influence, trust and agreement, you will be able to develop strategies of stakeholder communication and management.

Different stakeholders will require you to develop various and varying ways of communicating and engaging stakeholders. The different forms of communication (direction and depth) can and should be used to address issues arising in and within the different stakeholder groups as highlighted by the change formula.

6. Implementation

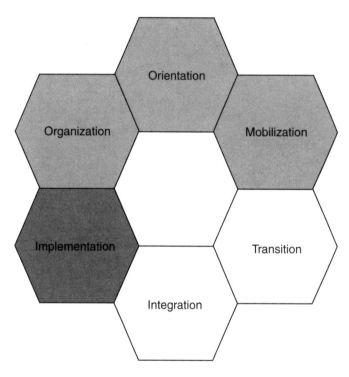

We accept the verdict of the past until the need for change cries out loudly enough to force upon us a choice between the comforts of further inertia and the irksomeness of action.
(Louis L'Amour)

Daring ideas are like chessmen moved forward; they may be beaten, but they may start a winning game.
(Johann Wolfgang von Goethe)

The illusion of progress can be achieved by simply rearranging the terms of description so that new acronyms are created.
(Scott Smith)

Introduction

The aim of this chapter is to continue our understanding of the change process by looking at some of the issues related to implementation of change projects. In Chapter 8 we will be looking at what change means from an individual and team perspective in terms of the nature of transition. In this chapter the focus will be more on the 'hard' aspects of change management:

- ensuring that the organization of change is followed through into implementation;
- highlighting areas of potential difficulty; and
- seeing what needs to be done to ensure alignment between the intended changes and the organization.

Project management implementation

It is perhaps useful to begin a discussion on implementation with some lessons learnt from projects that have encountered some disruption and deviations along the way. I will use two organizations, picked pretty much at random, by way of illustration. The first is a public body, a government department, investing heavily in IT change and working in partnership with a global consultancy firm. They held a joint review of a systems implementation in the summer of 2006. The outcomes are listed below.

From the client's perspective
1. Major business change programmes to be recognized as such, and they need to adopt a more realistic planning approach.
2. There needed to be a greater shared understanding of the different exit and entry criteria for each stage of the project.
3. Changes would be more manageable if there were 'clear islands of stability' built into the programme.
4. When managing risk it needs to be acknowledged which organization is shouldering what level of risk.
5. There should have been a process to ensure all the operational processes were aligned.
6. Re-engineer the business processes from the outset.
7. Skilled and experienced staff from outset would have helped.
8. Trials should not be underestimated and the change effort would benefit from them.

9. Integrated and co-located management teams would foster good working relations.
10. There needs to be better tracking of the development and changes to the programme objectives.
11. There needs to be a better link between the business change and benefits management... by looking at the benefits from a customer and business perspective.
12. Contract to have provisions to enable control and monitoring to be clearly accountable.

From the consultants' perspective

1. There needs to be a greater appreciation of the complexity of the client's customer relations.
2. Our (global) organization found it difficult to understand the needs of our client's individual customers.
3. The contract needs to be more pragmatic, realistic and less inflexible.
4. We need to agree boundaries, and provide a mechanism for changing these if necessary.
5. 'Scope creep' and its impact need to be well managed.
6. We need to ensure stakeholders' expectations are managed and aligned.
7. We need to insist upon having adequate time to look at the full impact of any changes requested.
8. We need to ensure that our client's contractual obligations are clearly defined and fully understood by both parties.
9. Consultants' and client's objectives must be fully aligned.
10. Ensure client's attendees at meetings are empowered to make decisions.

What was interesting about this review is that it reveals that even when organizations are experts in their field things will go wrong and very basic things not get done. Although the project turned out to be relatively successful and the team work and problem-solving ethos of the change team members worked exceptionally well, there were still problems with the process of implementation. In that sense good project management methodology is critical to the successful implementation of projects... though neither at the expense of over-engineering nor allowing emergent change to occur.

The second example is a financial services company which, having conducted a strategic planning process, decided to embark upon an extensive, cross-group reorientation. At one of their reviews they generated this list of concerns about project implementation:

1. Look for design faults at an early stage and then continue to look for them.
2. Always undertake a potential problem analysis.
3. Always build in a process of automatic review.
4. Be prepared to say no!
5. Don't just do learning reviews after each project, build the learning into the current project.
6. Ensure you have people with prior knowledge of implementation.
7. Have dedicated project management.
8. Maintain a network of people and resources.
9. Have an executive authority overseeing project implementation.
10. Have significant top-level commitment.
11. Have clear change objectives.
12. Differentiate between the what and the how.
13. Prototyping and piloting work.
14. Have dedicated people and a multidisciplinary approach.
15. Ensure time for team building.
16. Check for over-specification.
17. The project management capability in client and consultant needs to be good.
18. Managing the consultants and their capability is critical.
19. There needs to be a sound contract.
20. Research well and double check.

This review covers a number of aspects of change management. There were once again concerns to ensure that the management of the change project was well structured and organized, but there was also attention paid to the people side of change and the idea that the whole thing doesn't have to be planned upfront – some piloting and prototyping can occur followed by a review to see what was working and what wasn't. Throughout there was an appreciation that the project wasn't being done in isolation, hence reference not only to sponsorship and executive authority but also to ensuring the project was networked well into the organization and the change stakeholders.

Operationalizing the changes

When implementing change there are a number of different aspects that need to be borne in mind:

- Is the change plan on track?
- Are the changes actually being implemented?
- Is the organizational infrastructure being realigned to accommodate the changes?
- Is business as usual still being undertaken?

Ford and Greer (2005) looked at 22 organizations to see how well management control systems were used when implementing (planned) change. Their research suggested that managers used control systems less widely than other elements in the change process, although they found a clear correlation between the use of such control systems and change project success.

In their article on managing change, Pfeifer and Schmitt (2005) recognized the implementation phase to be the most problematical stage of the change process. They identified four barriers to success:

> the *management barrier* reflects the problem that the focus of management activities is dealing with daily business, not discussing new strategies. The *vision barrier* arises when visions and strategies are not communicated to employees in a comprehensible way... strategic objectives are not broken down by means of target definitions on the employee level, with the result that participation of those affected is not achieved. The *resource barrier* means that resources are not purposefully deployed for the implementation of the strategy. In strategic change, the endeavour to secure *acceptance* of changes by all employees as a whole usually fails.

 They recognized that the change process itself can stretch over a number of years and fatigue can set in amongst managers, or yet another priority can come along. In such cases they saw the importance of controlling mechanisms, but mechanisms that were not too constrictive:

> Although the implementation process has to be planned and controlled, it is important to understand that the planning of the implementation and the implementation itself cannot be separated strictly. A change process is dynamic and this dynamic always requires adaptations in planning. Therefore the management should be willing and flexible to adapt even the target definitions, made in the earlier stage of the change process, if changed boundary conditions require this step.

Sirken *et al* (2005) believe that some of the 'hard' factors rather than merely the softer issues (culture, leadership, motivation, etc) should take more prominence when implementing change:

> What's missing, we believe, is a focus on the not-so-fashionable aspects of change management: the hard factors. These factors have three distinct characteristics. First, companies are able to measure them in direct or indirect ways. Second, companies can easily communicate their importance, both within and outside the organizations. Third, and perhaps most important, businesses are capable of influencing these elements quickly. Some of the hard factors... are the time necessary to complete it, the number of people required to execute it, and the financial results that intended actions are expected to achieve.

They go on to look at four key factors which came out of their study. They mention in passing that since the original research, the Boston Consulting group have used these factors to predict outcomes in more than 1,000 change initiatives across the globe.

The four factors are duration, integrity, commitment and effort. The duration of the project needs to generate a process of review – 'a long project that is reviewed frequently is more likely to succeed than a short project that isn't reviewed frequently'. Whether this is a rigorous project management style review with specific milestones and 'gateway' reviews, or whether there is a more informal reflective review depends on the circumstances and the approach you are taking to change. In the organizations studied in this book the more IT-based and restructuring changes needed a clear, transparent and rigorous set of reviews as did those parts of changes which had legal implications (mergers and redundancies). However, a notable feature of the more emergent types of change was the regular reviews either encompassed in a management workshop (Aster); a stakeholder meeting (the primary school); the practice of developing dialogue, understanding and insight (Aarhus); or using a leadership development programme to review progress (Institute of Public Health).

They define integrity as 'the extent to which companies can rely on teams of managers, supervisors, and staff to execute change projects successfully'. This comprises the interesting mix of knowledge, skills and experience in getting changes done on time, to budget and the required quality. In each case study we saw that the change team comprised credible people (from a change management perspective and from those in the business) with access to a sponsor with power and authority. But we also saw in most of the cases that time and effort were spent in building the capacity, capability and cohesion of the team. They were also well networked into the parts of the business which were changing.

Commitment covers the demonstrable willingness of top management, the change team and the recipients of change to be engaged in the change. In some ways this is determined by the correct identification of the key stakeholders and the ability to manage them; by the ability to motivate employees to make a positive contribution to the change; and to manage the psychological transition as well as the actual implementation. Once again we can see good practice coming out in the case studies whereby top team support and sponsorship were evidently present and employees were actively engaged in a process, which meant they were less 'done to' than being willing participants.

The fourth and final factor is effort. Sirken *et al* define this as the effort required 'over and above the usual work that the change initiative demands of people'. If no allowance is made for this increased effort, or inadequate allowance, then the change initiative runs a higher risk of failure. This includes the focus by sponsors and senior management who will often have multiple time pressures on them or can move onto the next change initiative. The change team themselves might be fully focused on and resourced up to the 'go live' date and may not have the time, budget or people to continue the change process. Managers have the sometimes unenviable task of juggling business as usual, implementing the changes in their areas, and managing staff through the transition. They can also be the recipients of change them-selves, so undergoing both survival anxiety and learning anxiety (Schein, 2002). Finally, staff involved in implementing change need time to do so, either by a reduction in their normal workload, backfilling, or a recognition that there will be a performance dip.

Kotter (1995) looked at over 100 different organizations going through change and picked out eight key aspects of the change process which could either lead to a failed initiative or, if got right, lead to transformation:

1. establish a sense of urgency;
2. form a powerful guiding coalition;
3. create a vision;
4. communicate the vision;
5. empower others to act on the vision;
6. plan for and create short-term wins;
7. consolidate improvements and produce still more change;
8. institutionalize new approaches.

I think what is useful at the implementation stage is to continue to bear all of these in mind. If you don't want the momentum to slacken then the sense of urgency needs still to be evident; likewise the abiding vision, whether or not it has evolved, needs to continue to be articulated and communicated; the guiding coalition needs to be sustained and continued levels of empowerment enabled across the organization. Progress needs to be acknowledged as and when it happens and incorporated into the organization's way of doing things. In the process of doing these things you will be able to see whether you have drifted away from the vision or whether the vision needs to be fine tuned; you will have a greater understanding of the human systems at play and where you need to focus your attention in terms of possible resistance or blockages; and you will have a clear sense of whether you are on schedule according to your plan.

In a later article Kotter (2006) adds to his initial analysis by highlighting what he calls the 'four mistakes' that cause failure and the 'three key tasks' to ensure success. The four mistakes he sees as writing a memo instead of lighting a fire; talking too much and saying too little; declaring victory before the war is over; and looking for villains in all the wrong places. The first two of these relate to the way you communicate and engage with your stakeholders and employees and the way that you demonstrate leadership and commitment to the changes yourself. In terms of declaring victory too soon, Kotter is highlighting the fact that change takes time and a few quick wins don't signal that the task has been accomplished:

> When a project is completed or an initial goal met, it is tempting to congratulate all involved and proclaim the advent of a new era. While you should celebrate results, don't kid yourself or others about the difficulty and duration of transformation. Once you see encouraging results in a difficult initiative, you are only six months into a three-year process. If you settle for too little too soon, you may lose it all. Celebrating is a great way to mark progress and sustain commitment – but note how much work is still to come.

The following list is adapted from Kotter (1995):

- Establish a sense of urgency – ensure that the level of current dissatisfaction or future threat is sufficient to kick-start the change and maintain momentum.
- Form a powerful guiding coalition – ensure that key stakeholders are engaged and the change team has the necessary sponsorship, power and authority.
- Create a vision – have a clear understanding of what you want to achieve from the change and for it to be lofty, strategic and motivational.
- Communicate the vision – ensure people are informed and hopefully engaged with the change by having a shared understanding of and commitment to the direction of the change.

- Empower others to act on the vision – ensure that those people who are needed to make the change happen have the necessary resources, mandates and enabling mechanisms to achieve their goals.
- Plan for and create short-term wins – be clear that progress is being made towards the ultimate goals through the achievement of smaller goals along the way, thus demonstrating success and maintaining momentum.
- Consolidate improvements and produce still more change – build on improvements in the organization as and when they occur and continue to move forward with change.
- Institutionalize new approaches – ensure all changes are embedded in the organization and the organization is fully aligned.

Kotter also highlights the fact that you need to be wary of pigeonholing certain groups into being resisters to change. It is often not employees who resist change but senior managers who have their own motives for so doing. As a consequence Kotter is keen that the guiding coalition is seen as representing all employees.

The first of the three key tasks is to manage multiple timelines – noting that transformative change can take years and that short-term wins need acknowledging and communication is an ongoing task. I believe this ties into the idea that there may be waves of change (or ripples, if you prefer) each with its ebb and flow. Communication and engagement need to be attuned to these happening.

Kotter sees building coalitions as the next key task. As indicated above, the coalition isn't just the most senior or most powerful people in the organization but a grouping of necessary stakeholders. For this you need people with the right skills, or people who can learn them and people who work well together: 'The best partners have strong position power, broad experience, high credibility and real leadership skills.'

Another ingredient is to realize that the coalition builds as the change progresses. Back to the images of the wave and the ripple, where the network of people involved expands over time and as the changes take place and take hold across and throughout the organization. Kotter also underscores the need to invest in the change team throughout the change – we have seen different change teams from the case studies invest time and effort in building their vision, developing their operating principles and tackling issues collaboratively.

The third of Kotter's tasks is to build a vision and sustain it throughout the changes. Here he is not prescriptive; he understands that the process is more:

> emotional than rational. It demands a tolerance for messiness, ambiguity, and setbacks. The half-step back usually accompanies every step forward. Day-to-day demands pull people in different directions. Having a shared vision does not eliminate tension, but it does help people make trade-offs.

In *Making Sense of Change Management* (Cameron and Green, 2004) we introduced our own adaptation of Kotter – the Cameron Change Model – which highlighted and accentuated a number of other aspects of implementation.

Creating vision and values emphasizes the need to incorporate values at the heart of the change process, both in the sense of what type of culture you are developing and in terms of how you want to implement the changes. It will be counterproductive, for example, to have wonderful espoused values if you take a coercive approach to change.

Communicating, engaging and empowering others is an ongoing process as the change unfolds. This is particularly true if you are operating under a more emergent or organic premise where those you are engaging with are in dialogue with you as to how best to implement the unfolding changes.

Noticing improvements and energizing involves staying in touch with the change process and seeing what is working and what needs attention. This is more than just monitoring the project plan in a mechanistic way and actively directing attention, other people's as well as your own, to emerging themes. There's an underlying assumption that this thing called change cannot be fully controlled but somehow needs different sorts of interventions at different times.

Case study analysis

Both the technical and psychological aspects of the project management of the Aster grouping process were conducted with openness and no hidden agendas. The project itself was run along effective best practice project management guidelines with detailed plan of activities, all tasks having a responsible person owning it, and clear reporting procedures. During the period of change external organizational development consultants were brought in to help manage the people side of organizational change.

In order for the Institute to achieve its change goals it needed to become an influential body, by doing everything to a high standard, with a real attention to both task process and people process, ensuring clarity of agendas and outcomes and that all staff were supported.

With Biogen Idec the implementation process, though multifaceted, was relatively straightforward. The negotiation with French staff, managers and works council was achieved by setting up a process through a combination of legal advice, adherence to French labour law and agreeing a common set of objectives around the negotiating table. The project management of finding and acquiring a new building for HQ was achieved through the investigation of different locations and sifting them through pre-selected and agreed criteria. At the same time a detailed recruitment plan was put in place to ensure that any gaps left by those from the old HQ not wishing to move were quickly filled.

There was also a project plan for setting up centres of excellence across Europe. As resources were freed up at the centre, management teams across Europe were given additional resources (made available from the decentralization process) and greater local control allowed for regional decisions and marketing campaigns. These mandates were agreed through open discussion and further clarification when needed. The corporate body set the overall strategy but empowered the affiliate businesses to operationalize this.

The British Council implementation process started with what was called a 'mobilization and visioning' event. This two-day team workshop brought together the technical people, the business people, the change training team and the consortium. They spent time on task (the what) and process (the how) and striking a balance between the two, and the first outputs were a shared and understood vision and a set of guiding principles for the team working.

The implementation followed a normal systems project. However, alongside developing the software a key strand of the implementation process was getting staff to understand what the changes were for; how they would affect their way of working; and helping them learn what to do. Change management workshops were designed and run for all staff. Coordinators were appointed in all areas and all managers were asked to complete a business readiness grid which detailed the extent to which each section was prepared for the changes.

An effective project management structure was established with a clear line into the programme management board. There was business representation for all strategic discussions and a business assessment group assessing the blueprint, the training and user acceptance, and they reported directly back into the board. There was a clear governance structure with a senior responsible owner and clear responsibilities and accountabilities. An issues log and a risk management log were part of the everyday process.

The mobilization of the key managers at Aarhus went hand-in-hand with the task of restructuring. Principally it was the managers who either had the new jobs, new roles and responsibilities and different reporting structures, or who had to implement them within their areas of remit. Hence the process of having working sessions where they came together to address the issues, reflect, engage in dialogue and reach consensus enabled them to leave the sessions, go back to their departments to implement what had been discussed and then return to the next working session to raise and address any issues of implementation or highlight other issues that had emerged. In this way the format was similar to an action learning group but with the added dimension of an organizational perspective and a collective task.

Summary

Even if you have excellent project management methodology, not everything will necessarily run smoothly. When operationalizing the changes you need to make allowances for:

- management barriers;
- the vision barrier;
- the resource barrier; and
- securing the acceptance of the change by those affected by it.

In any change where there are human systems at work a key focus has to be on individuals, teams and other groups going through change.

Kotter identified eight things which can contribute to failure of the change initiative and eight antidotes:

1. Establish a sense of urgency.
2. Form a powerful guiding coalition.
3. Create a vision.
4. Communicate the vision.
5. Empower others to act on the vision.
6. Plan for and create short-term wins.
7. Consolidate improvements and produce still more change.
8. Institutionalize new approaches.

Learning from previous internal change projects and best practice guidelines will help reduce the risk of failure, though the uncertain nature of change suggests that mistakes, taking wrong turns and abortive attempts are part of the process. An effective change monitoring process – of task and of emotion – is an important component of change.

7. Transition

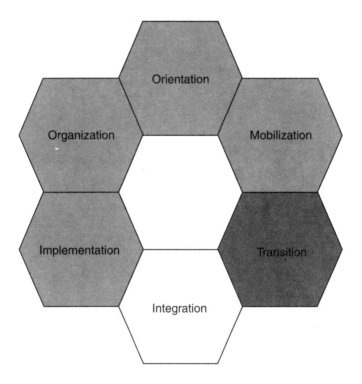

Bounds should be set
To ingenuity for being so cruel
In bringing change unheralded on the unready.
(Robert Frost, 1874–1963, US poet)

Tis a strange place, this Limbo! – not a Place,
Yet name it so;–where Time and weary Space
Fettered from flight, with night-mare sense of fleeing,
Strive for their last crepuscular half-being; –
Lank Space, and scytheless Time with branny hands
Barren and soundless as the measuring sands,
Not mark'd by flit of Shades,–unmeaning they
As moonlight on the dial of the day!
(S T Coleridge)

The evidence is mounting that real change does not begin until the organization experiences some real threat of pain that in some way dashes its expectations or hope open to the possibility of learning.
(Edgar Schein)

Introduction

The aim of this chapter is to look at how change affects individuals and teams and some of the key things that managers and change agents need to be aware of and do.

The change might be to restructure the organization of 20,000 from nine divisions into five whilst at the same time increasing customer focus; or it might be to divide the company into four separate business units with devolved powers but some shared central services; or it might be to introduce a new performance management culture into the organization in response to declining market share. The causes and types of change are endless, but whatever they are they will involve people and the need for people to change their attitudes and behaviours. One of the most critical issues in change management is how you manage people through this transition and help them adapt to their changed circumstances. Much has been written over the last 30 years about the psychological impact of change on people, and this chapter seeks to explore some of the findings and suggests some practical things that change agents need to be doing to ensure that the transition is as smooth as it can be.

 Virginia Satir, who practised and wrote extensively on change, once said that 'change happens one person at a time' (Satir *et al*, 1991). So if you are the chief executive and your goal is to get the whole organization of 20,000 moving in a new direction, you may not pause to reflect upon the fact that each one of those 20,000 people will need to go through a psychological process. Each one of those 20,000 will experience the change differently, for a variety of reasons, as we shall see. A key challenge for you is to be able to pick any one of those people and to be able to answer yes to the following questions:

- Does that individual know the nature of the change and what is required of him or her before, during and after it?
- Are there mechanisms in place that will enable that individual to make the transition in a relatively smooth and trouble-free way?

● Do we know what that individual needs to be able to psychologically and professionally adapt to the new situation and are we meeting those needs?

Individual change

Personality and change

We have already seen in early chapters how an individual's personality can influence how they respond and adapt to change. We have used ideas drawn from the MBTI® to explore this. We know that 39 per cent of the UK population, for example, are thoughtful realists; 37 per cent are action-oriented realists; 9 per cent are thoughtful innovators; and 15 per cent are action-oriented innovators (figures for the United States are similar). We know that the make-up of the managerial population differs from that of the general population; see Table 7.1.

Table 7.1 UK population and UK managers compared

IS Thoughtful Realists	IN Thoughtful Innovators
Are concerned with practicalities Learn pragmatically and by reading and observing Focus their change efforts on deciding what should be kept and what needs changing Their motto is 'If it isn't broke don't fix it' UK Population: 39% UK Managers: 21%	Are concerned with thoughts, ideas, concepts Learn conceptually by reading, listening and making connections Focus their change efforts on generating new ideas and theories Their motto would be 'Let's think ahead' UK Population: 9% UK Managers: 20%
ES Action-oriented Realists	**EN Action-oriented Innovators**
Are concerned with actions Learn actively and by experimentation Focus their change efforts on making things better Their motto would be 'Let's just do it' UK Population: 37% UK Managers: 26%	Are concerned with new ways of doing things Learn creatively and with others Focus their change efforts on putting new ideas into practice Their motto would be 'Let's change it' UK Population: 15% UK Managers: 33%

Source: UK population, OPP Ltd (1996); UK managers, Curd et al (2005)

You will note that UK managers have a much greater population on the future-focused (right side) of the table when compared to the population at large. If you compare the IS thoughtful realists you will see that over 39 per cent of the UK population are more likely to be wanting change only if there is a good enough reason for moving from the status quo. This compared to only 21 per cent of managers. Interestingly, when looking at the EN action-oriented innovators the situation is reversed, with more than twice as many managers concerned with new ways of doing things than the general population.

The difference in preference when it comes to change means that there may be a tendency to skew the communication and management of change along the preferences associated with the managers. It is therefore important to be able to expand one's repertoire to accommodate all types. Barger and Kirby (1995) have identified what each preference needs during organizational change (see Table 7.2).

Table 7.2 Preferences and associated needs during organizational change

Extraversion	**Introversion**
Time to talk about what's going on	Time alone to reflect on what is going on
Involvement – something to do	To be asked what they think about things
Communication, communication, communication	Thought-out, written communication and one-to-one discussions
To be heard – to have a voice	Time to think through their positions before discussions or meetings
Action, getting on with it, keeping up the pace	Time to assimilate changes before taking action

Sensing	**Intuition**
Real data – why is change occurring?	The overall rationale – the global realities
Specifics and details about what exactly is to change	A general plan or direction to play around with and develop
Connections between the planned changes and the past	Chances to paint a picture of the future – to create a vision that works for them
Realistic pictures of the future that make the plans real	Options – a general direction, but not too much structure
Clear guidelines on expectations, roles, and responsibilities – or the opportunity to design them	Opportunities to participate in designing the future, to influence the changes

Table 7.2 Preferences and associated needs during organizational change
continued...

Thinking	Feeling
The logic – why?	Recognition of the impacts on people
What systemic changes will there be?	How will people's needs be dealt with?
Why?	Inclusion of themselves and others in the
Clarity in the decision making and the	planning and implementing of change
planning	What values underlie the changes? Are
What are the goals? What will be the	they the right ones?
structure?	Demonstration that leadership cares
Demonstration that leadership is competent	Appreciation and support
Fairness and equitability in the changes	

Judging	Perceiving
A clear, concise plan of action	An open-ended plan
Defined outcomes, clear goals	The general parameters
A timeframe, with each stage spelt out	Flexibility with lots of options
A clear statement of priorities	Information and the opportunity to gather
No more surprises!	more
Completion – get the change in place	Loosen up, don't panic, trust the process
	Room to adjust goals and plans as the
	process continues

Anxiety and change

In Chapter 5 on mobilizing for change we looked at Schein's ideas on the need for survival anxiety to outweigh the individual's learning anxiety, and that the process should generally be one of reducing the learning anxiety rather than raising the anxiety levels about survival. Individuals faced with the need to change may well have a number of fears associated with it:

- Will they be losing their work identity through losing their current role?
- Will they be losing their set of formal and informal work relationships?
- Will they be able to cope with the demands of the new way of doing things?
- Will they be competent enough to perform adequately?

Questions such as these exemplify the natural concerns of individuals facing change. There is often a performance dip across the organization when change is implemented, partly due to the extra focus needed on installing the changes in terms of resources, energy and effort, but also due to the need for people to acquaint themselves with the new way of doing things – be it a new system or a new way of interacting with the customer. This performance or learning dip can be seen in different stages. The first stage is when the individual moves from unconscious competence (previous status quo) through a growing awareness that things need to change because they are not necessarily doing the right things or the things right (from unconscious incompetence to conscious incompetence). It is at this point people can have doubts about their ability to survive the new regime. With the right support people can move through to learning how to do things the right way up until the point is reached when it's done automatically (from conscious incompetence through from conscious competence to unconscious competence). Clearly there are ways of supporting them through this phase. One of the ways in which you can manage people's anxieties is by ensuring that there is a motivating vision of the future in which they feel they will be a part and have a contribution to make.

Giving them a clear understanding of where they fit and what is expected of them is another commonsensical thing to do, along with equipping them with the right tools to do it. The right tools include the resources and the necessary training. In some of the case studies we saw different ways in which these capabilities were encouraged – through practice areas, general and specific training, management development, help desks, coaching and other support mechanisms. A culture of not blaming people when they don't quite get it right also helps.

Beyond this, as we have suggested in Chapter 6 on implementation, the organizational infrastructure such as reward systems, IT systems, structures and shared values need to be in place and aligned.

The change or transitions curve

Kubler-Ross's initial research (1969) into the psychological process of those facing traumatic change, together with those management researchers who have extended her model to organizational change situations (for example, Adams *et al,* 1976) indicates that individuals go through a number of stages when dealing with change.

The change or transitions curve (see Figure 7.1) describes a typical trajectory through these stages though we should recognize that not everyone will necessarily experience all these stages nor necessarily in this sequence. Indeed it is possible for people to get stuck and not move on, or move through the curve and then find themselves back at the beginning.

Even when change comes as no surprise it is often experienced as a shock. The change may have been on the horizon and you had mentally understood that it was approaching, but this doesn't allow for the bodily and emotional feeling when it does come. It's the conversion into reality which makes people close down and switch off, resulting in a numbness. This can be experienced in expressions such as 'the walking wounded'. See someone who has just had bad news – say, that they have been made redundant – and they really have brought the shutters down between them and the world. This can then move into a stage of denial where somehow they haven't been able to take in the news or the consequences and it's somehow easier to pretend to themselves that it hasn't actually happened. These first few stages I believe are a prerequisite to people being able to begin thinking and feeling about the change. We are talking about change that can severely disrupt one's life and the means to having a livelihood. Change can challenge the notion of who you are and it can also turn your world upside down.

When individuals allow feelings about their circumstances to arise (and this isn't necessarily a conscious process, remember) then a typical emotion will be one of anger. People are annoyed at someone else for imposing this

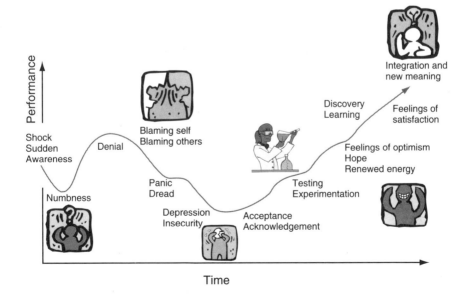

Figure 7.1 Change or transition curve

change, or taking away their role, or their prospects. They may well be angry with the organization, their line manager or their work colleagues, but they may also be angry with themselves for allowing this to happen. Even though it isn't their fault they may shoulder some of the blame – 'If only I had worked harder, or seen it coming'.

These feeling of anger, blame, irritation and frustration can then subside only to be replaced by feelings of anxiety. Once again the intensity may vary, but these feelings can range from the merely nervous through to dread and panic. We have already seen what Schein has to say about anxiety and some of the contributing factors. Clearly on this emotional roller coaster there will be real feelings of worry about the destabilization to the present and concern about the ability to survive into the future, whatever it may bring. This will be accompanied by the anxieties about competence, the ability to learn and step into a role which they may not know about, and may not want.

These anxieties can run their course, and leave a sense of depression and perhaps apathy. There's a realization that what you have had has probably gone for ever and you may not have the appetite to accept anything new at this point. In some ways this stage replicates some of the qualities of the initial stages of numbness and denial, but this has been transformed into a sense of loss. There's often no inclination to do much about the situation, maybe just passing time or 'treading water'.

All of these stages are marked by an internal focus (of what's happening to me) and most likely rather negative emotions about the present and future. And then something happens. It may be the gradual realization that you have to continue with your life, or perhaps it's been the support or challenge of family, friends or even your manager. But at some stage you start looking outward and acknowledge that the past is over and there becomes an acceptance that something else needs to be done. This looking towards the future can take a number of guises but will generally be characterized by the idea that you can explore options and test some of them out. It might be a new role recently advertised, or a training programme that is particularly relevant. It might be going down the pub with some co-workers, and you find yourself with the new team. With this comes some optimism that the worst is over. Exploring these possibilities leads to learning more about what needs to be done and how well you can do it. Focusing on this leads to more of an immersion in the new order of things and a connection with the 'new' organization. As time goes by you find yourself integrating these new behaviours, ideas and attitudes into your world view.

The transitions curve can take many forms, but going through it is a normal and natural process. Knowing about it helps – but doesn't mean you don't go through it! Being someone responsible for others' well-being means that you can assist people in going through the process. Table 7.3 suggests certain generic strategies as you move through the curve.

Table 7.3 Strategies for moving through the change curve

Stage	Description	Strategy
Shock *Numbness* *Denial*	Characterized by a sense of disbelief and non-acceptance of the change and maybe 'proving' to oneself that it isn't happening and hoping that it will go away 'Let's keep our heads down; we don't need these changes; perhaps they'll go away'	Attempt to minimize shock Give full and early communication of intentions, possibilities and overall direction
Blame *Anxiety* *Depression*	Getting angry that you find yourself in this situation, blaming self, blaming others Attempting to avoid the inevitable Getting anxious about whether you'll survive or be exposed as incompetent Hitting the lows and responding (or being unresponsive) with apathy or sadness 'I don't want this to work; I don't think I'm up to it or up for it; and I don't want to be part of it'	Listen, empathize, offer support, protection Do not suppress conflict and expression of difficult views or emotions Help individuals weather the storm Recognize how change can trigger past experiences in individuals Try not to take others' reactions personally
Acceptance	The reality of the situation is accepted 'I guess those things have gone for ever; I wonder whether the changes will work'	Help others complete Allow others to take responsibility Encourage Create goals Coach
Exploration	The idea arrives that perhaps there are things 'out there' Perhaps some of these changes might be worth at least thinking about. Perhaps you might just ask to see the job description of that new job 'Maybe these changes are working; perhaps I could try something on for size; maybe I could contribute'	Encourage risk taking Exchange feedback Set up development opportunities

Table 7.3 Strategies for moving through the change curve   *continued...*

Stage	Description	Strategy
Optimism *Learning* *Integration*	As you enter this new world there's the discovery that things aren't as bad as you imagined, perhaps the company was telling the truth when it said there would be new opportunities and a better way of working	Discuss meaning and learning Reflection Overview of experience Celebrate success Prepare to move on...
	'It's not so bad after all; they're definitely working; I enjoy contributing'	

An important point again is to remember that different people will go along the curve at different speeds and different groupings of people will go through it in different time periods. Often the senior managers and the change team will be seeing how the changes can be fully integrated whilst middle managers are maybe only starting to understand some of the possibilities, whilst many staff may still be in the throes of anger, blame, anxiety or depression. No amount of inspiring communications about wonderful visions of the future will actually be received, let alone well received by these communities. Getting back to the questions I posed at the beginning of the chapter – if you picked any one person going through change would they have what they and the organization needs for them to survive and thrive through these changes?

Weinberg (1997), developing ideas from Satir *et al* (1991), also maps this process but gives it an additional slant. He highlights that point of inflection when the inwardly-turned person who has been feeling pretty low one day moves through acceptance of their situation to being a relatively outward-looking person. He describes this point when a transforming idea occurs, which can be from within or from another person. Up until that point the individual has tried in one way or another to reject the changes or find some way around them, but the transforming idea occurs and the person's world view enjoys a radical shift – such as occurs when you see something in a totally new way (like the picture of two head silhouettes turning into a vase). From the moment the transforming idea has occurred, the challenge becomes how to integrate this into your way of working. The beauty of this is that you can see how a whole group can shift once they've all 'got it' and how the old status quo is replaced by the new one.

Bridges' three zones

Bridges (1991) also spans the individual and the organizational when he talks about transition:

> *Transition* is about letting go of the past and taking up new behaviours or ways of thinking. *Planned change* is about physically moving office, or installing new equipment, or restructuring. Transition lags behind planned change because it is more complex and harder to achieve. *Change* is situational and can be planned, whereas *transition* is psychological and less easy to manage.

He picks up on this psychological process and segments the transition process into three – endings, the neutral zone and beginnings. These three can be readily mapped onto the transitions curve, with endings covering the space and time between news of the change and towards depression and apathy; the neutral zone is that period of time experienced at the bottom of the trough; whilst the beginnings start as the curve moves upwards.

Endings

Bridges made the rather perceptive observation that you can't actually start a new beginning without finishing what it was that you were doing. This ending can be large or small depending on the nature of the change and the attachment that you have to the current state of affairs. The greater the attachment then the greater will be the loss, and the sense of loss. Even when the prospect of change towards something else might turn into a positive experience you can still feel loss for what is – moving to a new home means leaving the old one.

It is normal for people to feel this sense of loss, and people can feel a range of emotions – indeed all those on the transition curve of numbness, blame, anger, sadness, anxiety, confusion, depression and so forth. In organizational terms there may be the loss of a number of things: people, ways of working and indeed events. Here are just a few:

- your boss;
- your peers;
- your team;
- the informal network;
- your job role/description;
- your job objectives and targets;
- office location;
- desk;
- other teams;
- other departments;

- the monthly team meeting;
- the weekly one-to-ones; and
- the annual departmental picnic!

There is also a process that can occur around letting go through what Bridges describes as disenchantment with the old way of doing things; disengagement from the previous situation and people; and a dis-identification with what was by stepping outside the situation, though this can result in a disorientation and unease about the direction in which you may be heading.

The neutral zone

The neutral zone is that limbo land which Bridges calls that 'nowhere between two somewheres'. Everyone knows that the changes are taking place but very few people have adjusted psychologically to this. They know that things will never be the same again but they don't quite know what shape the future will turn out to be. Emotionally, people may well be exhausted from what they've already been through and they may be rather depressed, not knowing quite what is happening. Some of their islands of stability will have been lost – for example, their regular routines may well have been disrupted, an old boss replaced by a temporary manager who has different, as yet unknown, rules of engagement. Resources might be being reallocated, job descriptions being revised, people appearing and disappearing. Both the formal and informal ways in which they used to get their work accomplished have shifted and people are doing strange things for unknown reasons. Energy and motivation can ebb and flow, communications can become blocked. Indeed Bridges suggests that normal rules do not apply in the neutral zone, and there can be little chance of finding out what does apply.

Beginnings

To get to the beginning you have to have gone through the ending and endured the neutral zone. The beginning phase is the time when people are more outward-looking and engaged in creating the future. Once again, remember that different personalities will reach this stage earlier than others as will different members of the organization's hierarchy. The 'early adopters' may well be here whilst the laggards are quite a way away.

Strategies for managing transition

Bridges identifies a number of things you can do at the different stages (see Table 7.4). They are all concerned with understanding the psychological and emotional needs of people and designing interventions that will address those needs.

Table 7.4 Leading through Bridges' three stages

Endings	The neutral zone	Beginnings
Identify who's losing what by understanding what is going to change and how	Normalize the neutral zone by preparing people for the experiences often felt and letting them know that is a normal and natural part of the change process	Explain the purpose behind the outcome that is sought, as communication is always needed at this stage
Accept the reality and importance of the subjective loss by not discounting individuals' emotional reactions	Redefine it by accentuating that it is a normal and healthy part of the process and not overly negative	Create a picture of how the outcome will feel and look by using a combination of very practical analogies along with engendering a sense of inspiration and imagination
Don't be surprised at over-reaction as you don't know the extent to which they are unsettled by these changes	Create temporary systems in the neutral zone by compensating for those things that have been lost: the forming of temporary relationships, having shorter term targets and milestones, parallel communication channels	Lay out a plan for phasing in the outcome; this will appeal to many who need a route map and some milestones
Acknowledge the losses openly and sympathetically by not denying them and by enabling people to discuss their reactions if they wish to	Strengthen intra-group connections through proactively managing the informal and formal networks, which will be in a state of flux	Give each person a part to play in the outcome and the plan to get there, which continues the philosophy of engaging with those you want to be part of the future
Expect and accept the signs of grieving even if this is uncomfortable or taken as a sign of resistance to the changes	Use a transition monitoring team, which can be drawn from people immersed in the changes, to act as a conduit for feedback and taking the emotional temperature of the organization	Be consistent in the way you communicate and what you communicate, remembering that the words are only a small part of the information conveyed. Ensure managers are role-modelling new behaviours

Table 7.4 Leading through Bridges' three stages   *continued…*

Endings	The neutral zone	Beginnings
Compensate for the losses by acknowledging them and seeing if something can be given in return: tangible, intangible or symbolic	Use the neutral zone creatively by allowing and encouraging different ways of doing things: there's often less rigid strictures and structures at this time so make good use of the opportunity	Ensure quick successes through establishing short-term goals and selecting actions with a good chance of success
Give people information, and do it again and again by remembering that the right communication is key but also that it may not be heard the first or second time		Symbolize the new identity in communication, artefacts and rituals
Define what's over and what isn't as some people need to know exactly what is changing and what isn't		Celebrate the successes when they occur as a way of marking the beginnings, reinforcing the changes and sustaining momentum
Mark the endings symbolically, ritually and emotionally		
Treat the past with respect by not denigrating it, as it has its own validity and value		
Let people take a piece of the old way with them which connects with valuing the past and seeing change in the context of the past		
Show how endings ensure continuity of what really matters by connecting into the core values that will prevail whatever the new direction		

Source: Adapted from Bridges (1980, 1991) and Social Sciences Institute, North Carolina A & T State University People, Partnerships, & Communities (1998)

Teams through change

The majority of individuals work in teams towards organizational goals. A number of significant things can happen to individuals within teams and the teams themselves during transition. The psychological processes occurring within individuals mean that their attitude to team working can vary from the norm – some will want more contact, some less. Some will be working harder within the team, some less so. The team itself can be affected by the change – losing members, gaining members, being dispersed or becoming a new team. Glaser and Glaser (1992) identified five elements that contribute to the level of a team's effectiveness or ineffectiveness over time. Each one of these is disturbed during times of change. The five elements are:

1. Team mission, planning and goal setting, which is the clarity of understanding of the team's purpose, overriding objectives and general direction.
2. Team roles, which is the allocation of roles and responsibilities and the degree to which they are clear for each individual and for the team as a whole.
3. Team operating processes, which are the processes by which the team will go about its duties together and engage in problem-solving and decision-making activities.
4. Team interpersonal relationships, which is the level of cohesiveness and collaboration amongst the team members in pursuance of the team goals.
5. Inter-team relations, which is the degree to which working across boundaries occurs within the organization.

At any time during change all five can be disrupted. With the company's strategic direction shifting, the team's goals may well change, giving rise to the need to refresh and reconfirm what they are. The organization of work may need reconfiguring, with different people taking on different roles with new responsibilities. Levels of training and competence may present an issue here. Given what we have described occurring in the neutral zone, a team's way of working may shift, with team members being called away on projects, regular team meetings being disrupted, management information being delayed, etc. All these things will impact on team relationships as people go through their own transitions curve and make sense of the changes for themselves. Issues of rivalry and competitiveness may arise, though pulling together to face a common threat is just as likely. Finally, the relationship between the team and other groupings will typically shift. Even if there was no internal change for this particular team, the rest of the organization in both its formal and informal structure and power base may have changed, resulting in the need for team members to connect, reconnect and forge new links across organizational boundaries. Table 7.5 lists some of the strategies you can adopt when managing teams through change.

Table 7.5 Leading teams through change

	Task	**People**
Team purpose	Establish purpose of change and team objectives in relation to change Review progress on team purpose and objectives, adjust as necessary	Ensure understanding and commitment from team about change purpose on an intellectual and emotional level Check out individual engagement to purpose (enrolment, enlistment, compliance, resistance) Discuss differences Review progress, recognize achievement Review team performance against purpose, recommit as necessary
Team roles	Establish and ensure clarity of roles and responsibilities of whole team and individual members Review roles and responsibilities, adjust as necessary Develop strategies for improving performance	Ensure individuals understand their roles and those of others Establish whether there are any overlaps or grey areas Establish the degree of 'comfort' with individual roles and establish levels of support and challenge required Highlight areas of team tension Review progress, recognize achievements and development areas Review individual role performance and structure, recognize achievement and provide development
Team processes	Highlight the need for team processes in times of change Establish processes for decision making, problem solving, conflict resolution if not already in place Review team processes, adjust as necessary Develop strategies for improving performance	Establish ground rules for team working Check out levels of trust and agreement Surface areas of team tension Review level of team efficiency, adjust as necessary Develop strategies for improving performance

Table 7.5 Leading teams through change *continued...*

	Task	People
Team relations	Highlight the need for team development processes Ensure team is agreed on purpose, objectives, roles and processes Review team relations, attend to if necessary Develop strategies for improving performance	Establish ground rules for team working Build safe environment for team to openly express thoughts and feelings Review progress, recognize achievement Reflect upon level of team effectiveness Develop strategies for improving performance
Inter-team relations	Establish dependencies on and with other organizational teams going through change Establish process for communicating with other teams going through change Review level of inter-team working, plan negotiations if necessary Implement actions from review if necessary and develop strategies for improving performance	Highlight the need to establish protocols with key organizational groupings Engage with other groupings on how they will work together Review level of inter-team working, engage others in negotiating better relations if necessary Continue to foster good working relations with other organizational groupings

Shadow side of organizations

to light a candle is to cast a shadow

(Ursula K Le Guin)

Given the nature of change and its innate capacity to disturb, it's little wonder that seemingly irrational things will happen during change. We have seen how change can affect individuals and teams and evoke a range of emotions. As an individual or within a team or larger group, or within an organization, there is always what is going on above the surface, but invariably there is what is going on below, too, and change situations can stir these up more than at other times.

For an individual it is what lies in the subconscious or in the unconscious – those bits of yourself you'd prefer to disassociate from, perhaps not reveal, or maybe fear. Although you might be unaware of them, it can sometimes be obvious to colleagues when they take the trouble to look.

Within the team or group situation the shadow side manifests itself in the thoughts, feelings and behaviours that people just don't want to discuss. When the team is described as or felt as being dysfunctional, more than likely there are things that are going on below the surface which are getting in the way of the task in hand being done effectively.

Within organizations the shadow manifests in many ways – it's the hidden, the unspoken, the undiscussable, the power plays, all the things that sap the energy from an organization and divert it from achieving its objectives and addressing the issues that are holding it back.

Individual shadow

Whether alone or with others we are all a complex mix past, present and future. We bring with us into any situation bag and baggage from the past. Our formative years have a critical affect on who we are, how we present to the world and how we react to situations. Our earlier relationships with significant figures (mother, father, siblings and the like) can cause us to repeat patterns that might have been useful then but most likely are inappropriate now (Freud, 2002).

We have seen how our innate personality can cause us to respond to different types of communication and put us under stress in different way – all these things can happen below the level of awareness and can be a great source of synergy, or more likely, conflict, with people of a different type. Our life experiences cause us to enter into current situations with a set of predispositions, and indeed prejudices that then get us behaving as if they were true – with the consequential reactions from others.

So the key is to surface the individual shadow by discovering where your blind spots are, by increasing your self-awareness and by checking out how you interact with others and where you come into conflict with them.

Team shadow

In any team or small group situation, not only do we all bring our respective individual shadows but we can and will often display even more seemingly non-rational behaviour as the team shadow manifests itself. Bion (1961) suggests that various phenomena might be observed. For example, the group look towards one person to solve all their problems (the messiah), or they exhibit fight or flight behaviours, either way avoiding the task in hand.

Often people will scapegoat one person, either in or outside of the group, and because there are power and politics at play (beneath the surface) there can be all sorts of 'hidden agendas' which bear little resemblance to the agenda on the table. Sometimes a team will 'park the elephant' in the corner, that is, they've recognized there is an issue which needs addressing but no one has the appetite to address it.

Information itself is power and not all information gets communicated. So how can we make the best decisions either for the business or for ourselves? As people can be preoccupied with the consequences of the change, the actual agenda is the last thing on their minds. Different people can manifest political behaviours – someone does everything to please the boss, especially telling him or her what they think they want to hear, whereas another person who has suffered in a previous change isn't going to risk saying anything out of turn, so doesn't engage in dealing with the change or the transition.

Organizational shadow

Like individuals and groups, organizations too have a shadow side. With organizations this can be inextricably linked to its culture, 'the way things are done around here'. It can manifest in various guises but you know when you've encountered it by certain feelings and observations:

● Things don't seem to get done very easily.
● People say one thing but do another.
● The informal organization is better equipped than the more formal organization.
● There are higher levels of frustration, lack of motivation and more 'walking wounded'.
● People are put into impossible situations – damned if you do, damned if you don't.

There can be something about the culture that gets people not to achieve the task they are there to do or engage in the changes that are everyone's responsibilities, no matter how skilled or motivated they are. The values that the organization espouses are not the values that are enacted or rewarded – 'the customer is king' and 'people are our greatest asset' bring forth a shrug or a hollow smile. The top team, rather than bringing stewardship to the organization, are seen to be individually motivated, mal-aligned and out for their own ends or for their own areas and not for the good of the company, its customers, shareholders or staff. Potent symbols and artefacts around the place accentuate the shadow rather than the vitality of the organization – customer-facing staff stand talking to themselves; the reception area is full of dirty ashtrays; the stories people tell are ones of failure, gossip or to the detriment of the organization.

A lot of these things go on below the surface and are not discussed – as Argyris (1990) points out, we cover up certain things and then cover up the cover – there are things in this organization we don't discuss and we don't discuss the fact that we don't discuss them.

Surfacing the shadow

Egan (1994) discusses the shadow in organizations in some depth and a number of practical things you can do to surface the shadow and deal with it. He suggests you need to focus your attention on the shadow side of things during times of change as well as all the other things you are doing:

- Legitimize the search for and naming of blind spots.
- Ask the questions behind the questions.
- Welcome new perspectives from others.
- Think about ways you might be in the dark.
- Sit up when you are surprised by behaviour or events.
- Identify the consequences of not discussing the issue.
- Use a confidant to discuss fears about negative consequences.
- Identify issues that you're reluctant to discuss.
- Identify issues that others are reluctant to discuss.
- Develop the ability to name the issue, having put yourself in the recipient's shoes first.
- Turn embarrassment into learning.
- Monitor self-interest.
- Use shared problem-solving methodology.

You need to choose viable political strategies, whilst always having the business needs in mind.

Egan uses the analogy of sport – learning the nature of the game that is being played, who the key players are and what their motives and motivations might be. You need to access these networks, developing lines of communication and forming alliances and coalitions as necessary. This is very much in the realm of the political metaphor, and Egan certainly uses that language. It is about negotiating your way through and around the various competing interests, knowing which are the issues to remain firm on and which you can yield a little on.

Baddeley and James (1987) discuss political skills for managers on two axes, one which runs from the individual being politically aware to being politically unaware; the other from psychological game-playing through to acting with integrity (see Figure 7.2). The first axis is really about how emotionally intelligent (Goleman, 2000) you are in being aware of your self and being able to pick up on what is going on around you in the organization. Clearly when operating within a political metaphor, or when the shadow side is rising, being politically astute is important. The other axis is really concerned with the values that you hold and the values of the organization. Acting with integrity would be the natural aim for managers in most organizations and as such is a good model for enacting change, as the 'how' of the change is as important as the 'what', and the how of the change needs to be aligned with the organization's future vision and values.

Case study analysis

At Aster a number of binding and bonding interventions helped the different sections operate alongside each other, managing the 'what's tight – what's loose' tension between each other and the centre. An expanded management

Source: adapted from Baddeley and James (1987)

Figure 7.2 Political skills for managers

development programme brought the senior managers together on a number of occasions and clear signs of a new Aster culture emerged.

The pace of change was such that on an emotional level there were a lot of feelings to deal with and on a task level there were quite a number of things that needed doing or clarifying. There was a degree of cooperation and genuine willingness of managers to fully engage together in working on their collective challenges – an indicator perhaps that the pre-merger work on managing the fit between the people, the culture and the business objectives had been repaid.

What helped people during this time was the development and communication of a clear strategy; the reflection back of a core set of values which were role-modelled by senior mangers; and a sequence of staff briefings and cascades and the establishment of an annual staff conference to celebrate success, involve and engage staff in the future direction and test out ideas.

For the Institute the main focus of managing the changes was ensuring that all the stakeholders were on board and engaged. This was done through the many joint initiatives created and also the continual networking of the managers and staff with the communities of interest across all of Ireland. The leadership development programme – which members of the Institute themselves attended – was an impressive way of developing, learning, sharing best practice and enhancing overall leadership capability in furtherance of the shared vision.

Biogen Idec communicated a lot on creating a positive and alluring vision of the future for the location of the new HQ, for the centres of excellence across Europe and for the greater devolved powers.

At the British Council the Change Communications Manager's main tasks were to ensure excellent communication to and from the business, ensuring business readiness and aligning communication to enable change management. It is important to note that those areas of the business which were under-represented demonstrated a lower level of engagement and readiness for change.

Throughout the transition period communication and engagement were paramount. From the first global 'web chat' on the company intranet at inception through to feedback reviews after go live there was a forum for two-way communication – information dissemination and addressing any queries or concerns.

The coordinators' network was set up at an early stage with the aim of acting as a formal communication conduit between the programme team and the affected areas. They had a key communication role in being the eyes and ears for the programme team and, having their fingers on the pulse, they could be an integral two-way communication channel. The coordinators also had a key role in ensuring that the relationships between business and project were managed effectively. Later on they transformed into 'Power users' or coaches and were on hand in situ available to support people through the learning process.

At Aarhus the implementation and transition went hand-in-hand. The process for gathering data, making decisions and agreeing actions allowed those involved in the change to surface emotional issues and highlight areas of tension and conflict. The change team built this into the programme with a series of interventions focusing on the leadership, primary task and collaboration across the organization. At the same time managers had individual time to reflect upon, discuss and plan their support and development needs. Issues related to leadership, shared understanding, relationships and communication were raised and time and space created for them to be fully aired and resolution or routes to resolution agreed.

For the kitchenware company, staff were treated as colleagues, with an open-door policy giving them the ability to contact managers at any time. The significant policy changes were communicated early, and conversations and discussions had around important company issues and any customers' needs. The sales force was fully engaged with setting the sales plan, using a bottom-up process.

Changes to product, product lines and structures within the company, acquisition of other companies, and taking on other companies' accounts all impact on stakeholders' perceptions, create instability and can generate anxiety. Managing customers, employees and suppliers through the changes required deliberate focus and energy.

The changes at the primary school were framed in a very positive light – the new school building and the appointment of a young credible, dynamic head inspired confidence amongst staff, children and parents. On the one hand the change process created involvement and engagement (for example, the vision-creation sessions), which allowed people to begin to feel much more a part of the process. On the other hand the head needed to have some frank discussions with individual members of staff as to what was expected of them in terms of their performance and what they could expect from the head in terms of support. Parents as a key stakeholder group were invited to contribute in various ways.

A number of things were symbolically changed, such as the old style annual general meeting where the head and governors sat in a long line and spoke at those parents who had made the effort to turn up. These meetings became a 10-minute report on historical events and the rest of the meeting was used to talk about changes that were planned over the coming year and how the future could be co-created. Parents were also invited to contribute through a newly revitalized Parents' Forum.

Summary

Change happens one person at a time and you need to identify the range of different personalities who might be involved in change and manage their particular needs. The MBTI® personality indicator is one method of tailoring your approach to different personality types.

Schein identifies different types of anxiety (survival and learning) which need to be addressed in order to allow change to progress. The more you can reduce the learning anxiety which prevents movement, the more effective the change will be.

The change or transition curve is a representation of an important psychological process that identifies key stages which individuals will progress through during the transition. This is a normal and natural process and should not be underestimated. Strategies to manage people's distress will make the changes smoother. However, remember people disturbed by change are less likely to hear what you are communicating and will need time to adjust, and those initiating change or at the forefront of change will be at a more advanced stage of the change curve. Those you are communicating with may well be further behind and more inwardly focused.

Bridges described three zones (endings, neutral, new beginnings) which people will go through during the change process. Different interventions are called for at each of these times. It is much harder to create a new beginning if the organization hasn't fully managed the previous ending.

Teams experiencing change also need to be supported by addressing their change needs along the following five dimensions:

1. team purpose;
2. team roles;
3. team processes;
4. team relations;
5. inter-team relations.

Unconscious processes may become overt during times of disruption, with the shadow side of the organization appearing on an individual, team and organizational level. This needs to be spotted and addressed.

8. Leading Change

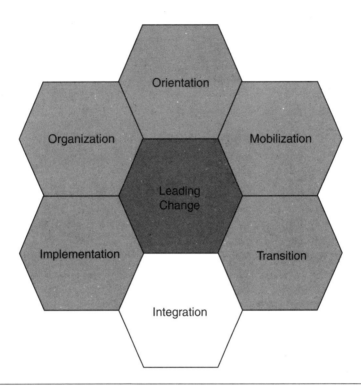

We'd be the first to admit it. We're in serious need of some inspirational and focused leadership. We need to promote a strong sense of purpose in teams whose morale and confidence are low… we need to develop a clear strategic vision if we're to deliver the kind of services this great town and its people deserve.

Which is why we need a credible and highly accomplished change manager like you. Someone able to champion a new vision while focusing all our resources on the things that matter most. Not least the delivery of our ambitious yet realistic goals.

It's obviously not going to be easy. But it will present you with the kind of challenges your talents deserve. And make full use of your proven ability to raise aspirations, expectations and performance levels.

Here, you'll do this with the support of a senior management team which you yourself will shape, and by strengthening relationships with our many partners.

> You're a radical thinker who's bold but not reckless. A hard-edged decision maker and skilled negotiator. A charismatic ambassador and customer champion. And an inspirational leader with experience of transformation in a comparable organization. But most of all, you'll be able to take us from being one of the biggest to one of the best.
>
> **(Job advert for a chief executive, 2006)**

Introduction

The aim in this chapter is to bring together some of the themes discussed in previous chapters to establish what it is that needs leading and how leaders go about this successfully. The job advert above suggests a number of things:

- leadership is needed to manage change;
- leadership is complex;
- leadership requires a considerable skill set; and
- leadership might be an impossible task... for one person.

This chapter looks at ways in which leaders can help ensure that change is managed successfully within their organizations. In our definition of leaders we include change agents at all levels within the organization, for reasons that will become apparent.

Characteristics of leadership

Here are three quotes about leadership from three prominent leaders and leadership researchers which display some of the different aspects of the complexity of the subject:

> Leaders must be seen to be up front, up to date, up to their jobs and up early in the morning.
>
> (Lord Sieff, Marks & Spencer)

> Managing is helping to make happen what is supposed to happen anyway; leadership is making happen what isn't going to happen anyway.
>
> (R Pascale)

> A crucial difference between managers and leaders lies in the conceptions they hold, deep in their psyches, of chaos and order. Leaders tolerate chaos and lack structure... managers seek order and control.
>
> (A Zaleznik)

The first quote suggests following the line of the classical leader who is out in front of his troops and on top of everything and moving forward fast. Of course this definitely has its place in leadership, but we shall see that there are a number of styles you can choose from and a number of situations in which different styles might be more appropriate. The second two quotes distinguish between what managers do and what leaders do, but they come at it from different angles. Although there is great discussion about whether one can separate the two roles, or whether there is someone who just manages or someone who just leads, what we shall do is to separate the two for the sake of analysis whilst registering that they usually go hand-in-hand within the same person.

Pascale is making a clear statement that leadership is fundamentally about change – effecting change in the organizational world, whilst Zaleznik is more concerned with the idea that it takes a certain sort of person, a certain sort of perspective to lead. We have seen that often change takes the form of emergence or evolution as plans start to be put into action, and Zaleznik is suggesting that living with the sense of chaos (Bridge's neutral zone?) and helping others through it in a confident fashion is a sign of leadership.

In the introductory chapter we presented a model that looked at leading outcomes, interests and emotions with the self at the centre (see Figure 8.1). When we have asked senior managers and political leaders to populate the boxes with leadership characteristics they came up with the statements in Table 8.1.

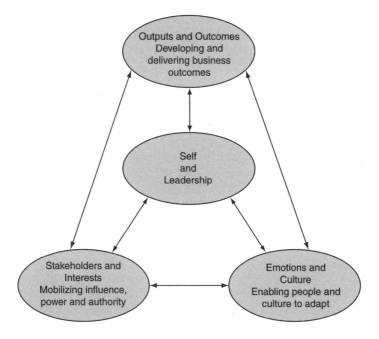

Figure 8.1 Leading outcomes, interests and emotions

Table 8.1 Characteristics of leadership

Outcomes	Stakeholders	Emotions	Self
Scanning the environment	Stakeholder identification	Communicating	Maintaining personal values
Developing vision, values and strategy	Involvement and engagement	Enrolling	Developing self-awareness and knowledge
Deciding priorities, resources, performance	Drawing together diverse views	Developing	Developing self-management skills
Planning and performance framework	Negotiating a way forward	Supporting emotional movement through transition	Developing interpersonal and organizational awareness
Structures, systems, styles	Incorporating diversity	Inspiring	Developing leadership skills
Ensuring delivery, evaluation, learning	Partnership working	Adapting cultures	Coping with complexity, uncertainty, ambiguity and risk
Decision making	Championing	Enabling and empowering	
	Sharing leadership and power	Changing behaviours	Developing resilience
	Being an ambassador	Spotting and nurturing talent	
The leadership task in this area is defining outcomes and developing strategies to delivery them	*The leadership task in this area is ascertaining what interests and voices there are about this change and negotiating a way through and forward*	*The leadership task is to spot the challenges possibilities and dilemmas individuals and groups will face and enable the to be addressed*	*The leadership task is to spot the task and make use of the appropriate leadership style*

The leadership task

If we return to the adapted change equation and Kotter (1995), we can begin to see some of the tasks to which the leader or change agent needs to attend.

Ensuring that there's pressure for change and establishing a sense of urgency are key elements in alerting people that change needs to happen and will be happening. The style can vary depending on the situation, but what is needed is communication with relevant stakeholders in a convincing way. In may need the leader to be challenging:

> Followers want comfort and stability, and solutions from their leaders. But that's babysitting. Real leaders ask hard questions and knock people out of their comfort zones. Then they manage the resulting distress.
>
> (Heifetz and Laurie, 1997)

Creating a vision is sometimes the domain of the executive team, sometimes the whole organization may be involved, but being able to draw on people's ideas and imagination to then craft a vision which is lofty and strategic is a leadership task. The degree to which it is a shared and understood vision is a function again of style and inclusivity, but it will depend on the level of buy-in that it receives. Remember too the different personalities – lofty visions are inspirational for some of us, what it actually means 'on the ground' is motivational for others of us.

Developing the capacity and capability for change involves a number of tasks. There is ensuring that the mechanics of change are in place – change team project management methodology, resources, etc – and the need for the 'powerful guiding coalition' which can involve clear sponsorship and varying levels of stakeholder connection. Capacity can be both about resources in terms of the implementers of change and also allowing for the performance dip associated with organizational change. Capability is concerned with ensuring that there are the necessary levels of skills and competence within the organization or brought in from outside.

Actionable first steps can ensure that the change is taken seriously, that it has started and, when linked to planning for and creating short-term wins, that it has momentum. But leadership is not always about being at the helm, and one of the tenets running throughout the book, backed up by some of the research quoted and demonstrated by the case studies, is that stakeholder involvement, inclusion and engagement support the change process. Continuous communication of the vision and empowering others to act on the vision allows this to happen, as does noticing improvements and energizing areas that are flagging.

Spotting where there is resistance to change, understanding why there is and acting appropriately (by redoubling efforts, altering course, communicating, challenging or supporting more) are key leadership duties.

One of the complaints levelled at leaders is their propensity to move on to other things after the change is in train but not yet achieved. Leadership can be about ensuring that improvements are consolidated, change is integrated and then further change can happen.

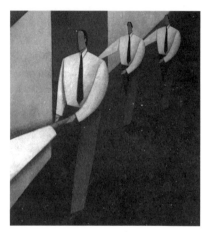

Heifetz (1994) sees the leadership task as first 'getting on the balcony' to know what's going on strategically and operationally, what's happening now and what's on the horizon. From that perspective you can then decide what the 'adaptive challenges' are. He differentiates technical change, which is probably accomplished with minimal effort or disruption, from adaptive change, which will challenge, disturb or destabilize the organization and those in it. Given this propensity to knock people out of their comfort zones, part of the leadership task is to manage that process by recognizing the psychological component of change and transition and help people through it. Maintaining disciplined attention is about getting the right balance between being on the balcony, focusing attention on the adaptive challenges and ensuring business as usual. Giving the work back to the people is ensuring there is distributed leadership across the change initiative and understanding that a leader's task is not to do it solely on your own but to involve others in the change effort. A leader's role is also to ascertain feedback – what's working what's not – and acknowledge that you haven't got all the answers and others have valid points of view.

Table 8.2 The leadership task

Get on the balcony	See the whole picture, the environmental challenges, the boundaries and relationships within the organization and between it and other providers, suppliers, communities and stakeholders. Make sense of and see the connections between changes, pressures and objectives

Table 8.2 The leadership task   *continued…*

Identify the adaptive challenges	Identify those challenges that cannot be met by continuing to work in the same way – challenges to the underlying beliefs and culture of the organization. Recognize when the values that made us successful are becoming less relevant and we need to develop different ways of thinking and behaving
Regulate distress	Understand the impact of change on people's work and help them to make sense of the purpose and outcomes of the change, to see the big picture. Provide clarity even if you cannot provide certainty. Do not inflict change unnecessarily
Maintain disciplined attention	Ensure that even in times of change the detailed demands of customers and other stakeholders are met – do not lose sight of the real business
Give the work back to the people	Ensure that people are able to get on with their work without 'interference' from above, build trust, support people in reaching up to take on bigger challenges and do not lean down to do the work of more junior people (just because you can do it well)
Protect the voices of leadership from below	Recognize that the people who challenge are demonstrating a concern for the organization and a commitment to its goals – take care of the people who bring contentious issues into the open: they may have an important perspective

Adapted from Heifetz (1994) and Heifetz and Linsky (2002)

Leadership roles

Senge sees leadership occurring at different locations within an organization. There are the executive leaders who have the traditional hierarchical positions who exercise the more formal leadership, but there are also the more local leaders who have the job of translating the vision into tangible actions, and network leaders who adopt a role of connecting different parts of the organization involved in change. In the machine metaphor you will have leaders who are the architects of change and probably operate through a project management methodology, ensuring plans are implemented with allocated roles and responsibilities, with project manger and project sponsor in place. The other metaphors would bring forward other skills – the leader as negotiator, the leader as coach, and the leader as facilitator. Bate (1995) generates an amazingly long and varied list of leaders in cultural change drawn from his idea of five dimensions of cultural leadership:

1. the aesthetic, dealing with ideas about change – 'the sensate, the ideational, and the idealistic; the spices of culture';
2. the political, dealing with the meaning of change – 'putting the idea into words, and giving the ownership of that idea to the organization community';
3. the ethical, dealing with the standards within the change – 'a guided learning process';
4. the action, dealing with the practices around change – 'converting cultural meanings into cultural practices – and back again'; and
5. the formative, dealing with the structures around change – 'the architecture of culture'.

Leaders as: Artist, Poet, Rebel, Adventurer, Jester, Utopian, Inventor, Storyteller, Myth-maker, Gossip (but not quite of the usual sort), Pathfinder, Rule-maker, Teacher, Coach, Mentor, Whistleblower, Critic, Devil's Advocate, Advocate, Champion, Salesperson, Implementer, Architect, Designer, Draughtsman, Builder, Sculptor.

(Bate, 1995)

Higgs (2003) and Higgs and Rowland (2005) identified three distinct groupings of:

1. shaping behaviour: by communicating what specific behavioural change was necessary and by holding people to account;
2. framing change: by establishing the parameters of change in terms of defining the why, the when and the how, covering both the mechanics and guiding principles; and
3. creating capacity: by ensuring the necessary resources and focus are available along with enabling connections and communications across the organization.

The strategy implementation team of a financial services organization undergoing major change generated a set of competencies for their local change leaders. In addition to the general project management ones they included the following.

Role model/framework provider

Embodies confidence in the way that they manage the change process, has a handle on the current situation, demonstrates what needs to be done to keep the change progressing, gives a sense of being on top of things.

Wider context

Has the ability to see current changes in the wider context of team, division and organization. Not only sees how change fits with overall organizational strategy but transfers that understanding to others.

Empathy

Has the ability to see how others are experiencing change, understands and acknowledges what they are going through and takes this into account when managing the change process.

Communication/being straight

Communicates facts about current and future changes in an appropriate and timely manner. Keeps their people fully informed. Differentiates between fact and opinion. Links overall purpose of change with the likely consequences at a local level.

Is straight with both good news and bad. Can be relied upon to be open and honest about change and how it affects individuals and groups.

Counselling

Adopts a supportive stance towards those going through change, with a demonstrated understanding that the emotional component of individual change needs to be acknowledged and respected.

Challenging

Is able to confront individuals and groups with the reality of the situation and to identify and communicate what are unacceptable attitudes and behaviours and work towards acceptable solutions.

Involvement

Actively demonstrates the belief that those going through change have a contribution to make in ensuring that the change is successful. Encourages individuals and teams to engage fully in the change process.

Reframing

The ability to see the situation from a range of different perspectives and within the wider context, and get others to do likewise. To proffer and provoke creative solutions in order to put the current situation into a more coherent framework.

Enabling learning

Acknowledgement that changing situations require the acquisition of new skills, knowledge and behaviours. Enables their people to attain these.

Reviewing
Recognizes that true learning takes place only when past experience is linked to new behaviour through reflective activity. Ensures that regular reviews occur as part of the normal management process.

Recognition
Sets a positive 'can do' environment, acknowledges progress at all stages and gives positive feedback to individuals and groups when they have accomplished their objectives.

Leadership style

Goleman (2000) quotes research by the consulting firm Hay/McBer drawing on a sample of 3,870 leaders that found six distinct leadership styles, each building from different components of emotional intelligence. The different styles correlate positively and negatively to the overall organizational climate and performance of an organization, with the facets of organizational climate studied being clarity, commitment, flexibility, responsibility, rewards and standards. Goleman found that the most effective leaders were those who could use the styles flexibly by developing competence in more than just one and by deploying different styles, dependent on the challenges of any given situation. He found that the most effective leaders had access to not one, two or even three of the styles, but were able to demonstrate at least four of the styles, which was optimal.

The coercive style, later relabelled 'commanding', is characterized by the leader telling you what to do. Useful in situations which require immediate compliance (like an emergency), it doesn't allow for followers to think for themselves or be creative. The authoritative style, later relabelled the 'visionary' style, is one concerned with vision building and demonstrates authoritativeness by establishing respect and credibility and being able to bring people with you due to your ability to engage with others and be clear about the direction. The affiliative style is one used mainly when the focus is people rather than task. Often used when there is conflict or discord, its primary purpose is to get people aligned and cohesive. The democratic style is best used when you want or need people to be engaged in the decision-making process. It's not focused on the people as such but on what they can contribute. The pacesetting style is one often seen in organizations that have big change agendas and energetic and committed people (often at the top). As the name implies, it's leadership from the front with a clear idea of where the change is going. It gets change moving but can result in burn-out of the people leading change or leaving the rest of the organization (ie the followers) behind. The coaching style of leadership is used appropriately when bringing on people and developing the organization's capability by developing the people. It is best used when there is time and space to invest in the process.

Leaders who have mastered four or more – especially the authoritative, democratic, affiliative and coaching styles – had the most positive impact on climate and performance. Each style, if deployed appropriately, had short-term uses and benefits but over time the coercive and pacesetting styles produced a negative impact on climate and performance.

Effective leaders were seen to be flexible in their deployment of the styles and sensitive to the impact such styles had on others within the organization. Very few leaders demonstrated all six styles and even fewer, according to Goleman, know when and how to use them.

Different leadership styles appear to be appropriate at various points in the change process, as Table 8.3 suggests.

Table 8.3 Leadership styles and their appropriate use in change situations

Leadership style	Change situation
Coercive	When there's an organizational crisis and action needs to be taken immediately. The leader needs to have the necessary competencies to make the right decisions
Authoritative	When a vision needs to be articulated and moved towards. People need to be engaged and the leader needs to have credibility
Affiliative	When people are going through transition and need support. When different interest groups need conflict resolution or coalition building
Democratic	When stakeholders need to be engaged in creating the solution or when the complexity of the change is such that solutions will be achieved through collective endeavour and collaborative problem solving
Pacesetting	When the change needs kick-starting and there's the willingness and enthusiasm to initiate and implement the changes. When there is a community of change champions
Coaching	When the underlying ethos is one of learning, growth and development. When the organization needs to build its leadership capability and is willing to invest in it

Source: Goleman (2000)

Case study analysis

At Aster the previous rather coercive style shifted to a more pacesetting style. Richard engaged in regular and open conversations with staff and all managers, using staff briefing, conferences, small group and individual discussions. He demonstrated that he knew where he wanted the organization to go, had the intellectual firepower to argue his corner and encouraged people around him to participate in creating the future. What was interesting was how the culture as a result shifted from one of 'We don't normally do this' to one of 'Let's give it a try.' In the longer term leadership needs to spread across the senior management and down into the organization. The challenge is to sustain the success by becoming a leader who is primarily a facilitator or enabler and also to continue to build the leadership capacity throughout all parts of the Group.

The leadership style exhibited by the Institute's Director and her senior management team was a balance between being affiliative, democratic and authoritative. The Institute needed to get close to all of its stakeholders, build trust and discover what the needs and ideas were of all of these bodies and the constituencies that they represented. It then had to craft a vision and a strategy which would command respect, be authoritative and encourage engagement. These needed to be underpinned by a set of core values which permeated everything it did – tackling health inequalities in an inclusive way, setting out a motivating vision, setting consistently high standards, being collaborative, building relationships and fostering networks wherever and whenever possible.

Biogen Idec adopted an authoritative style of leadership which relied on it having clarity of direction, an understanding of the needs and wants of the various stakeholders, a certain credibility with staff and business partners but also an openness to incorporate different views and new data as they emerged, but always within predefined parameters.

Its treatment of staff was based on fairness and equity. There were no special cases or exceptions when it came to redundancies, promotions or relocations. It tried to achieve the balance between being clear, consultative and direct.

The leadership styles of the key players at the British Council focused on balancing the different aspects and demands of the programme. Involvement of all stakeholders every step of the way, was a guiding principle. At critical decision points it had to hold its nerve and balance the need to be authoritative with the need to be both democratic and affiliative. Going through periods of turbulence it sometimes had to focus more on the people than the task. Leadership throughout the project was variously described as 'firm but responsive' and 'honest but robust'. With the organization facing changes that it had never managed before, an overly directive style would not work. Accessing the shared wisdom of all the key players was crucial. The leadership style was based on the context, on the level of complexity of the project and the levels of shared knowledge and wisdom.

The three Aarhus managers had quite different personality types, with a consequential variation in leadership styles. One was a quiet thinking type of person who had quite a few ideas but also always allowed the time for reflection before a decision. The second also thought things through but was more outgoing and translated ideas into creative possibilities. Interaction with others was important for him as, through his questioning approach, he was able to discover new avenues of thought and action. To complement the first two, the third manager was much more focused on the here and now; he had an eye for detail and required proper ways of doing things. Rules-driven might be one description; another would be attention to the quality of the process and the procedures. He had a handle on the resources and allocation of those resources.

Nick and Dennis demonstrated the quite classical leadership style of leading from the front and showing and sharing their enthusiasm and commitment to the project. What was striking though was their willingness to listen, learn and act on what customers, suppliers, staff and the Chairman had to say. They were extremely focused on the moment and for the long term, but had the flexibility to alter their tactics if people or the environment intervened.

The head's leadership style was very much symbolized by three pictures that had struck her as encapsulating the task ahead:

1. A woman having to juggling many things of different shapes and sizes.
2. Someone trying to get a flock of penguins to move in the same direction.
3. Being on a high diving board, ready to take the plunge!

These three pictures symbolized to her the need to be very clear about what she was embarking upon (in terms of vision and strategy); to be aware of all the different, and sometimes competing, interests amongst the stakeholders; and to recognize that going through change oneself and leading others through change can be a scary, anxious but exciting experience.

Summary

The key leadership questions through change are:

- Are you addressing the different dimensions of leading change?
- Have you identified the leadership task within the change?
- Do you understand the leadership roles within this change?
- What are the key competencies of change management?
- What are the most appropriate leadership styles?

During change leaders need to juggle the different dimensions of:

- outputs and outcomes – developing and delivering business outcomes;
- stakeholders and interests – mobilizing influence, power and authority;
- emotions and culture – enabling people and culture to adapt; whilst
- maintaining the appropriate authenticity and congruency in their leadership style.

Leaders can use the adapted change formula to ensure they are fulfilling their task. What are the leadership tasks in each of the following variables:

- pressure for change;
- a clear shared vision;
- capacity to change;
- capability to change;
- actionable first steps; and
- spotting resistance to change?

Heifetz suggests the following are the key leadership tasks when managing change:

- get on the balcony;
- identify the adaptive challenges;
- regulate distress;
- maintain disciplined attention;
- give the work back to the people; and
- protect the voices of leadership from below.

Bate identifies a number of leadership roles in culture change:

- the aesthetic, dealing with ideas about change;
- the political, dealing with the meaning of change;

- the ethical, dealing with the standards within the change;
- the action, dealing with the practices around change; and
- the formative, dealing with the structures around change.

Higgs and Rowland identified three distinct groupings of:

1. shaping behaviour: by communicating what specific behavioural change was necessary and by holding people to account;
2. framing change: by establishing the parameters of change in terms of defining the why, the when and the how, covering both the mechanics and guiding principles; and
3. creating capacity: by ensuring the necessary resources and focus are available along with enabling connections and communication across the organization.

One change team developed the following set of competencies for their local change leaders:

- role model/framework provider;
- empathy;
- counselling;
- involvement;
- enabling learning;
- recognition.
- wider context;
- communication/being straight;
- challenging;
- reframing;
- reviewing; and

Goleman's research suggests effective leaders need to access at least four of the following styles:

1. coercive;
2. authoritative;
3. affiliative;
4. democratic;
5. pacesetting;
6. coaching.

9. Integration

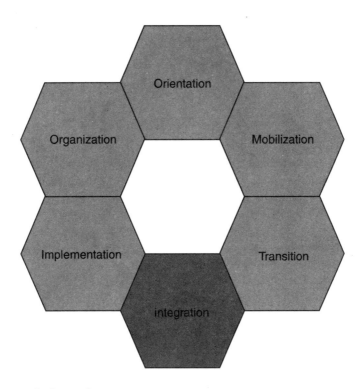

The completion at last
We were once only the embryo, implanted by faith
Cultivated from ideas, some old – and some new
Nourished with a desire – to seek our fate
Beginning to flourish – from dreams, left – from the cool
Morning dew –
If we survive the drought in the summer, of prejudice and hate,
Where lack of love – threatens to cut us down, like an unwanted
Weed
Providing winter's cold heart, – doesn't uproot us in war, only –
To fill – its own selfish plate.
Then perhaps – the following season, will bring us the promise
We so desperately need

For spring may bring us warm hearts, to expose our unstable
Petals, to a whole new light,
With April's tears of remorse, for discrimination, and ignorance,
Which, created such gloom
Replenished with hope – we continue to grow, there's no stopping
Us now, for now, – it's all done right.
From here it unfolds, – the completion at last, for all of God's care,
Will soon be in full bloom

(Dave Tanguay, 'The completion at last', © 2006 Dave Tanguay. Reprinted with the kind permission of the author. davesplace@suwanneevalley.net)

Introduction

The aim of this chapter is to look at how change becomes embedded in the organization and the degree to which learning has occurred and how changes can be sustained going forward.

Looking through the lens of the machine metaphor, the changes will be completed once the project plan is done. If the diagnosis, design and implementation were effective then the change will have occurred. In terms of Lewin's unfreeze, change, refreeze model, integration occurs at the time of refreezing the organization. If part of the design was to move from one state, as described in the From > To analysis, to the future state then this end state will be achieved when, for example, the strategy is in place, the new structure and systems are functioning, the staff with the appropriate skills and the management with the appropriate style are all working in line with the shared values. This will have been achieved though the organization and implementation of the changes, and the mobilization and transition of the stakeholders.

From the perspective of the organism metaphor, we can see that integration has occurred when the organization has fully adapted to its new environment. Integration will have occurred within the political metaphor when the new configuration of the power base has settled in and a new status quo has been negotiated. Within the flux and transformation metaphor, integration isn't necessarily the prime concern. Given that the way the changes have evolved has allowed scope for emergent themes to take hold and take shape, it may well be that some things which work, or which have 'stickability' have become a part of the way of life whilst other things have faded away. In some of these other metaphors it is as if the organization were in free-flowing mode and for change to occur it had to be frozen and then unfrozen – the mirror image of Lewin's original idea. From a task point of view, integration occurs when the project plan is completed and the change team goes home. From a personal perspective, integration occurs when people have gone through the transition curve individually and entered Bridges' new beginnings zone.

Embedding change

In a sense we are back at the beginning, because if we have orientated ourselves, organized and mobilized, implemented and made the transition, then we will have achieved our aims. Roberto and Levesque (2005) interestingly say:

> the seed of effective change must be planted by embedding procedural and behavioural changes in an organization long before the initiative is launched... to achieve effective institutionalization, core process and enabling conditions must be embedded into the organization well before the change initiative is rolled out... to embed change in an organization, managers have to create the conditions that enable employees to take ownership of the new procedures and systems and integrate and apply the key principles of the initiative to the way day-to-day work is done... These enabling conditions occur in three contexts: structural, procedural and emotional.

By 'structural' they mean the way in which the organization structures itself to enable its people to focus where and on what is needed, which links into the way they will be rewarded for the behaviours and the outcomes that are preferred. The 'procedural' context is the degree of fairness with which the change process is initiated and implemented, as perceived by the employees. Depending on whether the organization is doing it commensurate with its stated values and with an attempt to involve and engage staff, there will be more or less integration of the changes into the fabric of the organization. The 'emotional' context refers back to many of the aspects of transition that we have previously discussed. If preparation for the change does not seek to address the fears and anxieties of those who it will affect, there will be less support and mobilization.

As a precursor to these embedding mechanisms, Roberto and Levesque define four antecedent processes which contribute towards an enabling environment in which change can occur; see Table 9.1.

Table 9.1 Four antecedent processes

Chartering	The process by which the organization defines the initiative's purpose, its scope and the way people will work with one another on the programme: • Boundary setting – definition of scope of initiative • Team design – definition of roles, responsibilities, norms and ground rules for teamwork
Learning	How managers develop, test and refine ideas through experimentation before full-scale rollout: • Discovery – data and information gathering to define goals of initiative and means of achieving objectives • Experimentation – testing and refinement of initiative prior to full-scale rollout
Mobilizing	The use of symbolism, metaphors and compelling stories to engage hearts as well as minds in order to build commitment to the project: • Storytelling – use of stories and metaphors to create compelling accounts about need for initiative and explain specific changes • Symbolic action – use of symbols to reinforce credibility and legitimacy of core team and its message
Realigning	A series of activities aimed at reshaping the organizational context, including a redefinition of roles and reporting relationships as well as new approaches to monitoring, measurement and compensation: • Job redesign – alteration of underlying structures and processes that support jobs • Performance management – invention of new metrics to measure the effectiveness of initiative and incorporation of the metrics into employee performance appraisal process

Source: Roberto and Levesque, 2005

Learning

However, in all cases learning will have happened and it is this ability to learn new things and learn about the process that allows change. Weinberg (1997) describes this well in his model of how transformation occurs. Often the status quo is so strong or the prevailing paradigm so hard to shift that any attempt to introduce something new (what he calls 'the foreign element') is resisted. Initially, resistance takes the form of outright rejection, but if that fails then there is an attempt to absorb the new element into the existing state. If a new counter-culture leader comes into the organization then there may be attempts to undermine them; if that fails then there are attempts to get them to play by the existing rules. It's only when that fails that there's an attempt to adapt to the new element and transform the organization, and this attempt can either succeed or fail. If the latter then the cycle begins again; if it succeeds then we can see that the organization has shifted.

We have seen that a key capability of the organizations that manage change successfully is to be learning as they make the changes. They may pilot something and see what the consequences are, and then adapt their change initiative accordingly. But they may be doing something in addition: they may also be looking at the way they take those decisions, implement those initiatives and review their practice. This is what Argyris and Schön (1978) call 'double-loop learning'.

Single-loop learning happens when an action is taken and the intended outcome achieved or, when there is some deviation from the outcome, you try something different to achieve the outcome. There is not any thought about how you went about this or the underlying assumptions you may have. With double-loop learning you seek to understand why these actions are not working and then develop other strategies – with that knowledge – to remedy the situation. The additional thought process is about gaining some understanding of cause and effect and insight into prevailing assumptions or beliefs.

A further loop can be incorporated if the change principles themselves come under scrutiny. The challenge might be what kind of organization we want to be. If single-loop is concerned with whether we are doing things right, and double-loop concerned with whether we are doing the right things, then triple-loop learning is concerned with how we decide what is right. It is similar to the transforming idea in individual change since it involves a paradigm shift – a shift in the way you perceive the world around you.

As an example, the IT department wants to install a new system in the finance department. It meets with resistance in the shape of certain processes not working. It rewrites the processes (single-loop). It continues to meet resistance and recognizes that maybe it hasn't gone about it in the right way and decides to make sure that stakeholder discussion is part of the project plan (double-loop). It continues to meet resistance and realizes that it is operating within the machine metaphor when what is really called for is for it to fit with the prevailing political metaphor. It shifts its paradigm (triple-loop).

The learning organization

Senge *et al* (1999) suggest that for organizations to sustain change through learning and learning through change, there are five disciplines they need to master:

1. *Personal mastery.* Formulating a coherent picture of the results people most desire to gain as individuals alongside a realistic assessment of the current state of their lives today.
2. *Mental models.* Discipline of reflection and inquiry skills focused around developing awareness of the attitudes and perceptions that influence thought and interaction.
3. *Shared vision.* This collective discipline establishes a focus on mutual purpose... by developing shared images of the future they seek to create, and the principles and guiding practices by which they hope to get there.
4. *Team learning.* Through techniques like dialogue and skilful discussion, teams transform their collective thinking, learning to mobilize their energies and ability beyond the sum of individual members' talents.
5. *Systems thinking.* In this discipline, people learn to better understand interdependency and change, and thereby to deal more effectively with the forces that shape the consequences of our actions.

Pedler *et al* (1996) identified five dimensions of an organization's operations with 15 supporting aspects that would characterize a learning company. It is interesting to note that there is a focus on flexibility, permeability, participation and, of course, learning, which correlates well to the aspects of good change management within the case studies.

1. Strategy would include a *learning approach* with regular reviews, pilot projects and plans modified and built on as progress is achieved. Also within this category would be the notion of *participative policy making*, which would involve all members of the organization and other key stakeholders, with policy being co-created rather than being driven purely from the top down.
2. Looking in to the organizations would be areas such as the use of information technology to inform and empower people and their actions (*informating*); accounting and control mechanisms which enable learning and freedom to act within less rigid compliance and risk averse regimes (*formative accounting and control); internal exchange* covers the idea of their being mutually productive relationships between internal suppliers and customers with a free flow of information across the organization; and *flexibility of reward* allowing for more creative and flexible ways of motivating staff, with a degree of involvement from all.
3. Structures and how work is organized is flexible enough to allow creativity, innovation, development and responsiveness to occur (*enabling structures*) to meet current needs as well as preparing for the future.

4. Looking out covers the use of *boundary workers as environmental scanners* and *inter-company learning*. Both these areas allow for permeable borders and are aligned to that of a healthy organism where information flows between customers, suppliers, partners and others with a stake in improving the business.

5. Learning opportunities address the *learning climate* and the opportunities for *self-development* for all. A climate is fostered whereby people can experiment, take risks, make mistakes and learn through doing. This would be supported by the necessary training and development opportunities. There would be a two-way contract here, with the organization enabling learning but with individuals encouraged to take responsibility for their development as well.

Case study analysis

At Aster, after the change process, it needed to address some key issues:

- how to hold a strategic view across the Group whilst attending to operational issues within one's own business;
- how to spot and transfer best practice across the Group;
- how to build one's own identity as a business but be true to the Group ethos; and
- how to equip managers to be able to manage still more change in the future.

A series of workshops were designed to address these issues:

- to help managers share knowledge and understanding across the whole Group;
- to develop skills to better manage change;
- for managers to understand their management style and the impact it has on others; and
- to address the important and pressing issues arising from a dynamic and changing organization.

Managers and staff were involved, in a variety of ways, with developing the ongoing agenda for change. In addition to the workshops there were staff briefings, staff discussion groups and staff conferences where the forward agenda was communicated, ideas generated and potential obstacles highlighted and worked on collaboratively. Over time a number of working groups were set up to address different organizational development themes as they emerged:

- Develop practical ways in which people will 'buy-in', own and act out the values.
- Develop ways for managers to keep their 'finger on the pulse' – know the key issues emerging for staff and the organization to take action on.
- Generate ideas as to how people can take on responsibility and grasp opportunities.
- Direction – guided by Aster's vision and values and taking account of the strengths and weaknesses of the Group, where would you want Aster to be in five years' time?
- Improvement – examine current service improvement practices to confirm, a) whether they are appropriate for Aster Group, and b) how they can better engage and be made more meaningful to staff and customers.
- People – taking account of the staff surveys across the organization, examine and made recommendations of what we need to do to make the Aster Group a better place to work.

The Institute wanted to embed the changes by broadening and deepening the networks across all of Ireland, which would lead to better health for all. By developing the network and having open dialogue with all stakeholders, the vision of health equality could take hold across the island.

The leadership programme was a good case in point as its aim was to build leadership capability and capacity across all organizations working on the island. Four programmes have been run with 100 people from all health sectors nominated or self-selected to attend, including academics, public health doctors and community health workers as well as managers from local government.

The programme didn't just focus on individual leadership development but also on the impact on their respective organizations – creating a cadre of leaders, making wider connections and operating in an all-Ireland system. The ongoing peace process has helped, creating more porous borders, more fluid, less threatening. Likewise this increased level of communication and understanding has helped the peace process.

For Biogen Idec there were four key things that needed to happen as a result of the change:

1. a new fully functioning headquarters in Zug;
2. a more devolved and autonomous culture;
3. centres of excellence established in specific specialisms and functions across Europe; and
4. greater empowerment and autonomy to the affiliates.

The physical movement from Paris to Zug coupled with the reduction in staff ensured that the changes would last. The old way of doing things clearly could not be sustained. Likewise, movement of some of the key functions away from the HQ and the establishment of these functions (centres of excellence) in locations that were naturally better placed to operate them – international regulatory, clinical research, data management and pharmaco-vigilance centre close to the European drugs regulator and logistics at Hoofddorp, building on an already established centre with a central location, excellent transport and distribution facilities. At the same time the company's resources were devolved to the centres and the affiliates. Reporting lines were reconfigured to put power and authority in local operations rather than a controlling centre. All the changes were monitored, not just for effectiveness of execution, but also for how well they were received by staff, customers and investors.

At the British Council the programme office had created stabilization criteria for each part of the process and used a traffic light system to track progress. From the implementers' point of view they needed to manage the balance between focusing on the next phase – rolling the system out overseas – and addressing the stabilization issues in the UK.

System users had to manage the tension between accepting the new system with limited knowledge and creating 'workarounds', and gaining the necessary expertise to fully exploit the system. Management attention was needed to ensure business optimization and exploitation of the system, by attempting to engender inquisitiveness and to stop any backsliding by, for example, minimizing the amount of paper that was printed out.

Business process ownership resided within the business, within the process itself. This idea fitted with ensuring empowerment and indeed ownership where it belonged, but it did require specific responsible managers to be appointed and also enough resources attached to those roles. As often happens within organizations, managers with a full load of duties and responsibilities are asked to take on the additional responsibilities. Unless the role is reconfigured around the process, the role might be either too large or cumbersome, or deflect from giving the process adequate focus.

The programme support office worked on establishing a set of key performance indicators (KPIs) to have a reasonably objective measure of how things were going and which were used to:

- decide on areas that needed following up;
- decide which areas were a priority for action;
- illustrate and illuminate where things were going well; and
- manage expectations of the stakeholders.

Managing expectations helped at this stage in introducing the new system, as it addressed the following key questions:

- Does each part of the system function – yes or no?
- Are we able to process sufficient volumes at sufficient quality?
- Are we operating more efficiently than before?
- Are we demonstrating best practice?

The KPIs need adjusting as you pass through these phases. By focusing to start with on 'Does it work, yes or no?' you indicate that this is the level of your expectation. Going straight into assessments of whether you are immediately more efficient is unrealistic and can be dispiriting, as the answer can often be a no. The reviews of KPIs themselves can form the basis of an understanding of what has worked well and what now needs to change.

Within the kitchenware company the strategy continues to work well, with customer orders continuing to grow. The UK kitchenware market, however, is declining, so standing still is not an option. It needs to grow organically or through acquisition, and this growth can be through existing or new products. It had demonstrated it could grow organically through greater customer relationship management and fulfilment; it had responded to customers' needs and suppliers' ideas and enhanced the brands and developed the product range. In the last 20 months it has made two acquisitions of companies with similar product profiles (low value, high volume) covering similar accounts. The challenge for Dennis and Nick is how to embed the current success into a sustainable growing business. As the company grows there is probably the need for more formal training and development, more formal soft management skills and perhaps more attention being paid to sustaining an entrepreneurial culture. Such a large expansion will require different skills and capabilities across the organization; issues both of organizational capacity and capability will have to be addressed.

For the primary school the key ways that the changes were embedded were through the continued use of the processes that had been set up. These processes became part of the cultural shift and tapped into all the major stakeholders:

- All the power originally invested in the head was devolved to the leadership team, and further devolved to curriculum heads.
- The establishment of the children's representatives through the School's Council and Pupil Voice became ongoing parts of the termly cycle.
- Parents' Forum and the forward-looking annual general meeting became regular events, along with focused working groups looking at key aspects of the school and its curriculum.

- Discussions with the Local Education Authority led to the school being able to have greater degrees of decision making as it was deemed to be operating effectively.
- Links were made with a newly funded group of networked schools that exhibited many signs of sharing the same ethos, with an action inquiry approach to learning and a growing international dimension.
- Links were established with the National College for School Leadership's Leadership Network of over 250 heads engaged in similar innovation and reform in their schools and informing national policy development.

Summary

Paradoxically, integration processes need to be designed, developed and implemented at the beginning of the changes.

Roberto and Levesque suggest you have to install enabling conditions in three contexts: structural, procedural and emotional. As a precursor to these embedding mechanisms they define four antecedent processes that contribute towards an enabling environment in which change can occur: chartering, learning, mobilizing and realigning.

Sénge suggests for the learning organization to take root, organizations need to practise the five disciplines of:

1. personal mastery;
2. mental models;
3. shared vision;
4. team learning; and
5. systems thinking.

Pedlar, Burgoyne and Boydell identified the following components of a learning company:

- strategy, with a learning approach and participative policy making;
- looking in to the organization, with informating; formative accounting and control; internal exchange; and flexibility of reward;
- structures, to include enabling structures to meet current needs as well as preparing for the future;
- looking out, covering the use of boundary workers as environmental scanners and inter-company learning;
- learning opportunities that address the learning climate and provide opportunities of self-development for all.

10. Conclusion

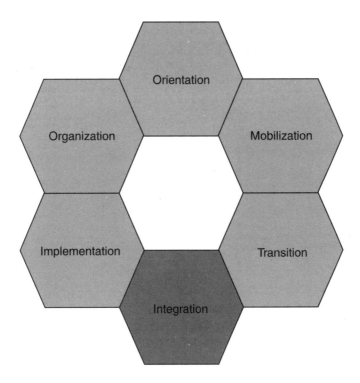

Managing change – best practice

Hiatt and Creasey (2003) highlighted findings from three Prosci research studies (www.prosci.com). These looked at change management in more than 400 companies worldwide and found that the greatest contributors to success were:

- effective sponsorship from senior management in terms of active visible support; ongoing support throughout the life of the initiative; acting as role models for the change; communicating and being ambassadors for change;
- buy-in from front-line managers and employees, which got the change moving and kept momentum going;

- continuous and targeted communication throughout the project, tailored in depth and breadth to the different interested communities;
- an exceptional change management team taking the form of an experience credible team who maintained good internal working relations and also networked into the organization; and
- a well planned and organized approach that is best fitted to the type of change being managed.

The major factors that contributed to change failure were:

- poor executive sponsorship;
- employee and staff resistance;
- middle management resistance;
- corporate inertia and politics; and
- limited budget, time and resources.

What was interesting in the research was that staff wanted to hear about the changes from two people – the most senior person involved in the change and the local line manager. It is as if they need to hear the overarching vision and strategic direction from someone who means what they say, and they need to hear about the change in a way that is translated into the local context. They also need to know that their manager is committed to what's happening. In addition, the sooner they hear about the change the better, linked to the sooner the organization planned for the change the better.

Given that staff and middle manager resistance were factors in project failures, the reasons for this resistance are important. Reasons for employee resistance were they do not actually know about the changes, or not being told enough about the implications of the changes; the fact they were unsure of what the future held for them and the organization; and also a proportion of them were not dissatisfied with the way things were.

Middle managers resisted change because they often had too much business as usual to occupy them, and so their current pressures, priorities and general workload meant they couldn't get engaged with the changes. Also, a fear of losing control was expressed, which manifests itself in terms of a loss of power. Looking back at Chapter 7 on transition, it is easy to understand where this fear comes from when you are losing your current way of doing things and unsure of the future state because you are in the neutral zone.

Lessons from the case studies

Key elements for organizations managing change successfully through the change process were as follows.

Orientation

There needs to be a good process for addressing both external and internal drivers for change, together with openness for change backed up by detailed data gathering and a rigorous decision-making stage.

In the majority of cases there was a co-creation of direction with key stakeholders. By connecting with them, a motivating shared vision could be built. An important component was having the end user – customer, client, pupil – always in mind and also the ability to refer back to them when deciding on what changes to make.

After the future state – outline or specific – had been mapped, it needed to be supported by a clear and convincing business case. This means ensuring that the drivers for change do lead to improvement coupled with a set of principles for the way the changes will be handled.

In each case holding the organizational values in mind and referring back to them as a 'touchstone' was a natural and integral part of the plan. What you do and how you do it emerged as an important concept. Clarity of vision and commitment to a core set of values was crucial in direction setting and/or in execution.

Those organizations where stakeholders felt a sense of readiness for change seemed to make the transitions more smoothly.

Organization

There was an imperative to address both the task issues (project implementation) and the process issues (the group/team dynamic). The projects were run by dedicated, credible people with meticulous planning on the things that needed to be got right.

There tended to be a credible project team with ongoing top level sponsorship. Where appropriate (eg systems change, due diligence) a well thought out project management methodology with a very clear decision-making and problem-solving process was evident.

In all cases the business and other stakeholders' needs were represented on the team and they fed into the design process and the solution generation. Being responsive to the customer, listening to the staff and suppliers or consultants aided the process.

Mobilization

Entering into real dialogue with key stakeholders took longer but ultimately enhanced the chances of successful outcomes. Taking the time upfront to create a 'facilitating environment' enabled change agents to allow tensions and potential conflicts to be raised and addressed. This reduced the possibility of these conflicts being 'acted out' negatively during the change process itself.

Involvement and engagement of all stakeholders with targeted communication according to need was demonstrated time and time again to be an indispensable factor in the successful management of change. Part of this was by ensuring that managers were engaged, involved and trained for the change and staff had many opportunities to feed back their views. Even those initially against the changes could be engaged in this process.

Holding onto the vision and having visible involvement of senior management supported the Prosci research findings. The combination of visible sponsors and top team commitment increased momentum and reduced organizational drag.

Communication channels were established really early on and a series of continuous and targeted communication occurred throughout the process. The various change teams engaged people in all of their relevant networks – especially the operational side of the business.

Engaging stakeholders was best achieved through attentive and active listening. Creating a motivating vision that all communities can get behind and then demonstrating that you can and will deliver builds short-term credibility and enables mobilization to happen more readily.

Recognizing and acting on the fact that different personality types like to be communicated with in different ways doesn't have to be an overly planned affair. But you do need to shape your strategy accordingly – for example, a series of one-to-one, group, team and stakeholder 'events' can tap into everyone's energy and enthusiasm and allow everyone to make contributions – first in terms of the direction, and second in terms of commitment to action.

Implementation

Providing coaching, supervision and development for the management population – linked to strategic objectives and operational realities – enhances management capability and provides emotional support (and challenge) during times of change.

As the changes take place, parts of the organizational infrastructure will change in line with the change direction – for example, a new structure and new locations went hand-in-hand with devolving power and budgets.

A very effective project management structure was established when the nature of the change required a more planned, top-down approach. This always came with a clear line into the programme management board. There was business representation for all strategic discussions and a business group assessed the blueprint, the training and user acceptance and reported back to the board. There was a clear governance structure with a senior responsible owner and clear responsibilities and accountabilities. An issues log and a risk management log were part of the everyday process.

Understanding the politics of the situation always helps as does going where the energy for change is. Spotting where the changes were being disrupted or where help was needed was also a distinguishing feature.

Transition

Creating dialogue means everyone's voice is heard, thus increasing the possibility of 'buy-in' and engagement in the change process. It's important for issues to be raised so that they can be addressed.

Workshops for affected managers to address issues of concern and planning for the future were shown to be useful change interventions in a number of the case studies. If the changes are conducted openly and with a lot of communication then the change team are more likely to get valid feedback about progress. The more you can forewarn people and clearly link the changes to the strategy, the more understanding will be the people affected by change.

Building capability and capacity through development programmes and time out to review and reflect was a major plank in a number of the changes. The transition period tended to be managed through dialogue and engagement. There were some meetings where boundaries, such as performance management issues, were laid down, but generally it was the movement from one culture to another done though dialogue and engagement.

That is not to say that change was always smooth. Disturbance is an inevitable part of the process and there will most likely be a period where the organization is in Bridges' 'neutral zone'.

Integration

Building staff and management capability and capacity, and getting structures, strategy and systems realigned and fitting with the new culture were key challenges for integrating the changes. It is important to recognize that additional resources are needed not only during the changes but most likely for a period of time after the changes have been implemented.

It is useful for senior management and the change team to ensure continued focus at the stabilization phase and to ensure learning reviews take place and are transmitted to the next change team.

Even if you are travelling at speed, do make sure from time to time that you put in the infrastructure to sustain the changes. You can also embed the changes by developing the leadership capability and the cohesiveness of the formal and informal organizational networks.

Leadership

Having complementary leadership styles in the top team creates a broader spectrum of leadership capability.

Creating the time and space for the change team itself to address (ie confront and work through) the 'emotional baggage' they may have picked up during the change process wasn't a universal theme, but did appear to ensure the lack of dysfunction of the change teams where it did happen. Having a project team being a cohesive unit helped the effectiveness of the team during the implementation process.

There doesn't seem to be any need for a particularly visibly charismatic leadership, but there does need to be a variety of leadership styles adopted at different points in the change process. Understanding the nature of the leadership task during these different phases was highlighted as a key element. A low key but authoritative style in keeping all stakeholders on board proved to be particularly effective in a number of the case studies.

In terms of Goleman's six styles of leadership, the most prominent ones that emerged in the case studies were the authoritative, affiliative and democratic, with some coaching style demonstrated. In a couple of organizations and in a number of situations the pacesetting style was prominent.

Conclusion

Managing change is no easy thing. Often, during the process, you may be accused of being too focused on the task, or too focused on the process. You may be consulting and communicating too little, or too much; you may be very clear about the end state, leaving no room for emergent possibility, or creating unease in the organization because you haven't fleshed out the specifics of the change.

This book has been an opportunity for change managers and others interested in managing change successfully to look at change from a number of different perspectives; to understand how other organizations have managed change well; and to offer some ideas and insights into the change management process. In summary, there is no one right way, but there are a number of frameworks within which you can find a way that is right for your change today.

Bibliography and References

Adams, J, Hayes, J and Hopson, B (1976) *Transition – Understanding and managing personal change*, Martin Robertson and Company, London

Ansoff, H I (1991) 'Strategic management in a historical perspective', in (ed) D E Hussey, International Review of Strategic Management, **2** (1)

Argyris, C (1990) *Overcoming Organizational Defences: Facilitating organizational learning*, Allyn and Bacon, Boston, MA

Argyris, C and Schön, D (1978) *Organizational Learning*, Addison Wesley, MA

Arnstein, S (1969) 'A ladder of citizen participation', *Journal of the American Planning Association,* **35**, 4, pp 216–24

Audit Commission, *Change Here!*, http://www.audit-commission.gov.uk/changehere/ [accessed 2006]

Baddeley, S and James, K (1987) 'Owl, fox, donkey or sheep: political skills for managers', *Management Education and Development*, **18**, pp 3–19

Balogun, J and Hailey, V (2004) *Exploring Strategic Change*, Prentice Hall, Harlow

Barger, N J and Kirby, L K (1995) *The Challenge of Change in Organizations*, Davies-Black, Palo Alto, CA

Barney, J B (1991) 'The resource based view of strategy: origins, implications, and prospects', *Journal of Management*, **17**, pp 97–211

Bart, C, Bontis, N and Taggar, S (2001) 'A model of the impact of mission statements on firm performance', *Management Decision*, **39** (1), pp 19–35

Bate, P (1995) *Strategies for Cultural Change,* Butterworth-Heinemann, Oxford

Beckhard, R and Harris, R T (1987) *Organizational Transitions: Managing complex change*, Addison-Wesley, Reading, MA

Beckhard, R and Pritchard, W (1992) *Changing the Essence: The art of creating and leading fundamental change in organizations*, Jossey-Bass, San Francisco, CA

Beer, M, Eisenstat, R and Spector, B (1990) 'Why change programs don't produce change', *Harvard Business Review,* **68** (6), pp 158–67

Bion, W R (1961) *Experiences in Groups,* Tavistock, London

Block, P (1991) *The Empowered Manager: Positive political skills at work,* Jossey-Bass, San Francisco, CA

Boddy, D (2001) *Managing Projects: Building and leading the team*, FT Prentice Hall, Harlow

Bowles, M (1991) 'The organization shadow', *Organization Studies*, **12,** pp 387–404

Bridges, W (1980) *Transitions: Making sense of life's changes*, Perseus Publishing, New York

Bridges, W (1991) *Managing Transitions: Making the most of change*, Perseus Publishing, New York

Brown, S L and Eisenhardt, K M (1997) 'The art of continuous change: linking complexity theory and time-paced evolution in relentlessly shifting organisations', *Administrative Science Quarterly,* **42,** pp 1–34

Buchanan, D and Huczynski, A, (2003) *Organizational Behaviour: An introductory text,* FT Prentice Hall, Harlow

Cameron, E and Green, M (2004) *Making Sense of Change Management*, Kogan Page, London

Carnall, C A (2003) *Managing Change in Organisations*, Prentice Hall, Harlow

Cooperrider, D and Whitney, D (2005) *A Positive Revolution in Change: Appreciative inquiry,* Berrett-Koehler, San Francisco, CA

Curd, J, Dent, F and Carr, M, (2005) 'Development challenges: looking at the future', *Training Journal,* January, pp 36–39

Daft, R L (1997) *Management*, Dryden Press, Fort Worth, TX

Deal, T and Kennedy, A (2000) *The New Corporate Cultures,* Texere, London

de Caluwé, L and Vermaak, H (2004) 'Change paradigms: an overview', *Organisation Development Journal,* **22** (4)

De Woot, P (1996) 'Managing change at university', *CRE-action,* **109,** pp 19–28

Dunphy, D and Stace, D (1993) 'The strategic management of corporate change', *Human Relations,* **46** (8), pp 905–20

Economist (2005) 'Business: The cart pulling the horse? Management and IT', 9 April, **375** (8421), p 57

Edelmann, L F and Benning, A L (1999) 'Incremental revolution', *Organizational Development Journal,* **17** (4), pp 79–93

Egan, G (1994) *Working the Shadow Side: A guide to positive behind-the-scenes management*, Jossey-Bass, San Francisco, CA

Eisenberg, E M, Andrews, L, Murphy, A and Laine-Timmerman, L (1999) 'Transforming organizations through communication', in (ed) P Salem, *Organizational Communication and Change* (pp 125–50), Hampton Press, Cresskill, NJ

Flanagan, P (1995) 'ABCs of changing corporate culture', *Management Review*, July

Ford, Jeffrey D. Ford, J and Pasmore, William A. Pasmore, W (2006) 'Vision: Friend or foe during change?', *Journal of Applied Behavioral Science;* **42** (2), pp 172–76

Ford, M and Greer, B (2005) 'The relationship between management control system usage and planned change achievement: an exploratory study', *Journal of Change Management,* **5** (1), pp 29–46

Frahm, J (2003) 'Organizational change communication: lessons from public relations communication strategies', Australia and New Zealand Communication Association Conference, 11 July, Queensland University of Technology, Brisbane

Freud, S (2002) *The Psychopathology of Everyday Life*, Penguin, Harmondsworth

Glaser, R and Glaser, C (1992) *Team Effectiveness Profile*, Organization Design and Development, King of Prussia, PA

Goffee, R and Jones, G (2000) *The Character of a Corporation: How your company's culture can make or break your business*, HarperCollins, London

Goleman, D (2000) 'Leadership that gets results', *Harvard Business Review,* March–April

Grant, R (2003) *Contemporary Strategy Analysis,* Blackwell, Oxford

Handy, C (1981) *Understanding Organizations*, Penguin, Harmondsworth

Harrison, R (1972) 'Understanding your organizations character', *Harvard Business Review,* **50** (3), pp 119–28

Heifetz, R (1994) *Leadership Without Easy Answers,* Harvard University Press, MA

Heifetz, R and Laurie, D (1997) 'The work of leadership', *Harvard Business Review,* January–February

Heifetz, R and Linsky, M (2002); *Leadership on the Line*; HBS Press, MA

Hiatt, J and Creasey, T (2003) *Change Management: The people side of change*, Prosci Research, Colorado

Higgs, M (2003) 'Developments in leadership thinking', *Journal of Organisational Development and Leadership,* **24** (5), pp 273–84

Higgs, M and Rowland, D (2005) 'All changes great and small: exploring approaches to change and its leadership', *Journal of Change Management*, **5** (2), pp 121–51

Hofstede, G (1991) *Cultures and Organisations*, McGraw-Hill, Maidenhead

Huczynski, A (2001) *Encyclopedia of Development Methods*, Gower, Aldershot

I&DeA (2006) *Inside Top Teams – A practical guide*, I&DeA, London

Jacob, N (2003) *Intercultural Management*, Kogan Page, London

Janis, I (1972) *Victims of Groupthink: A psychological study of foreign-policy decisions and fiascos*, Houghton Mifflin, Boston, MA

Johnson, G and Scholes, K (1999) *Exploring Corporate Strategy*, Prentice Hall, Harlow

Johnson, G, Scholes, K and Whittington, K (2005) *Exploring Corporate Strategy*, Prentice Hall, Harlow

Jones, A and Hendry, C (1994) 'The learning organization: adult learning and organizational transformation', *British Journal of Management*, **5**, pp 153–62

Jones, J and Bearley, W L (1986) *Group Development Assessment*, Organization Design and Development, King of Prussia, PA

Kahane, A (2004) *Solving Tough Problems*, Berrett-Koehler, San Francisco, CA

Kay, J (1993) 'The structure of strategy', *Business Strategy Review*, **4** (2), p 17

Kent, M L and Taylor, M (2002) 'Toward a dialogic theory of public relations', *Public Relations Review*, **28,** pp 21–37

Kolb, D (1984) *Experiential Learning*, Prentice Hall, New York

Kotter, J (1990) 'What leaders really do', *Harvard Business Review*, May–June

Kotter, J (1995) 'Leading change: why transformation efforts fail', *Harvard Business Review*, **73** (2), pp 59–67

Kotter, J (2006) 'Transformation', *Leadership Excellence*, **23** (1), p 14

Kotter, J and Schlesinger, L A (1979) 'Choosing strategies for change', *Harvard Business Review*, March–April

Kubler-Ross, E (1969) *On Death and Dying*, Macmillan, New York

Leadership Development Commission (2003) *An emerging strategy for leadership development – the competing demands of leadership*, www.idea.gov.uk [accessed 2006]

Lewin, K (1951) *Field Theory in Social Science*, Harper and Row, New York

Lewin, K (1999) *The Complete Social Scientist: A Kurt Lewin reader*, American Psychological Association, Washington, DC

Lewis, R (2000) *When Cultures Collide*, Nicholas Brearley, London

Martin, J (1995) *The Great Transition*, American Management Association, New York

Maslow, A (1970) *Motivation and Personality,* Harper & Row, New York

McKinsey Quarterly (2006) 'Organizing for successful change management: A McKinsey Global Survey', 1 August 2006, http://wwwmckinseyquarterlycom/

Morgan, G (1986) *Images of Organization*, Sage, Thousand Oaks, CA

Office of Government Commerce (OGC), http://www.ogc.gov.uk/index.asp [accessed 2006]

OPP Ltd (1996) OPP commissioned the Office of National Statistics to collect data, including responses to the MBTI Step I questionnaire, from a representative sample of the UK population, www.opp.co.uk [accessed 2006]

Pascale, R (1990) *Managing on the Edge*, Penguin, Harmondsworth

Pascale, R and Athos, A (1981) *The Art of Japanese Management*, Penguin, Harmondsworth

Pedler, M, Burgoyne, J and Boydell, T (1996) *The Learning Company: A strategy for sustainable development*, McGraw-Hill, Maidenhead

Peters, T, and Waterman, R (1982) *In Search of Excellence*, Harper and Row, New York

Pfeifer, T and Schmitt, R (2005) 'Managing change: quality-oriented design of strategic change processes', *The TQM Magazine*, **17** (4), p 297

Porter, L and Lawler, E (1968) *Managerial Attitudes and Performance,* Dorsey Press, Homewood, IL

Porter, M (1985) *Competitive Advantage,* Free Press, New York

Prahalad, C K and Hamel, G (1990) 'The core competence of the corporation', *Harvard Business Review,* June, pp 79–91

Roberto, M and Levesque, L (2005) 'The art of making change initiatives stick', *Sloan Management Review*, **46** (4)

Sadler, P (2003a) *Strategic Management*, Kogan Page, London

Sadler, P (2003b) *Leadership*, Kogan Page, London

Satir, V *et al* (1991) *The Satir Model: Family therapy and beyond*, Science and Behavior Books, CA

Schein, E (1999) *Corporate Culture Survival Guide*, Jossey-Bass, San Francisco, CA

Schein, E (2002) 'The anxiety of learning', *Harvard Business Review,* **80** (3)

Schoemaker, P (1995) 'Scenario planning: a tool for strategic thinking', *Sloan Management Review,* **36** (2)

Senge, P (1990) *The Fifth Discipline*, Doubleday, New York

Senge, P *et al* (1999) *The Dance of Change*, Nicolas Brealey, London

Sidhu, J (2003) 'Mission statements: is it time to shelve them?', *European Management Journal,* **21** (4), pp 439–46

Simpson, D *(1994)* 'Rethinking vision and mission', *Planning Review,* 22 (5), p 9

Sirken, H, Keenan, P and Jackson, A (2005) 'The hard side of change management', *Harvard Business Review,* October

Stace, D and Dunphy, D (2002) *Beyond the Boundaries: Leading and re-creating the successful enterprise* McGraw-Hill, Ohio

Thompson, J with Martin, F, (2005) *Strategic Management: Awareness and change*, Thomson Learning, London

Tichy, N (1983) 'The essentials of strategic change management', *Journal of Business Strategy;* **3** (4), p 55

Trompenaars, F (2002) 'Reconciling cultural dilemmas for competitive advantage and cultural change', Seminar, Oxford, October

Trompenaars, F and Hampden-Turner, C (2001) *21 Leaders for the 21st Century*, Capstone, Oxford

Turner, J, Grude, K and Thurloway, L (1996) *The Project Manager as Change Agent*, McGraw-Hill, Maidenhead

Von Bertalanffy, L (1968) *General Systems Theory: Foundations, development, applications*, Braziller, New York

Wack, P (1985a) 'Scenarios: uncharted waters ahead', *Harvard Business Review,* **63** (5)

Wack, P (1985b) 'Scenarios: shooting the rapids', *Harvard Business Review,* **63** (6)

Waterman, R, Peters, T and Phillips, JR (1980) 'Structure is not organisation' *Business Horizons,* **23** (3), June

Weinberg, G (1997) *Quality Software Management: Volume 4, Anticipating change*, Dorset House, New York

Whelan-Berry, K S, Gordon, J R and Hinings, C R (2003) 'Strengthening organizational change processes: recommendations and implications from a multilevel analysis', *Journal of Applied Behavioral Science,* **39** (2)

Witherspoon, P D and Wohlert, K L (1996) 'An approach to developing communciation strategies for enhancing organizational diversity', *The Journal of Business Communication,* **33** (4), pp 375–99

Worrall, L and Cooper, C (2006) 'The quality of working life: managers' health and well-being', Chartered Management Institute and Workplace Health Direct, quoted in *People Management*, 29 June

Zaleznik, A (1963) 'The human dilemmas of leadership', *Harvard Business Review*, July–August

Index

ALSO AVAILABLE FROM KOGAN PAGE